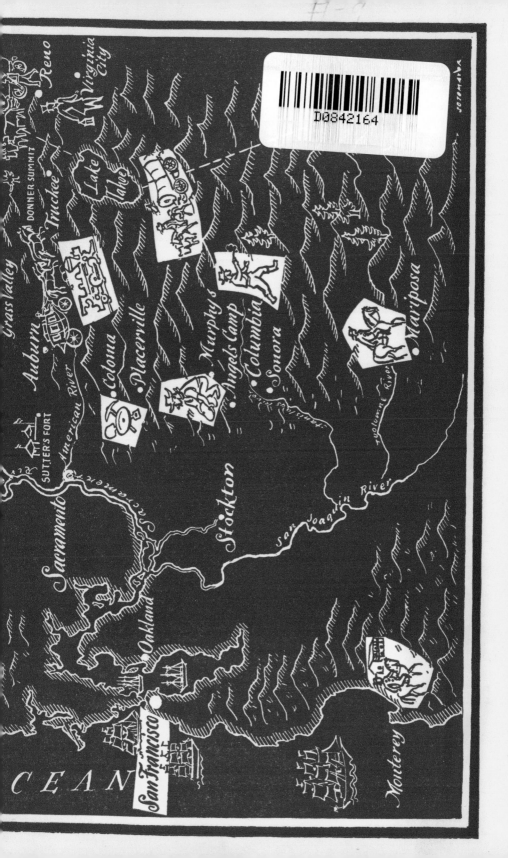

# CALIFORNIA CALLED THEM

Books by Robert O'Brien

THIS IS SAN FRANCISCO

CALIFORNIA CALLED THEM

# California Called Them

## A SAGA OF GOLDEN DAYS
## AND ROARING CAMPS

### BY ROBERT O'BRIEN

ILLUSTRATED BY ANTONIO SOTOMAYOR

McGRAW-HILL BOOK COMPANY, INC.

NEW YORK   LONDON   TORONTO

## CALIFORNIA CALLED THEM

Library of Congress Catalog Card Number: 51-12557

Published by the McGraw-Hill Book Company, Inc.

Printed in the United States of America

TO HARRY B. O'BRIEN

# Acknowledgment

Much of the material I have used was gathered primarily for "Riptides," the column which I write for the *San Francisco Chronicle*, and I am more indebted than I can say to George T. Cameron and Paul C. Smith, publisher and editor, respectively, of the *Chronicle*, for permission to draw freely and fully upon that material.

I also owe special thanks to the California Historical Society for permission to quote from *James Clyman, American Frontiersman*, edited by Charles L. Camp; to the University of California Press for permission to quote from *Expedition on the Sacramento and San Joaquin Rivers in 1817 —Diary of Fray Narciso Duran* (as it appeared in Publications of the Academy of Pacific Coast History, Vol. 2, No. 5); to the Oregon Historical Society for permission to quote from the *Peter Skene Ogden Journals*, as edited by T. C. Elliott for the Oregon Historical Quarterly (Vol. XI, No. 2); to the Houghton Mifflin Company for permission to quote from John Muir's *Steep Trails;* to Charles Scribner's Sons for permission to quote from *Mountaineering in the Sierra Nevada* by Clarence King; and to the Society of California Pioneers for permission to quote at length excerpts from the following articles which appeared in its Quarterly: "John Bidwell's Address to the Society of California Pioneers on November 1, 1897" (Vol. III, No. 1); "Journal of Pierson B. Reading" (Vol. VII, No. 3); "Shasta—An Address Delivered at the Pioneer Homecoming Day, Shasta, June 8, 1930," by Charles A. Shurtleff (Vol. VII, No. 2).

In the long preparation of a book like this, one becomes indebted to an ever-increasing number of sources and to what is, by the time the work is finally finished, a regiment of kind, interested, and helpful men and women who have, perhaps without even being aware of it, supplied to the author indispensable aid and encouragement.

This group, for me, includes literally hundreds of correspondents who, during the past six years, have generously volunteered to me, as a columnist, facts and impressions drawn from their own knowledge and experience and from the lore passed on to them by their fathers, mothers, and grandparents. It also includes others to whom, for many various reasons, particular thanks are due.

These are George Albro of Redding; Orbell Apperson, Sr., and Orbell Apperson, Jr., of Mount Shasta City; Walter Barrett of Truckee; Frank Bascom of Dunsmuir; Mae Hélène Bacon Boggs of San Francisco; Hubert Brady of Columbia; W. T. Davidson of Fort Jones; Eugene T. Dowling of Yreka; Mrs. Edna Behrens Eaton of Redding; Joel Ferris of Spokane, Washington; Miss Janie Hargreaves of Mount Shasta City; Phil Johnson of Twain Harte; Mr. and Mrs. Charles Masson of Dunsmuir; Jack Morley of Murphys; J. W. Schoonover of Fernbridge; Mrs. Jewel Smith of Fort Jones; and Joseph H. Wales of Mount Shasta City.

I shall always feel indebted to Philip and Paul Bancroft for aid and inspiration which, under the circumstances, could have come only from them; to Carl Latham, for saying the words which transformed the vague concept of such a book as this into plan and purpose; to William H. Hutchinson of Cohasset Stage, who has been a source of sustaining encouragement; to George and Isabel Schrader of Mount Shasta City, whose warm interest, hospitality, and willing assistance have endured from the very beginning of this work; to Antonio Sotomayor, for his loyal friendship and for his happy and sympathetic illustrations, and, finally, to my wife, the scope and depth of whose contribution can perhaps be comprehended only by another writer's wife.

The personnel of a number of institutions has been unfailingly helpful and cooperative, at times to a point far beyond the call of duty. In this connection I must express my gratitude to Mrs. Edna Martin Parratt, managing director of the California Historical Society; Mrs. Helen S. Giffen, secretary of the Society of California Pioneers; City Librarian Laurence J. Clarke, and Head Reference Librarian Dolores Cadell and her assistants—and of those assistants especially Miss Rose Suttey—all of the San Francisco Public Library; Dr. George P. Hammond, director of the Bancroft Library, and his assistant, Mrs. Eleanor Bancroft; Mabel Gillis, Librarian of the California State Library, and Caroline Wenzel of the

Library's California Room; and Librarian John C. Stump and the staff of the Mechanics' Institute Library of San Francisco.

For aid and guidance on a thousand and one occasions, I am deeply indebted to Larry Fanning, Joseph Henry Jackson, John Bruce, and Ben Macomber, all of the editorial staff of the *San Francisco Chronicle,* and to Mrs. Marjorie D. Brown and her assistants in the *Chronicle's* library.

In the absence of a formal bibliography, it is desirable to indicate certain sources upon which I have relied and which the reader may consult in the event his interest takes him beyond the range of the narrative.

The fundamental references are those volumes of Hubert Howe Bancroft's *Works* which are concerned with California, the Native Races, and the Northwest Coast; the files of the early-day San Francisco and north-country newspapers; and, in the book's final section, the *Siskiyou Pioneer* and *Yearbook,* the invaluable annual publications of the Siskiyou County Historical Society.

Anyone working on the background of the Mother Lode country to-day cannot avoid incurring a deep obligation to Joseph Henry Jackson for his *Anybody's Gold;* to the contributors to the California Division of Mines' *Geologic Guidebook—Along Highway 49,* prepared under the direction of Olaf P. Jenkins, chief of the division; and to Dr. Aubrey Neasham, regional historian of the National Park Service, Dr. Robert F. Heizer of the University of California's Department of Anthropology, and the late Philip Baldwin Bekeart, for research into the facts of the Gold Discovery.

As for the annals of the Mother Lode towns, you will find much material that I have used, and more, in Edna Bryan Buckbee's *The Saga of Old Tuolumne* and *Pioneer Days in Angels Camp,* and in Richard Coke Wood's *Murphys, Queen of the Sierra.*

For material in the section devoted to the Donner Country, I must especially acknowledge dependence upon the very readable and accurate *Sierra-Nevada Lakes* by George and Bliss Hinkle; *Ordeal by Hunger* by George R. Stewart; *History of the Donner Party* by C. F. McGlashan; *Seventy-five Years of Progress, a Historical Sketch of the Southern Pacific,* by Erle Heath; *California Highways and Public Works,* Centennial Edition; and papers of the Nevada County Historical Society.

In addition to those already mentioned, or referred to in the text, major sources for the final section on the Shasta Country include *Shasta County* by Rosena A. Giles; *Unwritten History: Life Amongst the Modocs* by Joaquin Miller; *Historic Spots in California* by Mildred Brooke Hoover and H. E. and E. G. Rensch; *Narrative of the United States Exploring Expedition During the Years 1838–1842* by Charles N. Wilkes, U.S.N.; *The Conquest of the Great Northwest* by Agnes C. Laut; and the files of the *Mount Shasta Herald.*

# Contents

# Introduction

In 1510, GARCIA ORDONEZ DE MONTALVO, a scribbler of Spanish romances, wrote in one of his fanciful novels:

*Know then, that, on the right hand of the Indies, there is an island called California, very close to the side of the Terrestrial Paradise, and it was peopled by black women, without any man among them, for they lived in the fashion of Amazons. They were of strong and hardy bodies, of ardent courage and great force. . . . Their arms were all of gold, and so was the harness of the wild beasts which they tamed and rode. For, in the whole island, there was no metal but gold. . . .*

When, years later, Spanish seafarers coasted down the long Pacific shore, they believed it the shore of an island on the right hand of the Indies, and very close, perhaps, "to the side of the Terrestrial Paradise," and so they named the land California.

A century passed. The true character and lineaments of the land emerged from the mist of wonder, dreams, and wild conjecture. It was not an island; there were no dark Amazons; a great sea separated it from the Indies; the Terrestrial Paradise was beyond the horizon, across another sea—who, now, knew where? But the name remained—the name and the one chimera, the most alluring of them all: "For, in the whole island, there was no metal but gold. . . ."

The Spanish seafarers and pathfinders died never knowing that the land they called California deceived them in all their hopes but this. It remained for a bearded, unschooled American carpenter to discover—by the banks of a foothill river and more than three hundred years after the novel was written—that the myth of Montalvo was not a myth, that the land would fulfill the promise it had seemed to hold out to the navigators who named it California.

As at last it gained substance, the discovery enfevered the world. Desire turned the faces and hearts of men everywhere toward the land of the

xiii

Pacific shore. California called them, and by the many thousands and from the corners of the earth, they responded.

To them and to their sons the land yielded two billion dollars in gold, and, in yielding it, wrought a change in America.

But what, meanwhile, took place in the wilderness arena, whose forests, rivers, mountains, and lonely reach of sky formed so proportionate a setting for so vast and sweeping a drama? What happened there?

To learn the answer, one must begin somewhere. One must begin with particulars. . . .

The particulars here, in this book, are seven little towns, and a mountain located 30 miles south of the Oregon border.

All but one of these seven towns were born of the California Gold Rush, and the seventh, you might say, is a Gold Rush grandchild. Their youth was riotous and reckless, like the men who made them; the evil they did, as well as the good, lives after them. As for the mountain, it survives in a realm beyond good and evil and the shifting designs of time.

These towns speak to us directly and indirectly of the great American mid-century excitement. Only geographically were they regional phenomena. In every other sense they represented a vigorous and vital phase of nineteenth-century America. Standing on the peak of a hundred years after and looking back, you can see them as expressions of a passage in our national life without which America would not be America.

This book is an attempt to relate them, as effects, to their cause; to feel for a meaning in them which transcends both cause and effect; to scan the mirrors that they held up; to follow their lives after the expansion they represented had been assimilated, and to see how they adapted themselves, or failed to adapt themselves, to a world that seemed no longer to have use or place for them.

The material presented here does not pretend to be the complete story of even these little towns. But it represents a valid fragment of the time of American youth and growing, a time of crudeness and strength, courage and a ruthless vitality, optimism, faith, and a dream of freedom and wide blue skies.

These qualities, this faith and dream are our heritage. We have but to recognize them to know that they are behind us, and within us, as we confront our destiny.

ROBERT O'BRIEN

# MOTHER LODE COUNTRY

# CHAPTER ONE

# Coloma–I

FOR TEN or twelve miles out of Sacramento, the road to Placerville—called even today the Trail of the Pony Express—is flat and straight, and takes you northeast past the gasoline stations, roadhouses, and motels that mark the perimeter of every California city and town. Across the countryside beyond them roll the broad acres of the Sacramento Valley truck farms and nurseries and orchards.

The road begins to climb just before you reach Folsom, where the State penitentiary is; then, leaving Folsom, you strike into the Sierra foothills, and the highway is flanked for mile after mile by the long tailing piles left by the gold miners as bleak and ugly memorials to their plunder of the California earth.

As you approach the 1,000-foot level, you may see (as I did a winter or two ago, when the air was still and the poplars, the wild apple trees, and the oaks stood bare and desolate against the gray sky) a bearded prospector panning for gold in a tiny stream that runs swiftly down a foothill meadow

beside the road—as startling and anachronistic a sight as would be the
sudden appearance of a Concord coach rocking along the smooth ma-
cadam highway, or an Indian hut of brush and skins, and a squaw mashing
acorns into meal between smooth brown rocks. If you do not see him
there, you will most certainly see him farther on, leading his patient pack
mule along the dusty shoulder of the road and walking swiftly, with head
and shoulders bent forward, his whole manner and gait expressing the
dark urgency that drives him from stream to stream, gulch to gulch, river
bar to river bar for the gold strike he must make before it is too late—before his stake and provisions dwindle, before his mule goes lame, before
winter comes, before his own legs and arms grow old and weak, before
hope itself flags, and despair fades the colors of the golden mirage that
lures him on.

In the meadow or by the road, he does not look up as you pass; he bends
to his pan, or strides along rapt and lonely, like a man who is late for an
appointment with destiny. As the car leaves him behind, you drive on
wondering whether you have seen a ghostly survivor of the Gold
Rush, doomed, like a sort of terrestrial Flying Dutchman, to haunt for
eternity the trails of the Mother Lode in quest of a will-o'-the-wisp bonanza.

At Shingle Springs, unless the winter fog is low, you can look to the
east and see the snow-covered Sierra Nevada—the Range of Light—so
remote, so far away, and so seemingly unattainable that they exert a
Shangri-La enchantment over you when you are seeing them for the first
time. The Spaniards saw them, perhaps from the very hillcrest along
which your car is speeding, and believed that somewhere in those mountains were caves whose walls were encrusted with virgin gold and flashing
jewels; Forty-niners gazed upon them and thought that they guarded
among their granite peaks a lake of gold.

And you and I, knowing today that these are but myths, are still akin
to them both: if we yielded to the mountains' spell, we too—like the
Spaniards, the Forty-niners, and the hurrying prospector back down the
road—would be bewitched, and believe that they hold out to us whatever
it is that we are seeking, be it gold or be it God. The Sierra in the distance
are a challenge and a barrier. They speak to courage, strength, and imagination, and promise his heart's desire to him who conquers them; and yet,
by their vastness and their mighty invulnerable crags, they deny that

promise, reminding man that he is but a puny infant in the timeless world of glaciers, seas, and continents under the seas, of snow falling for a century of days and nights, and volcanoes erupting at sunrise a million years ago. That is the paradox of the Sierra, and the paradox, perhaps, of snow-covered mountains everywhere.

But the road dips to the pines and winds on through the meadows; the mountains disappear from view and the horizon is once more limited by the familiar sight of houses and pastures and groves of willows and oaks, and across the countryside drifts the mellow tone of cowbells. Then, all at once, you are in Placerville, the "Hangtown" of the Gold Rush days. The noise and movement of traffic, the men and women on the sidewalks, the façades of stores, churches, bars, restaurants, and hotels, the neon signs glowing even by daylight, restore you to reality.

Some eight miles northwest of Placerville, along the twisting Mother Lode Highway, lies the sleepy foothill hamlet of Coloma, deep in a long valley and beside the rushing waters of the American River's south fork. Here are a river bridge, some cottages whose yards—in the springtime— are bright with flowers, a tiny post office, a meeting hall, a store or two. Here, also, along the silent and deserted streets and in the still shade of the China trees, are the house where the poet Edwin Markham lived while he taught school; the small, one-story brick buildings that once housed Ralph Bell's store and Bekeart's store; and the ruins of the granite-block jail—decaying relics of the days when 10,000 miners swarmed through the river fork's ravines and gulches seeking the glittering dust.

But, more than that, here is where it all began. In this peaceful valley— known to the Indians as *Culluma,* or "beautiful vale"—in the shadow of these ponderosa pines and towering hills, the pioneer James Wilson Marshall picked from Sutter's millrace the flakes of gold that revealed the secret of the Sierra and, in one moment of a wilderness afternoon in January, 1848, unveiled the future of California and all the West.

A cairn of stone beside the river marks the site of the sawmill Marshall was building that January for Capt. John A. Sutter, lord of the Sacramento Valley leagues of New Helvetia; and, high on a hill to the west, the tall Marshall memorial stands over Marshall's grave amid the cedars and the live oaks. Into its granite pedestal are chiseled a few words telling of the discovery:

*The first flake of gold was found in the race of Sutter's Mill in Coloma January 24th 1848.*

You can see that there have been two alterations in the original inscription. When the monument was erected in 1890, five years after Marshall's death, the word "nugget" was there instead of "flake," and the date read, "January 19th." Upon the monument's dedication, this lettering only intensified the old disputes which had resulted from the haziness of many of the details surrounding the discovery. Even Marshall and Sutter, the two most closely involved, did not always tell the same stories, and this fundamental confusion was multiplied by the varying accounts of others. Marshall said that he made the discovery,

*. . . on or about the 19th of January—I am not quite certain to a day, but it was between the 18th and 20th.*

There were many indications, however, that he was mistaken in his own mind, and in 1918 Governor Stephens appointed a committee to examine the matter and decide the true date, once and for all. This committee determined that Marshall was wrong: the true date was January 24. It was so fixed by an act of Legislature, and the inscription on the monument was altered to agree. After a similar investigation in 1931, and a similar act of the Legislature of that year, the word "nugget" was erased, and "flake" carved in its place.

Looming high above the monument's stone base is the bronze figure of Marshall, in miner's dress. He faces east across the valley; his left hand is extended with a finger pointing down the hill to the riverbank where he first saw gold gleaming in the millrace sands.

For three centuries before that 24th of January men had talked about the riches they believed lay hidden in the California earth. The Spanish explorers of the sixteenth century swore that layers of solid gold and vast storehouses of glittering gems were to be found within the depths of the Shining Mountains, as they, in their fables, called the Sierra Nevada.

In 1579, Francis Fletcher, chaplain of Drake's *Golden Hinde,* thought that these fables were true, although what made him think so is still a mystery. As historian Hubert Howe Bancroft says,

*. . . If gold and silver ever existed amid the rocks and hills in the neighborhood of Drake's Bay, the world has yet to know it.*

Later, as the land was colonized, the belief was kept alive by a tantaliz-
ing accumulation of bits of evidence: the discovery of silver deposits near
the Colorado River, for example, or tiny bits of precious metal in the possession of Indians. Jedediah Smith may have found placer gold near Mono
Lake in 1825, and other American exploring parties reported similar discoveries in the early years of the nineteenth century.

The first officially recorded discovery of gold in California happened
near Los Angeles in March, 1842, when a *vaquero* named Francisco Lopez
plucked a wild onion and in the earth thus dislodged found placer gold.
From $6,000 to $8,000 worth of gold was taken annually from the deposit
until the outbreak of the Mexican War in 1846 ended mining opera-
tions.

One of the strangest stories of early California gold—and it is perhaps
no more than a legend—has Paris as its setting. It is said that late one night
in 1837 a certain Le Carpentier, an antiquarian, was awakened by a loud
knocking on his door. Responding to it, he beheld on the doorstep a middle-
aged man whom he had never seen before. The stranger's clothes hung in
tatters from his gaunt frame. Dark, hollow eyes burned with a feverish light
in his haggard face, and he seemed faint with exhaustion. It was M. Le
Carpentier's impression that he was looking at a man who might have
traveled to his door through unimaginable peril and hardship from the very
ends of the earth.

Wild words burst from the stranger's lips: "Monsieur, you do not know
me, but I know you and your reputation as an antiquarian. If you will help
me get from the government a vessel and a hundred men, I will bring
back an entire shipload of gold. I assure you I am not mad. See here. . . ."
From the pocket of his ragged coat he produced a large fragment of quartz.

Convinced that the man was out of his mind, the kindly antiquarian
gave him something to eat, paid him a few francs for the quartz, and told
him to come back whenever he pleased. The stranger left the house, and
M. Le Carpentier never saw him again. But the quartz, when analyzed,
proved rich in gold.

Fifteen years later, in 1852, a boardinghouse keeper on a neighboring
street brought to M. Le Carpentier a small weighty package wrapped in
a torn handkerchief. With it was a letter addressed to the antiquarian. They
had been found, the landlord said, in the room of a man who had died in

the boardinghouse years before. They had been mislaid, had turned up again only the previous day, and now he was happy at last to be able to deliver them. He hoped that they were nothing of importance.

Puzzled and curious, M. Le Carpentier tore open the package. In it was a block of quartz whose color and texture he recognized at once as identical with those of the fragment given him by the mysterious stranger that night in 1837. He could see clearly where the fragment had been chipped from the piece he now held in his hand.

The letter, obviously written in urgent and trembling haste, was dated a few days after the midnight visit. "I am dying," it read. "You alone listened to me. You alone stretched out a helping hand. I bequeath you my secret. The country whence I brought this gold is called California."

The possibility has been mentioned that this may be nothing more than a diverting myth, based upon a folk theme as old as, or older than, the Bible. On the other hand, it may be fact: M. Le Carpentier's strange visitor may have been the true discoverer of the Mother Lode. But if he was, his deed cast no more than the outline of a shadow across the pages of history; even his name, now, is unknown. What we do know, instead, is that things began moving out of the realm of myth and legend in that summer of 1847 when Captain Sutter decided that he needed lumber for a flour-mill to be built on his property.

From Sutter's Fort on the Sacramento, James Marshall, a moody thirty-six-year-old carpenter and wheelwright who had crossed the plains from Missouri in 1844, made several exploratory trips into the foothills, and decided that the Coloma Valley and a bank of the south fork of the American River were the most promising for Sutter's lumbering venture. The two men entered into an agreement: Sutter was to furnish the men and materials, Marshall was to supervise construction of a sawmill and operate the mill when it was finished.

In August, with tools and supplies lashed to their creaking oxcarts, and driving a flock of sheep for food, Marshall and about a dozen men (most of whom had been members of the Mormon Battalion that had marched west from Council Bluffs, to fight in the war with Mexico) set out from Sutter's Fort on the 40-mile journey to Coloma. On the expedition's arrival there a week later, they began building log cabins, the sawmill, and a dam by which they could divert the flow of water from the river into the mill-race which was to supply the power.

Several months passed, until the bright sun failed to draw the nip from the pine-scented air and the days in the deep valley grew shorter. The cabins were finished, the frame of the mill was up, and the men were blasting and digging the race. By night they let water through to sluice out debris and earth that had been loosened by powder, pick, and shovel. By day they toiled on, unaware that all around them—in the rocks, in the gravel, in the river sands—lay the fabled wealth of the Shining Mountains that Spanish conquistadors had dreamed of three centuries before.

There are at least four versions of what happened beside the tailrace of Sutter's Mill on the afternoon of January 24, 1848. At the time the discovery was made, how could anyone there have known what it meant? Pebbles do not alter the course of a glacier; how could a few flakes of gold dictate the destiny of the West, or of America? And so no one took notes on what was said and done. Not one of them, at that moment, dreamed of the consequences. It was as George F. Parsons said in his *The Life and Adventures of James Marshall*:

*If we were writing a sensational tale, instead of a sober history, we might proceed to relate how Marshall sank pale and breathless upon a neighboring rock, and how, as he eyed the glittering metal in his hand, a vision rose before him of the mighty results of his discovery. But in fact nothing of the kind occurred. The discoverer was not of the spasmodic and excitable kind, but a plain, shrewd, practical fellow, who realized the importance of his discovery (though doubtless not of its full extent, since no one did that then) and proceeded with his work as usual, after showing the nugget to his men and indulging in a few conjectures concerning the probable extent of the gold field.*

In any event, a widely accepted reconstruction relates the discovery story as follows:

In the late afternoon of January 24, eight of Marshall's white helpers were working about the mill, either drilling boulders or felling and sawing timber. Marshall strolled along the tailrace with another workman, Peter Weimer (also spelled Wimmer and Wemer), whose wife had accompanied the party to Coloma as camp cook.

As he reached a point about two hundred yards from the mill, Marshall noticed some yellow particles that flecked a mound of excavated earth. He sent an Indian boy for a tin pan, and with it washed out the dust, perhaps a thimbleful. When the men finished work that evening, Marshall said to them, "Boys, I believe I have found a gold mine."

The men were good-naturedly casual and dubious. Most of them regarded the taciturn carpenter as a queer one, anyway: a visionary. It did not astonish them that he looked at a thimbleful of gold-colored dust and proclaimed it proof of El Dorado, nor did it move them to excitement. To take him seriously would have been to acknowledge themselves as queer as he was.

The next morning, Marshall took a closer look at the tailrace sands. He found a few flakes that had the appearance of gold. For a moment, he pondered over them. Were they sulphuret of copper? If they were, stones would crush them to powder. He hammered one of the flakes between two rocks. It yielded and bent, but did not break.

Marshall returned to the mill and called his men around him. He dented the crown of his hat and placed the hat on a bench. Then he dropped the flakes—tiny and thin, they were, weighing not so much as half an ounce—into the hollow of the crown.

"Boys," he said solemnly, "I've found it."

One of them compared the flakes with a five-dollar gold piece. They looked the same. They threw a flake or two into Mrs. Weimer's soap kettle and boiled them in a solution of potash. The metal stood the test. Two days later Marshall set out on horseback for Sutter's Fort.

He reached the fort on January 28 in a state of agitation. He insisted on seeing Sutter alone at once. Sutter led him to his private rooms. At Marshall's insistence, the door was locked behind them. "He was a singular man, and I took this to be some freak of his," Sutter said later.

Drawing from his pocket a white cotton rag, Marshall carefully unfolded it, and revealed his precious flakes. "I believe this is gold," he said.

Once more the metal was tested. They weighed it on apothecary scales, both in the air and under water. They applied nitric acid to it. Sutter consulted an encyclopedia to make sure that they were trying every means of analysis at their disposal. At last the lord of New Helvetia was convinced.

*"I believe this is gold," he said*

He said to Marshall, "I agree with you. I believe this is the finest kind of gold."

Marshall would not stay at the fort. He left immediately, in a driving rainstorm, for the mill and the wilderness setting of his momentous discovery.

Sutter tossed restlessly all night long.

*At once and during the night,* he recalled afterward, *the curse of the thing burst upon my mind. I saw from the beginning how the end would be, and the next day I had a melancholy ride of it to the mill.*

Meanwhile, Marshall had devised a curious and childish plot. At his suggestion, he and his men scattered on the tailrace sands all of the flakes and gold dust they had found. Sutter would see it, Marshall reasoned, and be so overwhelmed at the sight that he would produce his whisky flask and give everyone a free drink.

Thanks to one of Weimer's little boys, the plan failed. While Marshall accompanied Sutter to the tailrace, the child ran ahead of them, spied the gold with his sharp eyes and picked up every particle. "Father! Father! See what I have found!" he cried. Marshall and the others stood helpless, silently cursing the brat and saying good-by to their hopes for a swallow of the captain's liquor.

Nevertheless, they proceeded with the hunt, and when they had collected an ounce and a half of gold they gave it to Sutter. Later, he had it made into a ring. On it were engraved his coat of arms and the inscription, *The first gold discovered, in January 1848.*

The men at the little settlement at Coloma hardly gave the gold a second thought. They went back to work on the sawmill, and to felling the pines that it would rip into planks for the flour mill Sutter was building at Brighton, not far from his fort.

Sutter, however, was filled with uneasiness and doubt. If the news spread, what would happen at the flour mill? He was afraid he knew: his construction crew would drop their tools and desert him for the gold field, leaving the mill in whatever stage it happened to be when word of the discovery reached them.

He did what he could to protect himself, for he had his heart set on the completion of the flour mill. Estimating that the diggings probably extended some distance from the sawmill, he called a meeting of the Coloma Valley Indians and, on behalf of himself and Marshall, leased an area about twelve miles square from them for three years. In return for this lease he gave them some hats, shirts, and flour, and a few pleasing trinkets of trifling value. Then he urged the men at the sawmill to remain at their work for another six weeks, until the lumber he required was cut, and to promise that they would hold their tongues about the gold Marshall had found in the tailrace. Steady work, and not the risks of prospecting, was what appealed to the men: they agreed to both requests.

So the dry ax blows and the crash of falling trees once more echoed across the peaceful valley of Coloma and rose above the murmuring undertone of the river waters as they rushed from the canyon at the valley's head and flowed swiftly past the mill and the log cabins and wound along the valley floor west toward the mighty mother river the Sacramento. The foothills that stretched mile after mile north and south and the snow-capped mountains looming eastward were locked in silence, and 150 miles to the southwest the tiny village of San Francisco dozed by the shores of Yerba Buena cove and waited for the springtime, and the end of the winter rains.

But the secret of the Sierra troubled the hearts of Sutter, Marshall, and the rest. A thousand unuttered questions, impulses, fears, and hopes strove to force from them a word, a hint, a sly and oblique reference that would ever so slightly lighten the burden of their self-imposed silence. It was only a question of time before they would yield to them.

The first to give in was Sutter himself. Three weeks after the discovery he wrote to General Mariano G. Vallejo at Sonoma, *I have made a discovery of a gold mine, which, according to experiments we have made, is extraordinarily rich.*

The second to talk was Charles Bennett, one of Marshall's workmen at Coloma. About the time that he wrote the letter to Vallejo, Sutter sent Bennett to Monterey to obtain mining privileges in the Coloma Valley from the American military authorities then administering the affairs of the territory of California. Bennett took with him 6 ounces of American Fork gold in a buckskin pouch as evidence that the request was both serious and warranted. Although Sutter swore him to secrecy, Bennett progressed no farther than Benicia, some sixty miles south of Sutter's Fort and less than half the distance to Monterey, before the urge to speak proved irresistible.

As he tarried there in a store, a Benician burst through the door with news that coal had been discovered on the slopes of Mt. Diablo twenty miles or so to the southeast. The announcement created a sensation. A hubbub of excited conversation filled the shop. Bennett's promise took wing. His voice rose above the others.

"Coal!" he scoffed, and reached inside his shirt. "I'll show you some coal —the kind they mine on the American River!"

The buckskin bag thumped to the counter.

The hubbub abruptly ceased. Everyone stared at the bag. Bennett, one elbow on the counter, lounged at ease, enjoying the effect of his gesture.

"Go ahead," he grinned. "Take a look."

A few days after Bennett's departure for Monterey, a Swiss teamster arrived at Coloma with supplies from Sutter. One of the Weimer children said to him brightly, "We've got some gold."

The teamster laughed.

"What the boy says is true," Mrs. Weimer said sharply. "Look here"— she showed him some dust—"what do you call that?"

The teamster obtained some of the gold, returned to Sutter's Fort and swaggered into the store operated by the Mormons Sam Brannan and George Smith, who more than once had refused him drinks on credit. With a cavalier flourish he tossed his poke to the bar.

"A bottle of brandy," he said. "Make it the best in the house."

Smith eyed him suspiciously. "How many times do I have to tell you?" he snapped. "No money, no drinks."

"This time I have money," retorted the teamster, patting the poke. "Gold."

Smith threw up his hands. "Don't bother me. I have no time for foolishness."

The teamster grinned. "If you don't believe me, go to the fort and ask Captain Sutter."

Smith decided that he would call the bluff of this buffoon. With the poke in his hand he hurried to the fort and Sutter. "Your man came to me with this and said it contained gold—from Coloma. I think he's a liar and told him so."

Sutter thought for a moment, wondering, perhaps, at the way in which the devil, by putting words in the mouths of men, gave the very metal itself the power to speak out and proclaim the Sierra secret. "Nevertheless," he said at last, "it is gold."

Back at Coloma, in the long foothill valley, the wind riffled gently through the pines. The men bent to their saws and axes, all but one of them unimpressed by the discovery. He was Henry Bigler, a Mormon. On the pretext of hunting ducks or deer, he would go off with a rifle over his shoulder; then, when out of sight of camp, he would drop his gun and hunt for gold. Toward the end of February he wrote to three Mormon friends employed at Brighton on Sutter's flour mill. *Keep it to yourselves and do not tell anyone,* his letter said, *but gold has been found in the Coloma Valley.*

The Brighton mill builders could keep it to themselves no better than Sutter, Bennett, Mrs. Weimer, the teamster, and Henry Bigler. A week later, three other Mormons to whom they had confided the secret arrived at Coloma to try their luck at prospecting.

Two weeks after that, the discovery emerged from the realm of the whispered word, the knowing glance, the half-believed, the half-unbelievable. The *Californian,* a weekly published at San Francisco, gave it form and substance in a sixty-one-word paragraph headed, GOLD MINE FOUND.

*In the newly made raceway of the sawmill recently erected by Captain Sutter on the American fork, gold has been found in considerable quantities. One person brought $30 to New Helvetia, gathered there in a short time. California no doubt is rich in mineral wealth; great chances here for scientific capitalists. Gold has been found in every part of the country.*

Sutter and Marshall were like explorers of strange and unfamiliar seas who see the shape of an approaching ship emerging from the mist. They discern its vague, looming outlines and observe its deliberate advance half in alarm and half in wonder. What flag does it fly? they ask each other. Is it a good ship, or an evil one? Uneasily they watch it as, seeming to seek them out, it draws nearer. . . .

In the month of April, 1848, some ten weeks after the discovery, E. C. Kemble, editor of the *California Star* of San Francisco, decided to take a sight-seeing trip to the Coloma Valley. His trip, he notified his readers, had nothing to do with gold; he was merely planning to *ruralize among the rustics of the country for a few weeks.* On his return a short while later, he had only a perfunctory, travel-poster report to make to his subscribers:

*Great country, fine climate; visit this great valley, we would advise all who have not yet done so. See it now. Full flowing streams, mighty timber, large crops, luxuriant clover, fragrant flowers, gold and silver.*

By twos and threes, curious San Franciscans drifted quietly out of town, bound for the American Fork to learn for themselves what was going on in Sutter's valley at Coloma. Some of them came back as quietly as they had departed, but with gold dust enough to buy hot toddies for the house in the saloons of Portsmouth Square. It remained for the Mormon Elder Sam Brannan to shake them, wake them up, and make them comprehend that what they had dug from the earth and traded for a drink was not mere metal and mineral dust: it was the substance of El Dorado.

"Gold! Gold from the American River!" he cried as he ran down Montgomery Street waving his hat and holding aloft a bottle filled with gold dust. And in that moment, they suddenly saw themselves transformed into potential millionaires. Brannan's words, the magic of his enthusiasm, swept them from the muddy San Francisco streets to the threshold of Paradise.

Within a week or two, at least a hundred and fifty of them—one-fourth of the town's male population—had nailed up their shops, traded their belongings for picks, pans, shovels, and bacon, and struck out for Coloma. Editor Kemble still would have no part of it. Toward the end of May he wrote, *Fleets of launches left this place on Sunday and Monday, closely stowed with human beings. . . . Was there ever anything so superlatively silly?* It was all a hoax, he cried, a fake—*a superb take-in as was ever got up to guzzle the gullible.*

But Editor Kemble was brushed aside in the pell-mell rush for the gold fields. His shrill warning echoed down deserted streets, and with amazed incredulity he saw his friends and readers turn into madmen before his very eyes. He saw them pay five hundred dollars for skiffs they could have bought in March for fifty, and he saw them pay fifty dollars for a two-dollar spade. He saw them trade their homes for bottles, quills, brass tubes, jars, and even barrels in which to bring back the gold dust they would shovel from the ground when they reached the rainbow's end in Coloma Valley. And it was all for a myth, a fairy tale!

"Fools!" he cried. But the cry went unheard and unheeded, and mingled with the harsh lament of the gulls that flapped and circled above the deserted shore of the cove.

The golden maelstrom whirled wider. Men of other settlements—San Jose, Monterey, Santa Barbara, Los Angeles—yielded to its irresistible sweep. Carpenters dropped their hammers, doctors deserted their patients and clergymen their flocks. Clamored the *Californian:*

*The whole country from San Francisco to Los Angeles and from the seashore to the base of the Sierra Nevada resounds to the sordid cry of gold! Gold!! GOLD!!! while the field is left half-planted, the house half-built, and everything neglected but the manufacture of shovels and pickaxes. . . .*

Trading ships brought word of the excitement to Honolulu, and it spread from there back to Oregon and Canada and Mexico. Couriers carried it over the Rockies to the East, whence it crossed the Atlantic to Europe. The eyes of all the world, alight with desire and hope, greed and golden dreams, turned to the long and peaceful valley of Coloma and the gravelly bars of the swift, singing river.

The great American Gold Rush was beginning.

# CHAPTER TWO

# Coloma-II

COLUMBUS DISCOVERS a New World, and dies in obscurity, his appeals for reparation neglected by an indifferent king. Balboa, from his peak in Darien, becomes the first white man to gaze upon the sparkling Pacific, and is beheaded in a Haitian jungle by a treacherous rogue. Centuries later, of six men who find a mountain of silver in Nevada, five die paupers or madmen, and the one whose name the fabulous lode bears to this day sits down beside a Montana trail and blows out his brains.

The curse of the discoverers was to fall also upon Sutter and Marshall, partners in the discovery of the great California gold fields. From the moment the dusky yellow specks caught Marshall's eye, the two were doomed. Before a year passed, the tide of the Gold Rush which they themselves had unwittingly brought about swept them ruthlessly aside and left them dazed amid the wreckage of their hopes and plans.

Sutter's employees, almost to a man, deserted his fields and shops for the

18

diggings. Half-finished leather was left to rot in the vats of the Sutter's Fort tanneries. His cattle roamed untended across the 76 square miles of his Sacramento Valley kingdom, and his crops perished unharvested in the fields. His mills stood silent, stripped even of their massive stones by plundering Argonauts. Agents whom he hired to protect his interests fleeced him, and he was forced to sell his vast acres, parcel by parcel, to pay the lawyers who were trying to save his property from the squatters.

*I was,* he later recalled, *the victim of every swindler who came along. I understood little about business and was foolish enough to have faith in men who cheated me on every side. . . . They [the miners] stole the cattle and the horses, they stole the bells from the Fort and the weights from the gates, they stole the hides, and they stole the barrels. . . . I could not shut the gates of my Fort in order to keep them out; they would have broken them down. Talking to them did not do any good. I was alone and there was no law.*

In 1849, Sutter moved to Hock Farm, his ranch on the Feather River, and from there tried to salvage something from the ruins of his fortune. But courts found flaws in his Mexican land titles, and years of expensive litigation yielded him nothing. Still another blow fell in 1865, when fire destroyed the Hock Farm residence and everything in it. Sutter moved to Washington, D.C., and then to Lititz, Pennsylvania, to spend the rest of his life petitioning Congress for indemnity. His claim, originally $125,000 but reduced by compromise to $50,000, went before Congress for the sixteenth time in the spring of 1880. On June 18, two days after Congress adjourned once more without acting upon it, the unhappy lord of New Helvetia died in a Washington hotel room, at the age of seventy-seven.

The ring he wore—the one made of the first Coloma gold—he had paid for with his whole world, and half a lifetime of despair.

Marshall's life and fate challenge analysis, and this analysis can lead you to your rock-bottom concept of history and, indeed, of life itself. If you believe in accidents, in the fortuitous concourse of events, then to you Marshall is simply a man who unwittingly stumbled over the end of the rainbow and thus, by destiny's caprice, had a hand in history. Sooner or later someone would have discovered the Mother Lode, but a man named Marshall happened to be building a mill in a certain valley where there happened to be gold, and he found it when he found it, and that's an end to it.

If you believe, however, in an operative law and in men as being agents of that law, then you may follow Marshall through his early years and mark how every step and every hour took him across the western wilderness and to that millrace bank on that winter's day in 1848, as surely and as inexorably as if he had been born only to lean down and pick up a thimbleful of gold dust—the shining key to the Sierra mystery. Regard it as law at work, and you can travel far back along a chain of related events and never find a yielding link. The wanderings of fifteen years led him and him alone to the valley of discovery.

To John Bidwell, for instance, it was clear that it had all been arranged by a Providence, and represented the smooth functioning of a detailed plan carried out by this Providence with Sutter and Marshall as its elected collaborators. Even Marshall's tendency to aberration, recognized by all who knew him, was accounted for and depended upon in the operation of the plan, according to Bidwell.

Bidwell, who had arrived in California in 1841, when there were fewer than a hundred and fifty "foreigners" in the territory, was, along with Pierson Barton Reading, an eminent pioneer survivor of the Gold Rush. Both he and Reading visited Coloma that winter; shortly afterward, they both made strikes of their own, Bidwell on the Feather River, and Reading in the Trinity fields. Both (in contrast to Sutter and Marshall) prospered on vast holdings of north-country land, and lived honored, respected, and contented until their deaths.

Looking back upon the pageant of California history in 1897, Bidwell told the Society of California Pioneers:

*It was preordained that gold should be discovered in this way.*

*Sutter's wants for lumber increased year by year, and it was his custom year by year to send men into the mountains to search for a place to build a sawmill on some tributary of the Sacramento or Feather Rivers. In 1846 he sent me. In 1847 he happened to send Marshall. Marshall the people usually called crazy. Certainly no sane man would have built a sawmill where Marshall did. It was an utter failure as a place to obtain timber. . . . Marshall intended to raft his lumber partly down the American River and then to Sacramento to the Bay of San Francisco to sell it. That thing has never been done to this day. No man has ever attempted to raft lumber down even the Sacramento, much less the American River, to the Bay. . . .*

*So Marshall built his mill and started the water through the wheel, but the mill wouldn't turn because the water wouldn't run uphill. This compelled him to dig a race through a gravel bank so as to conduct the water on down below the wheel into the river. The water was shallow and clear as crystal, and the bed of the race was perhaps decayed granite of the very color to show gold on the bottom to the best advantage. So Marshall saw and picked up the first piece of gold and became the famed gold discoverer.*

General Bidwell (to give him the title bestowed upon him in later years) concluded this passage with a recognition of Sutter's part in the discovery as Marshall's financial backer and active partner. It was Sutter's money and enterprise, he said, *which set in motion Marshall himself and all the conspiring conditions which converged in and unfolded that great discovery, under the eye of a guiding Providence.*

No matter how you explain Marshall and the Coloma flakes, you cannot escape the particular quality and timing of the event, which immediately pulled California into the broad stream of national affairs. (The pioneers drew upon Greek mythology to illustrate this phenomenon; on the State seal, adopted at the Constitutional Convention in Monterey in 1849, California is personified by Minerva, who sprang full-grown from the brain of Jupiter.)

Nothing but the discovery of gold in California could have inspired the westward surge of one of the greatest mass migrations in human history, or so swiftly have extended the American frontier from the Mississippi to the Pacific. In the next ten years, California raced through a century of growth. Her admission to the Union as a Free State at a moment directly conditioned by the discovery and her subsequent moral and financial support of the North were important factors in the beginnings, conduct, and results of the Civil War.

The discovery is a peak upon the map of human events; of it you can say, "Had it not been for this, had it not happened just this way, everything would have been different."

And so, before the effects of the discovery, the discoverer dwindles to insignificance—to a man on a monument. And when we see him there, looking down into the valley, pointing to the site, we remember only the deed. The man we forget.

As sweating, cursing, red-shirted Argonauts swarmed by the thousands over the bars and flats of the American River, pushing Sutter and him around, as they did anyone who got in their way, James Marshall became a little dazed. Nothing in his life had equipped him for this sort of thing.

Born in New Jersey in 1812, he had followed his father's trade, that of coach and wagon builder. At twenty-one, he had said good-by to his folks and roamed across the Alleghenies to Indiana and Illinois. He finally settled in Missouri, and there contracted fevers and ague so regularly that his doctor gave him only two years to live.

It happened that at this time, in Missouri, there appeared someone with a cure for Marshall's physical troubles. He was the Sante Fe trapper Antoine Robidoux, who returned from the Far West with the picture of California as an Eden, a fair, far land beyond compare, a land of fertile fields and everlasting springtime, where herds of wild horses grazed and played across green, sunlit valleys.

His glowing words stirred the bottomland Missourians, who lived half of their lives, it seemed, in the long damp days of dreary winters. But they were a practical people, and sought a basis of comparison in terms of realism and their own experience.

"What about the fever and the ague?" they asked the trapper. "Are there any in California?"

Robidoux smiled. "Friends," he replied, "you have asked me a direct question, and I must answer it truthfully. It so happens that several years ago a man living near Monterey had a chill. He was such a wonderment to the good people of Monterey, they traveled eighteen miles into the country just to see him shake."

If the trapper's words brought a wry laugh from Marshall's lips, their implications must also have given him cause for serious thought. He must have weighed over and over in his mind the hazards and dangers of the westward crossing against the promises of health and prosperity held out by this Pacific Eden. Hope tipped the scales and brought him to the Oregon Trail, facing the sunset—and Paradise.

Traveling with the great emigrant train of that year, Marshall reached Oregon in the autumn of 1844. There he remained for the winter. In the following spring, on a cloudy Sunday in June, he struck south for California with the McMahon-Clyman Party of thirty-nine men, one woman, and three children.

On the eighth day out, Clyman—James Clyman, trapper, mountain man, and the pilot of the party—noted in his diary, . . . *some Beautifull vallies are found that look allmost like enchantment the rapid little river Tumbling along one side rounded Hills of oak softining down to a vally bounding the others all covered in grass and flowers all wild as natures dream and covered with the light bounding deer.* . . .

On June 23 they crossed the Siskiyous and on the 25th the swift-running Klamath River, and fixed their eyes on the snow-mantled summit of Mount Shasta—the landmark that meant California and journey's end to so many trail-weary emigrants.

Leaving Shasta behind them, they pushed on down the rugged Trinity foothills; and now faraway glimpses of the vast Sacramento Valley, lying to the south in the distant haze of its summer heat, spurred them on by day and set them to tossing restlessly in their blankets by night. At length, on July 3, they attained their Eden.

*After packing,* wrote Clyman, *we again took to the Rocky hills the greate vally in plain view from the hills has occasionally been seen for several days all anxious to leave the Eternal mountains urged our Jaded animals to their utmost capabilities and about Three in the afternoon we entered the lower vally of the sacramento and threw ourselves under the shad of the wide spreading oak Trees that stand scattered promisquesly over this vally.* . . .

For the next few days, they made as much as thirty miles a day along the willows and sycamores of the winding riverbank, past the tawny summer hills, the groves of white oaks, and the broad fields of wild oats. Blue smokes drifted upward from the valley grass fires and hung motionless in the hot, dry air.

On July 15, Captain Sutter in New Helvetia wrote to Thomas O. Larkin, the American consul at Monterey:

*Dear Sir . . . I send you a News paper from St. Louis send to me over the Rockey Mountains, with a somewhat exaggerated description of California. The Company, which arrived the 10th ins$^t$ from the Oregon consists out 39 men, 1 Widow and 3 Children of which I send you inclosed a list.* . . .

The thirty-fourth entry on the list was, *James W. Marshal . . . Coach-maker & Carp* . . . *U.S.*

For a while, Marshall worked at Sutter's high-walled adobe fort, stocking plows, fashioning spinning wheels, and mending wagons. A streak of thrift and independence emerged, bringing with it hopes for a ranch of his own some day, and he managed to save enough money to buy a few acres on Butte Creek, to the north of New Helvetia.

Looking back, Bidwell would have contended that this private venture was doomed to fail. How could it have been otherwise, when Marshall was scheduled, according to the timetable of Providence, to be working for Sutter at Coloma on a day two years away? And Bidwell would have been right.

Stirred by the Bear Flag revolt of June, 1846, Marshall joined Frémont's raffish California Battalion and traveled south with it to drive the Mexicans out of California. He participated in several skirmishes and achieved perhaps the high point of his military career when, on sentry duty, he picked off a couple of Mexican scouts disguised as trees. Then, with the rest, he was mustered out in April, 1847.

He hastened back to his ranch in the foothills and there learned of a development that annihilated his plan for a life of independence: during his absence, his entire herd of cattle down to the last steer had been destroyed —some stolen, some slaughtered by bears, and the rest strayed into the wilderness.

Broke and discouraged, Marshall drifted back to Sutter's Fort and asked for work; there was no place else for him to go, and nothing else for him to do. A few months after that, he entered partnership with Sutter in the lumbering and sawmill project in the Coloma Valley. And that, until that autumn, when he set out for the valley with his oxcarts and tools and workmen, had been his life.

As for Marshall's general appearance and personality, you can picture him as of medium height, muscular build, brown hair, and dark eyes that were quick to register his feelings. His usual costume was, for his environment, equally undistinguished: white linen trousers, buckskin leggings, moccasins, a frontier shirt, and a Mexican sombrero.

*Nothing but gold in California would have inspired the westward surge*

He was a man of quicksilver moods; sometimes he was cheerful and companionable; at others he was, for no apparent reason, surly and cross. His associates noted in him moments of strange abstraction. Bidwell, who knew him well, speaking of Marshall before the discovery, said, *He was a man of exceeding eccentricity—a very curious fellow.* To Sutter, who knew him even more intimately, *Marshall was one of those visionary men who was always dreaming of something.*

But in spite of his tendency to brood and daydream, and his unpredictable temper—qualities which rendered him peculiarly unfit for frontier living —he was a competent workman. He was as honest as the day was long. He liked his liquor, and this was one trait which could be depended upon not to alienate the affections of his frontier comrades. He carried it, they say, as well as the next fellow.

If Marshall failed to realize at first what his discovery was going to do to him and his life, he received an acid foretaste about a year after he had picked the first fateful flakes from the millrace. In the early weeks of 1849, miners and other settlers wantonly ignored his posted notices against trespassing, overran the mill property, and squatted on its lands.

*Thirteen of Sutter's and Marshall's oxen soon went down the canyon,* he later recalled. *These cost four hundred dollars per yoke to replace. Seven of my horses went to carry weary men's packs.*

From this time on, Marshall lived in a nightmare world.

His millhands deserted him and scattered to the diggings. At nearby Murderer's Bar a band of whites on a spree slaughtered several Indians and raped their squaws. In reparation, the surviving redskins killed a few white men. A mob rallied, and, failing to catch these warriors, attacked innocent members of the Culluma tribe and shot seven, some of whom were employed at the mill. Marshall rose to the defense of the Cullumas, and so enraged the mob by this stand that in the end he had to flee the valley for his life. When he returned a few weeks later, squatters were laying out the streets of Coloma over his property. Once more, he was bankrupt.

Everywhere along the 200-mile reach of the Mother Lode men were taking thousands of dollars in gold from the Sierra streams and the foothill earth, some of them finding more in a week than Marshall had earned in a lifetime. He saw them brawling drunk, flinging the gold dust away on more liquor than they could drink, squandering at the monte tables and on the roulette wheels what it would take him months to make with his carpenter's tools. Gloomily he gazed upon their bulging pokes and despaired at their good fortune.

He tried prospecting, but wherever he went he was followed by superstitious miners who believed that Marshall, the Discoverer, was blessed with some magic divining power. They dogged his footsteps, pursuing him silently through the woods and across the ravines and gulches. When he arrived at what he considered a promising location, and drove his pick into the ground, they suddenly materialized from behind trees and bushes, pushed him aside, and dug frantically around the spot that he had selected. Marshall would glumly shoulder his pick, pack up his mule, and trudge on.

*Should I go to new localities,* he complained, *and commence to open a new mine, before I could prospect the ground, numbers flocked in and commenced seeking all around me, and, as numbers tell, some one would find the lead before me and inform their party, and the ground was claimed. Then I would travel again.*

In the depths of his bitterness, he began to take solace in spiritualism. He grew convinced that he was the favorite of certain benign spirits whose plans for his welfare were constantly being frustrated by greedy men. Soon, even the Indians were grumbling over his queer ways.

*Following the guidance of his spirit,* Sutter recalled, *he flitted hither and thither about the foothills. Once he asked me for help, and I gave him one or two horses and a few Indians. But they returned after several weeks very much disgusted and said that they would not go with him any more. . . . The curse of the gold seemed to last on him.*

At last, forsaking prospecting as a hopeless and humiliating waste of time, he tried to get work—any kind of work—but his applications were met with jeers from those whom he begged for employment.

"We hire you!" they exclaimed. "Don't be a fool. You found gold once, and you can do it again. Find us some, and then we'll hire you."

An angry mob threatened to hang him to the nearest tree unless he would tell them where they could find a gold mine. His life was saved by a friend who put him on a horse and got him out of town in time to escape the noose.

Still another thing rankled deeply, and he felt no less abused when he reflected, as he often did, that he was personally responsible for the great Australian gold strike. One day a discouraged Australian prospector named Hargraves had gone to Marshall at Coloma and loudly berated California for failing to make him rich.

"Look," said Marshall, "if you don't like it here go back home to Australia and do your gold digging. There's plenty of it there."

Hargraves thought it over; the Discoverer ought to know what he was talking about.

"Do you really think so?" he asked.

"I'm sure of it," replied Marshall.

Hargraves packed his bag, went back to Australia, and promptly struck a golden bonanza that yielded millions of pounds sterling to the British treasury. For this, a grateful Britain gave him a £5,000 reward, and Australia voted him another £10,000.

So, while others struck it rich, while Forty-niners took $600,000,000 in gold from the hills of his El Dorado, Marshall followed the spirit voices from mining camp to mining camp, up the lonely river canyons and across the barren gulches and river flats. *I wandered for more than four years,* he said, *feeling myself under some fatal influence, a curse. . . .*

He took to traveling about the country, making what living he could by giving lectures and telling the story of the discovery. At length, in 1857, an old man at forty-five, he returned to Coloma. There, on the hillside overlooking the valley, he built himself a rude cabin and supported himself by sawing wood, gardening, and cleaning wells. He tried to grow a small vineyard.

Now bitterness settled upon him in earnest, and he regarded his ungrateful nation with deepening gloom, for it owed him, he felt, a great debt. This was his frame of mind that first year back in Coloma: *The enterprising energy of which the orators and editors of California's early golden days boasted so much as belonging to Yankeedom was not national, but individual. Of the profits derived from the enterprise it stands thus, Yankeedom, $600,000,000; myself, individually, $000,000,000.* Morosely, he remembered Hargraves and added, *Were I an Englishman, and had made my discovery on English soil, the case would have been different.*

The editor of *Hutching's California Magazine* wrote to him at Coloma and asked him for his photograph. *I wish to say,* Marshall replied peevishly, *that I feel it a duty I owe to myself to retain my likeness, as it is in fact all I have that I can call my own; and I feel like any other poor wretch, I want something for myself. The sale of it may yet keep me from starving, or it may buy me a dose of medicine in sickness, or pay for the funeral of a dog, and such is all that I expect, judging from former kindnesses.*

Ultimately, more out of charity than in recognition of what he had done, the State granted him a tiny pension. He rented his cabin and land on the Coloma hillside for twenty-five dollars a year and moved to Kelsey, 3 miles away. He passed his last years waiting for his pension checks, which he would spend on drinks for himself and his cronies. Then he would earn enough to get along on until the next one by making and selling various household implements—potato mashers, candle snuffers, wooden bowls, clothes pounders—and by traveling to excursion grounds to write autographs with a shaky hand and peddle them to picnickers for a few pennies each.

He lived in this manner until he was seventy-four, and died in utter poverty at Kelsey, August 10, 1885.

<br />

CHAPTER THREE

# Angels Camp

SOME OF THE best and loveliest towns in Northern California are clearly in the grip of a deep conflict between the past and the present. This conflict torments, bedevils, and to some extent paralyzes San Francisco, Monterey, and those foothill villages which, by reasons of geography and commerce, have been drawn irresistibly into the current of twentieth-century life.

They have a rich vital background that is a romantic epic of Spanish dons and mission bells, mountain men and trappers, Forty-niners and vigilantes, clipper ships and covered wagons, thirty-mule freight wagons on the mountain trails and elegant Concords raising the red dust of the mountain coach roads.

For the sake of love and loyalty they must cling to this past, and, by preserving its symbols, do what they can to preserve its spirit. It is as if the past were to them a cemetery in which the truths and traditions of their

<br />

forefathers lay buried. They are the caretakers of the cemetery; they have guaranteed perpetual care of the old house, the old church, the ancient tree, the stone fence across a field that are its monuments.

Yet changing life and changing times frequently demand the destruction of the symbols. The towns and villages cannot go back, they cannot stand still; and the price they must pay for going forward wrenches their hearts in a most sad and bitter way.

In Monterey a weathered adobe stands on a valuable piece of land in the business district. Businessmen want to tear it down and erect in its place a modern restaurant or store that would perhaps represent both a profit and a credit to the community. To the keepers of the heritage of the old Spanish capital, the proposal is truly shocking. There is a clash. Desperate words. And the victory, no matter where it falls, is empty. In this arena, as in an arena the size of a continent, no victory is a victory when the vanquished goes down to defeat still believing in the principles for which he fought.

In San Francisco modern-minded transportation men propose to substitute busses for the cable cars, beloved relics of the Victorian days of Emperor Norton and the Comstock kings. San Franciscans by the thousand rally to the defense of the cable car, not as a means of transportation but as a symbol of the San Francisco heritage and the San Francisco spirit. So the bells of the quaint and antiquated "struggle-buggies" still jangle merrily up Powell Street and California Street and along the crest of Nob Hill, and a slender thread to the past remains, for the time being, intact.

In the Sierra foothill towns, it seems, the conflict is seldom so sharp or well-defined. The leisure of the pace of life, the respected and temperate hand of age and wisdom in public affairs, and a saving native humor keep it subdued and in check. Nevertheless, its existence is revealed in Main Street. Next to a little park shaded by cypress and locust trees that were planted by the Forty-niners stands a creamery, starkly white, with its milk-shake counter, juke box, and Coca-Cola signs. Across the street from a graceful pioneer church sprawl the pumps and oiling pits of a gasoline filling station. Diesel-powered busses roar away from the little stone building still pointed out by town historians as the station where the hell-for-leather riders of the Pony Express changed their mounts. And when evening comes, the neons cast a garish glow over the iron shutters and the delicate iron grillwork of the old Gold Rush buildings.

What makes the conflict so poignant here is that the Forty-niners who planted those trees and built those buildings were in many instances the grandfathers of the living; their voices are still remembered, their presence still felt. For the living to betray the past is for them to betray the sound of those voices and the work of those hands. The past is vivid and close and all around them: it is their father's father—the gulches he roamed, the creeks he panned, the stone he cut, the streets he walked, the chair he sat in, the bucket he made that still hangs in the well. Deny these and you deny him. Deny him and you deny the pioneers. Deny the pioneers and you deny everything they were and did; and to ask a native son of California to do this is to ask him to die, and die first he would.

There are several ways in which the Mother Lode towns have responded to the dilemma. One has been simply to perish, and all up and down the foothills desolate stone cellars, grass-grown beside the road, testify to the death of settlements that abandoned the struggle for survival. Another has been to reject not the past but the present, to dream trancelike through the long, drowsy summer afternoons, smiling, aware not of the car or truck passing through, not of the high whine or the air horn of the diesel-electric locomotive in the canyon over the ridge, but only of the faintly remembered sound of the sweet bells of the freight wagons, the footfalls of the Forty-niners, the fiddled strains of a barroom waltz and the smell of the pines that used to grow beyond the meadow. A few towns, a dozen, perhaps, are like this. The summer day will come when they will die contentedly in their sleep; their lineaments will crumble and decay; the manzanita will grow down the hillside and above them spread its dark sinewy arms, its fresh gray-green leaves.

Still a third way has been to make the best of it, retaining as much of the past as possible, accepting only as much of the present as necessary, and diluting the bitterness with resignation, the poignancy with humorous, and even whimsical, good grace.

Such a town is Placerville, whose citizens are still pleased and flattered by the visitor who calls it "Hangtown," and knows when and how it got the name. Such a town is Sonora, whose old-timers still refer to it proudly as the Queen of the Southern Mines. And such a town is Angels Camp, which, with frontier zest and pageantry, reminds the world at large every springtime that it is the home of The Celebrated Jumping Frog of Calaveras County. . . .

An Indian summer haze lay over the hills that late September in 1806 as the Spanish-Indian fighter Gabriel Moraga marched from Mission San Juan Bautista, a few miles northeast of Monterey, on an expedition of exploration into the wilderness beyond the broad valley of the San Joaquin River.

Moraga, his chaplain, Padre Pedro Muñoz, and his twenty-five soldiers traveled light and traveled fast, and with only two things on their minds: possible sites for new missions and the mood and strength of the foothill Indians.

They noted with interest the presence of many beaver and salmon in the San Joaquin, and pressed on past its tulares and black-willowed banks to the bare fawn-colored slopes of the foothill country. One day they came to an *arroyo* groved with oaks and willows. Hovering in the *arroyo's* still air were clouds of bright-winged butterflies, which, as the soldiers passed through, settled on their uniforms and faces. One even crawled into a man's ear. They named the place *Mariposas,* Spanish for "butterflies," and pushed on.

They turned north, crossed the canyons of the westward flowing rivers, toiled across rolling foothill meadows that were parched and sere because the fall rain had not yet come, and at length reached a broad field by a river. While the band rested on the riverbank, several soldiers wandered off in search of game. They returned with half a dozen bleached skulls.

Moraga followed them to their hunting ground, and there halted in amazement. Skulls and bones littered an acre and more. An Indian of a nearby *ranchería* explained that the field was an ancient battleground. A long time before, he said, invading warriors swarmed down from the Sierra to drive the tribes of the Sacramento and San Joaquin Valleys from their river fishing preserves. The armies had met on this field, and these skulls and bones were the remains of those who had fallen.

The explorer called the place *Calaveras,* or "Skulls," and the stream he named "River of Skulls," and these are the names the region and the river bear today.

At the end of a few days' further travel, Moraga and his men decided to turn back. They proceeded swiftly south, past Mariposas, along the rugged shoulder of the foothills, past the country of pines and sequoia, across the swift *Rio de los Santos Reyes* and through Tejon Pass of the Tehachapi mountain range. They arrived at Mission San Fernando on November 2. Padre Muñoz reported to the mission fathers that the expedition had been attended with famous success: on the journey to the foothills he had brought one hundred and forty-one heathen Indians into the Catholic fold and had baptized them in the faith of Christ.

The Land of Skulls was left alone for many years. During those years, changes came to the *pueblos* of the long California littoral. The flags of the Spanish monarchs fluttered down the plaza flagstaffs and in their place, for a while, waved the flags of Mexico. At last the flying banners were those of America, standing free in the offshore breeze. The battalions that raised them there during the Mexican War were mustered out early in '47, and the soldiers who had been Californians went back to what they had been doing before the war began. Among them, James Marshall, the moody carpenter of Sutter's Fort, hastened northward home to the wilderness ranch he had left beneath the Feather River pines.

On a day in June, 1848, a little less than six months after Marshall's discovery, James H. Carson, a Virginian, strolled down Monterey's Alvarado Street. Carson had been a sergeant in Company 3 of the Third Artillery and had come west with the New York Volunteers. They had arrived in Monterey aboard the U.S.S. *Lexington* in 1847, too late to see action in the Mexican War.

Now, no longer in uniform, Carson had an open mind about his future. Down at the end of the street, the blue waters of Monterey Bay and the open sea beyond flashed in the spring sunlight. A ship standing out between the headlands could take a man westward to Cathay, had he a heart for roving. And beyond the inland hills, sleek long-horned cattle roamed the *ranchos* of the valley. Had he a landsman's heart, a love of flowering mustard in the springtime and a cowboy's lament at dusk, he could saddle a pony, turn his back on the sea, and ride in a day to this other life that would keep him forever within the sight of oak trees and a *señorita's* smile.

But, as he pondered, Carson lifted his eyes from the sandy street.

*I saw,* he later recalled, *a form, bent and filthy, approaching me, and soon a cry of recognition was given between us. He was an old acquaintance, and had been one of the first to visit the mines. Now he stood before me. His hair hung out of his hat; his chin with beard was black and his buckskins reached to his knees.*

Upon his back this human scarecrow carried a leather sack. He opened it and held it toward Carson. "Put your hand in, and see what it brings out."

Carson did as the man said—and stood in Alvarado Street staring at a handful of gold dust.

"Where did you get it?" he asked in a trembling voice.

"Up in the hills, in the gold fields."

"How long did it take you to mine it?"

The man grinned and rubbed his stubble. "Longer 'n some. 'Bout a month, I reckon."

Guitar music was drifting from the open door of a *cantina* in Alvarado Street, the scent of oleander came from an adobe's *patio,* and that afternoon's sun fell rich and mellow on the red tile roofs of Monterey as James H. Carson rode swiftly out of town toward the northeast.

Two months later a weird procession entered the region Moraga had called Calaveras. Ninety-two were the members of this motley brigade, and they cursed in a dozen different tongues the chaparral and manzanita through which they hacked a trail for themselves and their sweating pack animals. Some were blue-eyed and fair, and some were dark-eyed and swarthy; some wore sailor dungarees and had the mark of runaway on them; some wore tattered Army uniforms stripped of insignia that would proclaim the deserted regiment; some were clad in the rag remnants of the once respectable garb of *alcaldes* and ministers, carpenters and masons, merchants and clerks; a few wore the boots and buckskins of frontiersmen. Sunburnt, bearded, and armed to the teeth, they toiled up the ravines and rugged canyons of the Land of Skulls until they came to the tinkling waters of a foothill creek.

Here, 60 miles south of Coloma and not far from where some Mexicans had discovered placer gold fragments the size and shape of melon seeds a few months before, the flimsy ties of convenience that had bound them together fell away, and they scattered with their crude implements to the hills that held their fortunes and the fulfillment of their wild and feverish dreams.

Carson, one of the leaders of the party, struck to the south, and 3 miles away pitched his tent on the side of a hill that still bears his name. In the earth all around him lay $26,000,000 in gold, and the heaviest nugget ever found in California. But these did not come out of the shafts and glory holes of the hill until years after Carson left it, with a pittance, for diggings that seemed more promising.

Two others of the party were John and Daniel Murphy, members of the great Santa Clara pioneer family of Murphys. At the breaking up of the expedition, they traveled seven or eight miles to the northeast and there founded the outpost that came to be known as Murphy's Camp or Murphy's Diggings.

A fourth fortune-seeker of this party resolved to remain, for the time being, at least, at the camp site beside the tumbling waters of the swift and narrow creek. There he kept his tent, and there in the weeks that followed he opened a small trading post for the miners who were panning the gravel of the nearby bars and flats.

This man's name was Angel—some say George and some say Henry, and the Pioneer Index of the historian Hubert Howe Bancroft lists him simply as "Angel." But his first name doesn't matter, for Angel's was what they came to call the little creek, and Angel's Camp became the name of the settlement that was soon ranged along the hillside above his trading post. In time, the apostrophe, as with Murphys, was discarded as superfluous.

Today, even the oldest old-timers in Angels Camp cannot say what happened to Angel. Their fathers have told them that he stayed beside the creek for a year, panning a little, but gathering the dust more comfortably and quickly over the counter of his trading post with his stock of red flannel, provisions, and tobacco. The story goes that he went up the Lode to Hangtown for a while, and then someone thought they saw him a few years afterward working behind the roulette table of a San Francisco gambling house. But no one from Angels Camp saw him, or even thought they saw him, after that.

By the next green grass and the blooming of the scarlet firebrush in the foothill meadow and the spring of '49, a tent village of 300 gold seekers clustered on the slopes about Angel's trading post. By 1853 the community's population was nearly five thousand. The main street sloped gently then, as it does now, from the north end of town to the south, from the foot of Dead Horse Hill to the foot of Mathew's Hill; and along this street stood ten wooden buildings, one and two stories high.

In that year, at the height of the Gold Rush, they represented the cold common sense of men who had gone to Angels Camp not for what they could dig there from the earth, but for what they could earn in the trade, barter, and commerce of a free-and-easy boom town.

Michael Cosgrove, a Dublin Irishman, was one of them. He rode into town one day in 1851, hammered together a sawmill on the banks of Angels Creek, and in no time at all had erected with the pine planks from his mill a hotel, a livery stable, a carriage house, three wooden dwellings, and a meeting hall.

In the year of Cosgrove's arrival, C. G. Lake spread an enormous canvas tent above the northeast corner of Main Street and Chinatown Road and called it Angels Hotel, and there, to the scraping of fiddles and the shrilling of fifes, the Forty-niners capered through the Spanish waltz and the quadrille with the caked red mud of a dozen creeks and gulches on their Wellington boots. Some wore knotted handkerchiefs on their heads or patches on their jeans to signify that for the purposes of the dance and the evening's entertainment they were to be regarded as female partners to remedy the absence—universal on the Lode in those days—of the real thing.

The Stickle brothers, Edward and George, who had come out from New York in '49, built a store on Main Street; and John Peirano did so well in a tented shop that a few years afterward he was able to put up a stone building for his establishment across Chinatown Road from the Angels Hotel and thus claim a rightful share of the respect due a Main Street frontage and association with Nunninger's Bakery, J. T. Fletcher's undertaking parlors, Scribner's drugstore, and Barkhorn's Beer and Billiard Saloon.

With the exception of the dark year of '52, remembered for a smallpox epidemic and famine so intense that the unmarried men left town to conserve the food supply for the women and children, these years and the years that immediately followed held the best bonanza days of Angels Camp.

At night the mountain lions screamed down from the pines behind the town, and in the wintertime the cold and drenching rains drove the miners cursing from their tents and their brush huts roofed with buffalo hides; but in the long, warm suns of the dry season the steam whistles of the quartz mills echoed cheerily across the town in the early mornings, and the pounding of the quartz-crushing stamps began to rattle and bang and shake the earth. For miles up and down the creek the overshot wheels and the flutter wheels commenced to turn, smoke rose from the dying breakfast fires, and the miners bent to their day's work over their picks and shovels and riffle boxes.

The children trooped into town from Scorpion Gulch and Slab Ranch on the spring and autumn mornings and filed into their schoolroom in Bennager Rasberry's residence on Main Street. During their lunch hours they played in the mined-out diggings behind the house.

Stages, bound north for Hangtown, south for Mariposa, or east for Murphys along Tom Matteson's Wingdam Stage Line, rolled along the dusty street past the tethered buckboards and buggies. And down the plank sidewalks, to the accepted accompaniment of the thudding of the stamp mills, the cries of the stage drivers to their horses, the shouting of the sidewalk peddlers, the strains of lively barroom fiddles, and the faint smell, perhaps, of burning sawdust drifting from the mill at the end of town—aware and yet unaware of all this that was the expression of the town's life the men of the town moved down the sidewalks in Palo Alto hats and checkered shirts, and the women in frontier poke bonnets and calico dresses, freer in their walk, somehow, and freer with their smiles than they had been on the streets of the New Hampshire village or the Pennsylvania town they had left behind for California.

Others mingled with them too, sometimes, bringing a touch of the glamorous and picturesque, a dash of the color of San Francisco's Portsmouth Square, to the busy little street: shuffling, blue-clad Chinese from Shanghai City, the Oriental settlement that was a little way out of town, along Chinatown Road; sharp-eyed and elegantly dressed gamblers off the river steamers, and the itinerant actors and actresses who, that night, would pack the miners into the pine-raftered Cosgrove's Hall or the Stickle brothers' theater on Circus Hill, and set them whooping with delight over rowdy performances of *Seeing the Elephant,* and *First Night; or the Virgin in California.*

Among that sidewalk crowd you could have found as well a young and bearded Angels Camper named John W. Mackay, who, as a hardware peddler, started a career there that would some day take him to Nevada's Mount Davidson and make him a silver king of the Comstock; and the beloved and respected Dr. William A. Kelly, a Forty-niner who went to Angels to hunt gold, but, what with all the cholera and smallpox, put aside his pick and Long Tom and became the town physician, never submitting a bill to his patients but letting them pay him as and when they wished, and, when he couldn't meet his own bills, inserting this personal advertisement in the local weekly: *All persons knowing themselves indebted to the undersigned will please call and settle at least a portion of their indebtedness, as I am very much in need of money. William A. Kelly, M.D.*

Another townsman of no more than local note was Jim Fair, who, like Mackay, had ahead of him a future as a Comstock king. In those days, he picked up what dust he could in the diggings around Angels Camp—Murphys, Whimtown, Shaw's Flat, and Carson Hill—and courted Theresa Rooney, the daughter of Tom and Alice Rooney, who ran a Carson Hill boardinghouse known for miles around as "Rooney's Cow Ranch."

When Fair finally married Theresa in 1861, it was the social event of the year, they say; and not long after that the canny miner sold his interest in the Invincible claim at the north end of town to James T. Boyd and Judge Delos Lake of San Francisco for $37,000. The mine (renamed by Lake the Utica after his birthplace in New York) did not begin to return a dividend until many years later, and old-timers in the hills back of Angels still wag their beards, lapse into silence, and stare into space when they recall the part Mrs. Robinson played in locating the broad rich veins of the Utica mine.

It happened that a certain Charles Lane eventually became superintendent and part owner of the property, which had stood abandoned and unworked for years. Lane took samples of the mine's ore to Mrs. Robinson, a San Francisco clairvoyant, and asked her what the spirits said about its possibilities. Mrs. Robinson closed her eyes, went into a trance, and at length spoke solemnly as follows:

"The spirits beyond the barrier have communicated with me. They tell me, and I tell you, that deep in the earth where this rock came from lies gold—gold enough for a Croesus."

Lane returned to Angels and ordered his men to sink the shafts still deeper. When his friends tried to persuade him to abandon the mine before he squandered all his own and his partner's money, he spurred his men on to even greater efforts.

"Everybody says no, but my ghost says yes, so we'll have to work a while longer," he would say.

One day in the early 1880s, as the miners picked and blasted their way toward the 550-foot level, the steam whistle at the head of the Utica shaft sent a long triumphant blast out across the town. Lane had struck his bonanza— a great vein of gold yielding $200 to the ton.

Lane, the old-timers say, hardly turned a hair. From start to finish he had believed what the spirits said. He had known it was there somewhere, all along.

In those other days, though, in the 1850s, the boys in Barkhorn's Saloon or at Ross Coon's bar in the Angels Hotel had plenty to talk about over their toddies and forty-rod besides the arrivals the stage had brought that day from the valley, or the show the night before at the Stickles' theater. The things that happened they told and retold and as the years went by the stories were woven into the Angels Camp legend as parts of the life, the history, the personality of this particular Mother Lode town of the Gold Rush. . . .

One day, two girls on their way to school delivered some milk to the cabin home of a pretty, dark-eyed Frenchwoman. She made a good living lending money to miners in need of a stake, and shared the cabin with a lover who spent his nights dealing monte in an Angels Camp gambling house. As the children called she came to the door with a fluting iron in her hand.

"I won't need any more milk for the next two weeks. I'm leaving this afternoon for a trip to San Francisco," she said cheerfully, and went back to her ironing.

Two days later, her body and the hatchet that had killed her were found on the cabin's bloodstained floor. Her gold dust was gone. They arrested the monte dealer, charged him with her murder, and then released him for lack of evidence. The identity of her assassin was never learned.

On another day, Bennager Rasberry, who owned the building on Main Street where the schoolroom was, threw away a keg of brandied peaches that had spoiled in the trip around the Horn. A neighbor's pigs found them and ate them, and four days afterward tottered and staggered around their meadow and filled the air with drunken squealing until they sobered up and returned to their slop troughs and acorns.

Rasberry himself provided talk enough for a winter of evenings. Once, while hunting, he jammed the ramrod in his musket. After tugging at it in vain for several minutes, he decided to blast it from the barrel. He aimed it at a gray squirrel and pulled the trigger. The ramrod left the musket in a cloud of smoke, flew off at an angle, and imbedded itself in the roots of a manzanita bush. Rasberry pulled the ramrod from the ground—and with it a fragment of gold-bearing quartz. From the vein thus uncovered, Rasberry that afternoon took $700 in gold. The next day it yielded $2,000, and the day after that $7,000. For months his Ramrod mine gave up immense profits, and when the vein finally petered out, Rasberry really didn't care very much. He was rich for the rest of his life.

On quite another afternoon, a procession of Angels Campers reverently carried to the Presbyterian cemetery the pine casket containing the bodies of Mrs. John A. Jackson, the Sunday-school teacher, and the infant that had died with her in childbirth. As they passed a Main Street fandango parlor, a gambler burst through the open door and sprinted down the street.

Hard on his heels, raising angry cries of "Hang the murderer! Lynch him!" a dozen others poured from the hall and collided head-on with the funeral ranks. For a few moments the two groups milled in shrill confusion in the middle of the street.

"Where's the gambler?" yelled the pursuers. "He just knifed a man to death in a monte game!" Reeling free of the turmoil, they regrouped and set off once more after the fleeing miscreant.

To a man, the pallbearers dropped the casket in the road, called on their fellow mourners to follow them in the name of justice, and joined in the chase.

A half hour later, having assisted in the capture, they returned. They rested to catch their breath, then picked up the casket and resumed the funeral. The moment the graveside services were over, they clapped their hats back on their heads and raced to Dead Horse Hill, where they seized the hangman's rope and yanked the gambling man to eternity.

"That's life in the mines for you—a funeral march one minute and a strangulation jig the next," they commented to one another as they lined up at the Angels bar for a refresher to cap the excitement.

Fire, which few of the flimsily built mining camps escaped, came to Angels in 1855 on a Sunday in June, and the mellow tones of the bell in St. Patrick's Church, across Main Street from the headframes of the Invincible claim, had barely died away before the strident clang of the fire triangles rose over Finnegan Lane and Chinatown Road. Shanghai City, in whose rickety shanties lived 200 Chinese miners and their families, was in flames. Twenty minutes later the spreading fire swirled high over Main Street. The frame buildings perished in fountains of sparks and billowing smoke. The bucket brigades and the feeble streams of the fire hoses were all but useless. When the fire finally burned itself out that night, not a building of importance was standing in Angels Camp.

The boys talked about the fire the whole summer long, and about the progress of the new stone buildings going up in place of the wooden ones that had been destroyed. Lake, for instance, was rebuilding his hotel in stone—rhyolite blocks cut from the Altaville quarry a few miles to the north by Allen Taylor, who had come around the Horn in '49. The same stone was being used in the reconstruction of the Stickle brothers' store and Scribner's drugstore, the Wells, Fargo office, and other Main Street buildings; and when they were finished, on them would be hung sheet-iron shutters and doors and beneath their roofs would be laid inches of sand, to keep them standing through any fire that ever threatened them again.

The year after the fire, the boys strung up a violent-tempered English tar named Colebrook who knifed a miner for calling him a hog thief. To get him away from the law they had to shoot out the courtroom lights in the middle of his trial, bind the judge and constable to their chairs, and whisk the sailor outside to the courthouse oak. But it was over in a twinkling and soon they were once more back at Barkhorn's and the Angels bar, warming their hands over a pine-knot fire and downing hot whisky toddy toasts to vigilante justice.

By this time the grass roots were no longer rich with dust and the Forty-niners were drifting away. The deep mines were working—the Invincible, the Cameron and Lightner, the Marshall, and the Sultana—but the bonanza boom was past; the smoke from a thousand campfires no longer rose blue against the dusk-blue hills at the day's end, and many water wheels hung motionless along the creek bed all year round. There wasn't much to talk about any more, and so the boys, when they gathered on those evenings in the '60s, steered clear of conversation, for the most part. The Civil War was on everybody's mind, but the subject could lead to bitterness and gunplay and no one wanted trouble any more—so they played cards when they met at Barkhorn's and the Angels bar.

The seasons rolled on, bringing the time of dry flumes and still pools and dry white boulders in the creek beds and hills tawny in the hot summer suns; the time of the poplar's April green and yellow autumn flame; the time of the snows, the footprints of foxes in the snow beneath the manzanita and the sound of ice-cold torrents rushing westward down the Sierra slope. These times came and went, and softly came again.

One night toward Christmas in 1864 Mark Twain—Sam Clemens, as they called him in those days—the newspaperman from over the hill in Virginia City, Nevada—dropped in from Jackass Hill, where he was visiting Jim and Bill Gillis. They were brothers of Steve Gillis, a printer whom Clemens had met and liked in Virginia City. A few months before, Clemens and Steve had gone to San Francisco. There, in a Howard Street brawl, Steve had broken a beer pitcher on his antagonist's head and Clemens had posted $500 bail to get him out of jail. When it began to look as though the blow might have been fatal, Steve quietly returned to Virginia City and Clemens just as quietly took the stage to the Mother Lode for a few months in the seclusion of Calaveras.

The branches of the ponderosas behind the camp hung heavy and white with snow on this December evening. A cold winter moon rode high above

Dead Horse Hill. Outside Angels bar an occasional buckboard went by, its wheels creaking on the packed snow of Main Street. Old-timers recall that their fathers have told them there was a lunar rainbow that night, arching luminous over the foaming waters of the swollen creek.

Inside the bar, thick waves of heat radiated from the black iron stove. Easy banter and the rattle of chips came from the tables where Mike Cosgrove, Phil Scribner, Doc Kelly, Jim Fair, and others sat over their card games. Tobacco smoke and the smell of drying mackinaws filled the air, and the steady light from the kerosene lamps in their wall brackets cast a warm glow over the comfortable room.

As the evening wore pleasantly on, Ross Coon, the droll Angels bartender, was prompted to pass along to the visitor the Mother Lode yarn about Jim Smiley's frog, Dan'l Webster, and how it lost a jumping contest because it had been loaded with a spoonful of quail shot. Clemens threw back his head and laughed, and blew an appreciative cloud of smoke toward the ceiling from his corncob pipe.

A week or two later, Clemens settled himself in his bunk in the cabin on Jackass Hill, and began to write, *There was a feller here once by the name of Jim Smiley, in the winter of '49—or maybe it was the spring of '50 —I don't recollect exactly. . . .*

Printed the next year in the *Saturday Press* of New York, the whimsical story delighted the nation, and Mark Twain, Dan'l Webster, and Angels Camp were famous from coast to coast.

Details that seemingly defied the order and unwritten laws proclaimed by their living environment impressed the people of Angels Camp, as they do the people of small towns everywhere.

Old-timers, sons of the first pioneers and now gray and bent, would sit on the front porch of the Angels Hotel on Main Street in the early 1920s, say, ransacking the almanac of their memory, and recall the year ('83, it was—or was it '81, or '82?) that Sam Gilman found the two white bear cubs in a mill shed. Such a thing had never been heard of before or since south of the Arctic, let alone on the Mother Lode, and the finding of the white bear cubs was an event to remember in the life of Angels Camp.

Not long after that Ike McCauley's hens created a sensation by laying eggs as large as turkey eggs, and for years afterward Angels Campers wherever they went boasted of the hens that laid the largest chicken eggs ever seen on the Mother Lode, from the Stanislaus River north to Auburn.

They would call to mind Old Jerome, the Indian who had been around Angels since anyone could remember. Claimed to be a hundred years old, even in the '80s, Jerome did, and there he was to prove it, sitting in the sun in his tattered coat and dusty black hat and silently gazing, like a Sierra sphinx, at the horizon.

They would remember, too, the December afternoon in '89 when the timbers of the Utica mine shaft cracked apart at the 400-foot level, and the falling tons of earth buried sixteen men of Angels Camp. Even after digging all that night their fathers and brothers hadn't reached the bodies. And only a year later a sharp dry report echoed like a cannon shot all over town and everybody rushed to the head of the Utica's north shaft, where the skip cable had snapped apart and slapped the gallows frame, sending the skip and nine men crashing down the shaft to the sump floor 350 feet below. Nine coffins were carried to the Presbyterian cemetery the next day and the men were laid to rest in the red earth they had known so well.

Years after that (it would have been in January of 1909) a cloudburst hit the hills back of Angels at three o'clock in the morning, and before dawn the surging creek was carrying trees, bushes, fences, and debris right through town, and the rain and hail were coming down in sheets and everyone got out of bed and went outside with a lantern to see what was to be done.

The bridge on the road to Carson went out, and the Chinese in Shanghai City hacked their way through their roofs to escape from their shanties before they were swept away by the crest of the flood. Horses standing knee-deep in their livery-stable stalls neighed with terror and kicked and thrashed as the water rose. By the washed-out bridge a blacksmith shop and a hardware store wrenched loose from their foundations and floated a mile down the stream before it left them stranded in a meadow. At Sequoia Springs a few miles away, where the cloudburst struck, it looked, they said, as if the Almighty had played a gigantic hydraulic monitor against the hillside, cutting a great raw gash in the earth, uprooting trees, and bringing down the hillside boulders in a mighty avalanche.

But within a few days Angels Campers had cleaned up the town and the creek banks, and had scraped the mud from their kitchen and living-room

floors and scrubbed them clean. The stages to Milton and Copperopolis·
and Jenny Lind went through on schedule again. By summer and the time
of still pools and dry white boulders in the creek bed, Angels Campers
were looking up at the hot blue sky, smelling the sere hill grass and wondering how long it would be before it rained again.

The old-timers sitting on the front porch of the Angels Hotel could look
up Main Street to the north end of town and see the great tailing dumps
of the Utica, which with its adjoining claims yielded $17,000,000 in gold be-
fore the veins petered out. They could remember when the hoists for this
mine reached town from San Francisco on freight wagons pulled by forty-
mule teams. They knew the days when the moss-grown foundations near
the now abandoned shafts trembled under the pounding thunder of a sixty-
stamp mill that worked day and night, crushing 180 tons of quartz every
twenty-four hours, month in and month out. They could see the cypress
trees and the ailanthus of little Utica Park, now sunken well below the
street level because of the caving in of the old mine stopes beneath, and
could tell you that they were growing over the site of the hoisting works
and the head of the Utica's north and south shafts, which dropped a sheer
3,000 feet into the earth.

They could look back down long-gone summers and remember the
voices, footsteps, eyes, and hands of their fathers, who rode up the foothill
trails in '49 and who built the stone buildings after the fire of '55. They had
a tiny spoon or a bit of ribbon in a drawer at home that they had saved from
a ball or a wedding in the '80s; in iron-bound attic trunks were the dresses
their mothers wore across the plains. How it happened was all clear in their
minds and memories as they sat on the porch, passing the time of day until
it was time to go home, and to sleep.

The decaying remains of the Utica, and the old-timers themselves, are
in a way temporal monuments to another era in the life of a Mother Lode
town. But there stand two others which proclaim to the tourist, the casual
passer-through, the twin legacy that Angels Camp has felt obliged to
acknowledge in more permanent fashion.

One is the undershot water wheel at the southern end of Main Street,
similar to those turned by the creek in Gold Rush days to operate the
primitive quartz-crushing mills of the Forty-niners; it is said to mark the

spot where Angel made his first gold strike. You find the other in a grassy open space in Utica Park. It is a life-size statue of Mark Twain that represents the author as standing hatless in a knee-length coat, and gazing, now, with intensity, at the blank white wall of the Calaveras Creamery a few yards away. At his feet several large carved frogs are poised in the act of leaping into space. *In memory,* says the lettering on the base, *of Mark Twain, who found inspiration here for his memorable story, "The Celebrated Jumping Frog of Calaveras County." Angels Camp—*1865.

Every May there comes a certain week end on which Angels Campers, with exuberant assistance from the rest of the Mother Lode, rededicate their town and themselves to the traditions of the Gold Rush and the Jumping Frog, and of the two it is clear that it is the frog, with all its absurdity, that has captured their hearts and fancy.

The Forty-niners are by no means forgotten. Above the broad and gently sloping Main Street, on clotheslines strung across from storefront to storefront, hang red flannel underwear, petticoats, cotton dresses, nightshirts, and pillowcases that have been handed down from generation to generation. Still vivid and bright, they flap in the spring breeze that wafts down from Dead Horse Hill, and provide an anachronistic Sunday-in-the-Mines touch that draws an appreciative cackle from the visitors down from the mountain towns for the jubilee.

The sign of the green leaping frog, however, is everywhere—on the business cards of Angels Camp garagemen and real estate salesmen, on official City Hall stationery, on the masthead of State Senator Jesse Mayo's weekly newspaper, the *Calaveras Californian,* which proudly announces that its home town is also "The Home of the Jumping Frog." Small ceramic frogs leer from shop-window displays, larger ones stare blandly at drinkers from the back bars of cafés, and still others are painted on the marquee over the entrance to the Angels Camp City Hall.

The town has been like this on this May week end ever since 1928, when the 2,000 citizens of Angels Camp decided to commemorate the historic Dan'l Webster with an annual Festival of the Frogs and a Jumping Frog Jubilee to determine the world's champion jumping frog. Delighted and intrigued, thousands of Californians from Mother Lode and San Joaquin Valley communities flocked to Angels Camp by buckboard and motorcar to witness the curious sporting event.

One year the enthusiastic attendance gave the late Arthur Brisbane a new bottle for his old wine of misanthropy. *Yesterday,* he wrote, *more than twenty thousand people gathered upon a Calaveras County hillside to watch a jumping frog contest. Last night, a mere two thousand five hundred gathered in Carnegie Hall to hear Albert Einstein lecture on the Theory of Relativity. Which proves that man is far closer to the frog than he is to Einstein.*

Californians did not dispute the statement, and turned out thirty thousand strong for the jubilee the following year.

The jubilee takes place a few miles south of Angels Camp, off the road to Carson Hill, in a shallow valley that was once a part of the old Stickle ranch. On one side of the valley is the slope that is still called Poverty Hill and that is honeycombed with gold-mine shafts that never yielded pay dirt. On the floor of the valley is a half-mile oval track, once used by the Stickle brothers to train and exercise their stable of racing horses. The other hillside that borders the valley rises sharply above the track, and on this are the buildings and pavilions of Frog Town.

Over these 60 acres of State-owned land, the Flag of the Frog flies high. It is a California State flag that has on it the leaping frog instead of the bear, and it flutters from the staff of the tiny headquarters building in open defiance of the State regulation that prohibits the display on State property of any flags but the American and the official California Bear.

(State Senator Mayo, to the candid horror of the Native Sons and Daughters of the Golden West, once introduced a resolution into the State Senate which would have permanently displaced the traditional bear in favor of the leaping frog. *California's bear has been chiefly employed in disturbing prospectors, sacking hen roosts, and frightening women and children, while the frog has greatly enriched the world's literature,* argued the Senator. The resolution was defeated.)

On festival days, the ferris wheel and the carnival thrill rides turn beneath Frog Town's dusty hillside oaks, and the smell of new-mown hay drifts from the meadows to mingle with the reek of frying hot dogs and hamburgers. Visitors, many of them in the brightly checkered shirts and the calico dresses of the pioneers, mill through the carnival grounds or sit on the hillside above the track.

The sun beats down from a cloudless sky. A confused medley of sounds

*The home of the celebrated Jumping Frog of Calaveras County*

provides an accompaniment for the scene—the clink of metal on metal from the horseshoe-pitching pits, the drone of roving planes overhead, the cries of the weight-guessers, the crackerjack venders, and the souvenir peddlers, the shrill wind-tattered screams of 'teen-age girls on the thrill rides, the racket of an exhibition two-stamp ore-crusher that recalls the Gold Rush days.

On a small stage facing the track's home stretch and the spectators, sleek, green, glistening frogs hop across a burlap jumping field for the world's championship and a purse that may mean as much as $1,000 to the winner.

The frogs have come from wherever frogs are found—from water-filled quarries of the Mother Lode, from foothill creeks and meadow ponds, from the muddy banks of the Sacramento, from the irrigation ditches and the rice paddies of the Central Valley. Some have been flown from Florida, Rhode Island, Minnesota, Hawaii, and arrive in strong, straw-lined little crates; but most of them are brought to Frog Town in shoe boxes, Mason jars, burlap sacks, tin cans, and even shirt fronts by hopeful entrants who range from grammar-school youngsters and university students to Mother Lode graybeards with leapers they have plucked from creek pools by the light of last night's moon.

Some one hundred and fifty frogs participate every year. They bear names scaled from the mundane to the fantastic, from just plain Joe and George to Heliotrope, Lana Turner, Sea Biscuit, and Atom Smasher.

Contest rules require that each frog be placed on the jumping field and started by his handler with a slap of the hand or a stamp of the foot on the stage floor. The frog is then allowed three leaps. Its distance from the starting-point at the finish of the third leap is its official jump. (The world's record is 16 feet, 2 inches, set in 1944 by Maggie, owned by Merlin Fisher, a Stockton, California, high-school student.)

Jubilee officials keep a sharp eye out for unorthodox practices. Starting a frog with an electric needle, for instance, is not permitted, nor is the use of stimulants. These never were effective: both adrenalin and benzedrine have been tried, without avail; alcohol, as in many humans, merely promotes in the frog a languor or stupor. Frequently frogs under the influence of alcohol have refused to jump at all.

Other bizarre practices have been noted. One year a schoolboy fed his entry a live bee in the hope that it would electrify the frog into leaps of prodigious length. The frog, however, swallowed the bee, blinked gratefully at the boy and went to sleep in the middle of the jumping field. Another year, the story goes, a frog with a curiously swollen appearance was placed on the stage by its owner, a nervous, cigaret-smoking college student. As the youth bent down to give the boards a starting slap, there was a small explosion, and the frog vanished.

Alarmed officials rushed across the stage. "What happened? Where's the frog?" they exclaimed.

The youth looked sheepish. "Guess he breathed on my cigaret. He was loaded with hydrogen."

But the years of experiment are over; the ways of science are not the ways of the frog, and old-time handlers swear that the frog to back is the frog that is flat-thighed, relaxed, and fresh from its native pool. This is the frog, they say, that will hop its heart out for the glory of Angels Camp and Calaveras County.

The day wears on. The spectators sit with newspapers on their heads to protect themselves from the blazing sun. They drink bottled beer and cokes peddled by the raucous venders that pass through the crowd. The bare shoulders of the bobby-soxed girls in jeans and halters deepen from pink to old rose to lobster red. The public-address system drones the names of the frogs, their owners, and the length of the jumps. It is perhaps five o'clock before the jumping is over and the winner announced. The crowd cheers, rises, and moves down the hillside to the track. News reporters and photographers from half a dozen papers crowd on the stage with the officials and the prize-winners. Holding their frogs aloft in their hands, the winning owners have their pictures taken. The cash awards are distributed. The longest leaper of them all, squirming in its owner's grasp, is lifted high for everyone to see.

"There he is, folks," cries the man at the public-address microphone. "The champion jumping frog of Calaveras County—and the world!"

With the end of the contest finals, the mountain pageant comes to a close for another year. The crowd scatters quickly, the departing cars and wagons throwing up long trails of red dust from the parking area and the road that connects Frog Town with Highway 49 and the road back to

Angels Camp. The carnival people begin the dismantling of their booths and rides, and grounds attendants start the dreary task of collecting the thousands of beer cans and bottles.

By the time the long sunset shadows lie across the valley and the distant slopes of Poverty Hill, Frog Town is deserted.

But up the road in Angels Camp, laughter and the lilt of "Oh, Susanna!" float through the open barroom doors, and with them the stamp of boots and slippers in the lively steps of the quadrille. The neons glow along the street, and on the dark hills east of town the night wind whispers through the pines.

# CHAPTER FOUR

# Murphys

On a drowsy May morning not long ago, Jack Morley, the seventy-seven-year-old town constable of Murphys, and I sat down on a wooden bench outside the iron-shuttered Murphys Hotel and had a talk.

We could sit there, beneath the overhang of the hotel's iron-railinged second-story balcony, and look up and down the main street, quiet and peaceful in the shade of its aged cork elms and locust trees, and see almost all there is left of what was once a boom town of four or five thousand, and one of the richest diggings on the entire Mother Lode.

Across and up the street was the tiny post office, and, on the corner of the road that led to Armory Hill, stood an ancient stone building, now vacant and with its black-and-green iron shutters closed and padlocked. It had been a Gold Rush food and dry-goods store. Down to our left was another stone building, painted white. Over the broad doorway was chiseled, *P.L. Traver—1856*. Jack, who now uses the building for the town garage, said there were 8 inches of sand, for fire protection, between its low ceiling and its metal roof.

If we rose and stepped to the corner of the hotel and looked south across Angels Creek, we could see there, about a hundred yards away, a low hill and a cavity in the earth under the hillside pines. The townspeople of Murphys still call this cavity "the million-dollar hole," because it yielded that much in gold to pick-swinging Forty-niners.

It was a fact, Jack said, that by the end of the first ten years of mining, Wells, Fargo alone shipped $15,000,000 in gold dust out of Murphys. Several more millions at least must have left the camps in the packs and buckskin pokes of lucky prospectors who were bound out of the diggings for the fandango parlors of Sonora, the gaming tables of San Francisco's Portsmouth Square, or even for a boat back home, and who preferred packing the dust themselves to exchanging it for Wells, Fargo cash.

Jack went to Murphys to live in 1893 after a couple of years as a Wells, Fargo shotgun messenger on the Milton-Sonora stage, the run on which, near Copperopolis in 1883, Black Bart committed his twenty-eighth and last holdup. From old-timers who had been there since Gold Rush days, Jack picked up what information he could about the beginnings of Murphys.

For years before the coming of white men, Jack said, the Indians from the foothills and the mountains, and some from the other side of the mountains, gathered annually on the eminence now called Armory Hill. There for many days, in a great roundhouse, they had what Jack called "the big cries," named that because of the wild shrills and whoops that ribboned the mountain silence as they ran their footraces and feasted and danced until they dropped exhausted to the ground.

The two Murphy brothers—they had crossed the plains with their father, Martin Murphy, Sr., in '44, in the first emigrant train to California— were trading with the Indians before James Marshall's discovery of gold, pitching their tents on the flats below Armory Hill during the great pow-wows, and exchanging beads and trinkets for valuable furs and buffalo robes brought to the roundhouse gatherings by the transmountain Indians.

"The squaws," Jack said, "wore buckskin strings around their necks. Tied to the strings were the butt-ends of quills. These quills were filled with yellow dust. The squaws would never part with the dust. They seemed to regard it as a charm."

The Murphys, according to this account (the first that I had ever seen or heard that placed them in the region before 1848), gave the yellow dust little thought until the strike on the American Fork, forty or fifty miles to the north. Then, in one way or another, they obtained a quill and had its contents tested in San Jose. It was, as by then they suspected, gold.

In June of '48, then, they returned to the foothills with Carson, Angel, and the other members of that expedition. After a month or so at the diggings to the north, they went back to the flats below the Indian roundhouse and there, on the banks of Angels Creek, hit a bonanza.

With 150 Indians to work their mining claims and a trading post that sometimes took in as much as $400 in dust in a single day, the Murphy brothers prospered. By 1849, John Murphy, then twenty-five, was said to own more gold dust than any other man in California. Once that year he led into San Jose from the Calaveras diggings a mule all but staggering under 350 pounds of dust.

At the end of '49, their fortunes made, the Murphy brothers packed up and left forever the boom town to which they had given their name. John returned to San Jose to marry Virginia Reed, a survivor of the Donner Party tragedy, and to become San Jose's mayor and for two terms sheriff of Santa Clara County. Daniel acquired vast cattle ranches in the San Joaquin Valley, Nevada, and Mexico. By the time of his death in Elko, Nevada, their acreage was far into the millions.

The town they left behind prospered, too. The news of their strike had brought 2,000 Forty-niners to the flats and the nearby diggings—Owlsburg, north of town; Algiers, south of the flats, where the French prospectors toiled over their Long Toms; Missouri Gulch and Pennsylvania Gulch; French Gulch, two miles to the west; and Skunk's Misery, near the Stanislaus River.

To bring more water to the flats for the washing of their gravel, the men of Murphys organized the Union Water Company, and by the end of 1852 a 15-mile canal of ditches and flumes tapped the Stanislaus in the mountains to the east and carried its waters across the canyons and sometimes even above the treetops to Murphys.

*The sun of Murphys' greatness has but just risen; a short time and she will take the sceptre of the mountain queen,* wrote an observer for the *San Joaquin Republican* two months before the canal's completion.

He credited the lively and busy town with 3,000 inhabitants; more than five hundred frame houses; a hotel in the process of construction that would boast *mattresses and blankets void of fleas;* eight taverns; two restaurants; one express and banking house; one livery stable; blacksmith shops, carpenter shops, bakeries, butcher shops, and markets; two steam sawmills; a cider and sirup factory; a bowling alley; and *dance and drinking houses innumerable.*

There was also, a little way out of town, a limestone-block jail. It is a Murphys legend, Jack Morley said, that the only miscreant ever to spend a night in it was one of the men who helped build it. On the day it was finished, he celebrated its completion so enthusiastically that he was locked up for drunkenness and disorderly conduct.

Three desperadoes, at any rate, managed through no fault of their own to avoid it. Two of them were strangers in Murphys, and confederates in burglary. In the winter of '52 they were captured, tried, and found guilty of robbery by a miners' jury. They were sentenced to death. Before the execution, the younger of the pair was permitted to write a letter. He created, under the circumstances, a masterpiece of restraint which is still preserved at the museum at San Andreas, the Calaveras County seat:

*Murphys Mines, Feb. 11, 1852*

*Dear Friend:*

*I take the opportunity of writing the few lines to you hoping to find you in good health me and Charley is sentenced to be hung today at 5 o'clock for a robbery good by give my best respect to Frank and Sam and Church*

*John Bucroft*

The third badman was Wild Bill Holt, who, somewhat later, would swagger into town on holidays armed with a shotgun and bristling with a portable arsenal of knives, daggers, and pistols.

One day Wild Bill broke loose in a sensational carousal at the height of which he reeled down Main Street emptying his six-gun at all the iron shutters in sight and making them clang like a row of shooting-gallery

targets. That night, as he stood swaying and belligerent in the doorway
of the Murphy's Hotel bar, Jack Morley said, someone else's pistol barked.
Wild Bill clutched his gun, but fell dead with five bullets in him before
he could fire.

"See," Jack said, pointing to the chipped facing of the hotel a foot from
our bench, "that's where one of the bullets missed Bill and hit the building."

The man who ambushed him was a Stanislaus River miner who had
argued with Wild Bill over a claim.

"They scolded him," Jack said, "and let him go. He'd done the town a
favor."

Wild Bill, of course, and the man who stood behind the locust tree between the sidewalk and the road and shot him were gone. Their times
were gone, and so were the miners, and the drivers of the twenty- and
thirty-mule lumber teams that came down the Big Tree road and rolled
to a stop before the barroom door in the years after the mines petered out
and gave way to the lumber mills. So also were the top-hatted actors and
the pretty actresses in their flounced dresses who came up from Angels
on the Wingdam stage to play in *Mazeppa* and *The Dumb Girl of Genoa*
at Judge Putney's Opera House. But the hotel whose hospitable bar they
knew and whose high-ceilinged rooms echoed to their voices was still there
on this May morning, with Maid of Portugal roses climbing its stone walls
to bloom above the second-story balcony, and it embodied those people
and those days in a way that nothing apparent in the town embodied the
present.

Built by James L. Sperry and John Perry, it was opened in 1856 as the
Sperry and Perry Hotel. Three years later a fire started down the street in
the Magnolia Saloon and before it had burned itself out nearly every
building in the business district was in ashes. Sperry and Perry rebuilt,
and were ready again for operation by the following spring.

There was a second fire in 1874 that stopped at the hotel's stone walls
after destroying nearly every other structure on that side of Main Street,
and that night a fantastic scene unfolded before the charred and smoking
ruins.

. . . *It seemed,* wrote one observer, *as though half of the wild Indians of*

*California and the wilder white men, had assembled to celebrate the de-struction of the village in a drunken night carousal.*

The hotel survived still a third fire in 1893 (by now Sperry and Perry had sold out to the Mitchler family, and it was known as the Mitchler Hotel), which got off to a spectacular start when a large quantity of kerosene and blasting powder exploded in a warehouse behind Jack Morley's garage, and blew the warehouse walls and roof to kindling wood. Jack, who was standing in Main Street, saw it go.

"It all lifted up and opened out like an umbrella," he said. As the smoke drifted away, other contents of the warehouse—dry goods, shoes, ribbons, stockings—fell slowly from the sky and came to rest in the branches of the nearby elms, transforming them into midsummer Christmas trees.

The heat from the blaze that followed warped the iron doors and shutters of the hotel, but left it otherwise undamaged and open for business as usual to the tourists who passed through Murphys on their way up the road to the giant sequoia stand of Big Trees, some fifteen miles to the east.

It was these tourists, in fact, who kept the hotel alive all those years after the decline of mining, and through the open door beside our bench was the old hotel barroom with its long mahogany counter, and its Anheuser Busch print of *Custer's Last Fight* behind the cracked glass of a gilt frame, and, on the old-fashioned gaming table, the photostated copies (the originals are in the San Andreas museum) of the last century's registers.

J. Pierpont Morgan and Mrs. Morgan, one of them notes, occupied the parlor suite on the night of August 4, 1869. Mark Twain, registering from Pike County, Mo., was there June 5, 1877, and two days later Horatio Alger, Jr., arrived on the evening stage in time for supper.

There are the signatures of *Italian Dave,* whose residence is listed simply as *Mountains,* and, farther down, of *U. S. Grant, Washington.* The next month, beneath the Sperry and Perry roof, slept an amiable and mild little man who signed himself in as *Carlos E. Bolton, Silver Mountain.* Not for another three years would he be unmasked as Black Bart, the stage bandit.

On April 10, 1880, the hotel was host to *Old Dan the Guide* from *God Knows Where,* and in the next September to Thomas J. Lipton of Glasgow, Scotland; and so the names go through the catalogue of mountain wanderers and world travelers who sought the warming fires, the bracing drinks,

*Dance-and-drinking houses innumerable*

the substantial food, and the rest to be found within the sturdy walls of
the Gold Rush inn.

The quiet shade of the old town, the space of green meadows between
the small white houses, the deserted stone buildings, the slow and deliberate
pace of the town's life, expressed in the silence of three old men sitting on
the post-office bench in the hot forenoon, in the stopping of housewives,
bound for the grocery store with shopping baskets on their arms, to gossip
beside a vacant lot on the main street, in the languor of a black-and-white
dog asleep in the dust beside the watering trough, in the slow and distant
clip-clop of a horse's hoofs receding down a road that is out of sight beyond the meadow—these that morning combined to wrap the village in
a peaceful, faraway mood, as still, as indifferent to the passing hours as a
stopped clock.

Jack, leaning forward, one forearm on his crossed knees, began to talk
about Joaquin Murieta and about the later days when he, Jack, had been a
shotgun messenger. There was nothing about Jack to suggest even faintly
the swaggering messengers of the tales of Bret Harte—no jeans, no boots,
no sombrero, no bright shirt, no picturesque frontier oaths, but instead a
slender, wiry, white-haired man of medium height wearing a blue serge suit,
a felt hat, a white shirt, and a tie with a stickpin. His voice was mild and
gentle, and there was so much of the past in the things he kept saying that
hearing him talk was like looking at the illustrations in an old book on the
Wild West.

On the Mother Lode scarcely a flat, gulch, hill, or town exists that does
not claim some association with the fabulous Joaquin. From Weaverville
in the north to Mariposa in the south, you can find at foothill crossroads
and villages signs proclaiming that Murieta once hid in a cellar here; here
he stole some horses; here he and his bloodthirsty outlaws hanged six
Chinese miners by their queues and then slit their throats; here he joined
a group of citizens who were boasting of what they would do to him if they
caught him, and suddenly, to their consternation and terror, stripped off
a false beard, cried, "I am Joaquin!" and then leaped on his bay horse and
galloped away, his mocking laugh ringing in the ears of the now pale and
quaking braggarts.

Murphys is one of the several communities in which it is said that Joaquin, embittered by the lynching of his half brother, swore vengeance against the Americans and launched his career as a highway robber and cutthroat. Jack believed Murphys was the place.

"When I came here in 1893," he said, "there was a man here named Joe Enos, a Portugee, who had been here since '51. He told me he knew Murieta and his brother and his brother's wife. The brother's name was José, and the wife's name was Rosie.

"José had a stolen horse. He claimed he had bought it, but the fellow he said he bought it from was in the valley or someplace else at the time, and so he could not prove it, and they hung him not far out of town. That was the reason Joaquin became a badman."

I asked Jack if he remembered any more of what Enos had told him about Joaquin.

"Joaquin was a gambler—used to play cards in the saloons and in a place that used to be up the road here, called 'The Blue Tent.' He played mostly three-card monte. As to what he looked like, Enos used to say, 'Joaquin was a regular dandy. Always wore fancy clothes, and a bright-colored neckerchief.'

"There was a story Enos used to tell on Joaquin—Joaquin couldn't have been around here very long, because he was killed in '53, two years, they say, after José was lynched—it was the story of Joaquin and the Mexican barber.

"Joaquin used to walk into a barbershop and say, 'I want a shave. I will pay you a dollar for the shave, but if you cut me I will kill you.' On these terms, none of the barbers in Murphys would shave him, except this little Mexican. His friends told him he was foolish. 'Joaquin means what he says,' they told him. 'If you cut him, he will kill you. Surely, your life is worth more than a dollar.'

"The little Mexican picked up his razor and ran his thumb along the sharp blade and gave them a big grin. 'I do not take chances,' he said. 'If I ever cut Joaquin, Joaquin will never get up out of the chair. I will give him one more cut—and he will be a very dead Joaquin.'"

"And that," Jack concluded, "was the only barber in Murphys who had the nerve to shave Joaquin."

A shotgun messenger was an employee of Wells, Fargo who rode on a stagecoach and was entrusted with the responsibility of guarding and delivering Wells, Fargo shipments of gold or money. He was called a shotgun messenger because he was always armed with a shotgun. He was supposed to use it only if absolutely necessary, on highwaymen or bandits who held up the stage.

Jack, one of the last survivors of his profession, was a messenger during the years 1889–1890, when he was eighteen and nineteen years old. He was on the Milton-Sonora run, which was about fifty miles long over an almost wilderness stagecoach trail through the foothill country. He traveled on a Priest six-horse stage from Milton to Copperopolis, then changed to a stage operated by John Shine for the run from Copper' through Columbia to Sonora. The stage would leave Milton at noon, travel the sixteen miles to Copper', and there stop overnight. The next day it would proceed to Sonora.

I asked Jack how Wells, Fargo selected its shotgun messengers. He replied that he didn't know about the others, but as far as he was concerned they just came to him and offered him the position.

"I told them I didn't want it; I was too young. But they kept after me, and finally I said I'd take it. The agent asked me, 'If a robber held up the stage, what would you do?' I said I didn't know what I'd do: I was never in that particular situation.

"'What!' he said. 'You mean you wouldn't protect Wells, Fargo's treasure?' And then I said, 'If any passengers were aboard, I wouldn't shoot. Wouldn't want any shooting going on; somebody might get hurt.' Well, I thought they wouldn't hire me, but he said, 'You gave exactly the right answers. You're hired. That's what Wells, Fargo wants—no danger to the passengers.' "

A man drove slowly down the shady street in an ancient touring car. Jack waved to him as he went by. "Hello, Charley," he called. The man waved back.

"I had my nineteenth birthday just after I went to work," Jack continued. "I had a shotgun—a Colt ten-guage with a sawed-off barrel—and a Colt forty-five. The shotgun shells were specially made for Wells, Fargo—brass, loaded with seven and a half drams of rifle powder and sixteen buckshot. On the stages there were two Wells, Fargo boxes, one a wooden one about 18 by 12 by 10, locked with a brass padlock, and another one, an iron box riveted to the stage frame. . . . But I was never held up, never had to fire a shot to protect them.

"The closest I ever came to it was this: One day we left Sonora at 5 A.M. It was dark. Flickering lights came from the coach lamps, one on each side of the stage with a candle in it and a reflector that threw the beam a little ways in front of the stage; but that morning they didn't travel very far because it was raining a little. I was sitting outside, up by Tom, the driver, with my shotgun ready in case we ran into trouble.

"As you left Sonora you came to a long hill, and the horses were laboring up that hill when we reached a large oak tree beside the road. Just before we came abreast of it, a man stepped from behind the tree and hollered, 'Hold up!'

"There'd be no danger to the passengers here; he was only a few yards away and I couldn't miss him. I raised my gun to let him have it. But just then, the lead horses became frightened and threw up their heads between me and the man. The man spoke. 'Hold on, Tom, and let me on that stage. I want to ride to Milton with you.' "

Jack cleared his throat and shook his head. "That fellow should have bought those horses and turned 'em out to pasture for the rest of their lives. If it hadn't been for them, he'd have taken sixteen buckshot right above the belt."

He showed me a photograph he carried in an envelope. It had been taken not long before, he said, by a short-story writer who wanted some information on Black Bart, the stagecoach bandit who terrorized the foothills in the late 1870s and early 1880s. The picture showed the trunk of a large pine tree, and, in the distance, a fence behind which, Jack said, now runs a dirt road. In the foreground was an expanse of field crossed by two faint ruts; these were what was left of the Milton-Sonora stagecoach trail. In the center of the trail near the pine tree crouched Jack, driving into the ground an iron pipe to mark the scene of Black Bart's last holdup. This point, near Funk Hill outside Copperopolis, was where Black Bart had held up the stage, had been frightened away, and, in fleeing, had dropped the handkerchief bearing the San Francisco laundry mark that led to his identification and capture.

"I knew where the spot was," Jack said, "because I used to drive the rig for Thacker and Hume, the Wells, Fargo detectives, when they came up here to investigate robberies. They pointed it out to me many times. Now, only one other man alive could have marked the spot—Charlie Fontana, who lives in Stockton and used to run a store in Copper'."

Tenderly, and with great care, he put the photograph back in the envelope, and returned the envelope to his pocket. As he did so, I could not help thinking that some day someone will find this picture in a box, in an attic trunk, perhaps, and wonder where and when it was taken, and who the man is in it, and speculate on the significance of the pipe he is driving into the ground beside the tree. He will try to decipher its meaning. "A pine tree, a fence, a field, and an old man with a pipe in the ground," he will muse. "It must have been important once. It must mean something," he will say, "but what . . . ?"

Jack gazed down the road. "Yes," he said, "that was the policy. One time Will Hendricks was the messenger on one of the stages around here. The stage left Murphys one morning and got to Angels all right, and then, six miles past Angels, Hendricks, from where he was sitting inside the coach, saw a man crawling under some live oaks beside the road. He stuck his shotgun out the coach window and shot him. But there was a second bandit on the other side of the road, behind a pine tree. He fired right into the stage, which had fourteen passengers on it, and a man named Holmes, who used to live right over there"—with a nod Jack indicated the other side of the street—"was hurt bad. His daughter, who was sitting beside him, lost an eye. And Wells, Fargo never hired Hendricks again."

Jack pushed his hat back on his forehead and leaned back against the stone wall of the hotel that began as the Sperry and Perry, became the Mitchler, and is now known as the Murphys Hotel. He looked out across the street and up the lane that led to a tall cedar tree and the white Congregational Church at the foot of Armory Hill. The thin hands that many years ago had carried a loaded shotgun over the stagecoach trails lay folded in his lap.

For a long time we were silent. Up the street, the three old men dozed in the sun. A bird sang in a nearby tree. Pretty soon the faint rhythmic sound of horse's hoofs came once more from the road beyond the meadow. The horse was walking slowly, pulling, probably, a wagon, or a buckboard.

Jack and I looked across the still, shady street, across the sun-bright meadow, and waited for it to come around the bend.

# CHAPTER FIVE

# Columbia

A NUMBER OF years ago Columbia was a Mother Lode ghost town of strange and brooding charm. It was, as it is today, two miles along the winding Columbia Road from Highway 49, and to travel them was to forsake people, traffic, and roadside filling stations for a deserted village that sat in the foothills a century away from everywhere, like a still life of the past.

As you reached the road's end, you came to a short, broad, main street shaded by tall locust trees. On each side of the street were one- and two-story buildings of faded brick. Some bore weathered signs—"Wells, Fargo, Express," "Bank," and "Stage Drivers' Retreat." But there was no one on the street, or on the short side streets. There was no one in the buildings.

You saw the ivy shining in the sun, where it climbed the wall of a ruin. You saw a crested jay break from an iron-grilled balcony and fly away.

On a hillside beyond one end of the street stood a gaunt brick school-house; beside it was a cemetery with rusty iron gates and gray, mottled stones. Not far away, on the bare summit of another hill and stark against the sky, was a brick church with Gothic windows.

As you stood there in the trancelike stillness, you had the feeling that you were being watched by a hundred invisible eyes.

There could be few places in all the world where the presence of the unseen was more palpable, where you knew more surely that reality lay not in what you saw, but rather in something all around you in the air, in the shadows at the street's end, behind the closed doors and staring windows.

The place was utterly yours, yet all things in it silently collaborated to name you a trespasser. You were in a realm in which you did not belong, a realm alone and apart, where life was the creeping of the ivy up the ruin wall, where time was measured by the fall of a decayed limb from a decaying tree, by the loosening and crash of a windowpane in a house that had been abandoned seventy years ago.

Later, looking back, it was difficult to recall the details. They grew blurred and hazy, until you half believed that you had been there in a dream, or that you had never been there at all. . . .

Carson Hill, Jimtown, Slumgullion Gulch, Sonora, Angels, Murphys, and other camps of the Mother Lode's Southern Mines were wide open and in full swing in March of 1850, when the site of Columbia was a glade of stately oaks, clear springs, and green grass, covered with a bright expanse of wildflowers.

There are two versions of how it came about that gold was discovered in the red earth and bedrock of Calaveras limestone which lay beneath the sloping terrain of this natural park. One is that it was found by Mexicans camped on Santiago Hill, a mile to the northwest. They mentioned their discovery to a group of prospectors that included Dr. Thaddeus Hildreth, his brother George, William Jones, John Walker, and Alexander Carson. Proceeding no farther, this party pitched camp, tried its luck and made a strike before dark. After a few days of digging they left temporarily to obtain more supplies, and returned to settle down in earnest. They named the place Hildreth's Diggings in honor of Doctor Hildreth, who came from the state of Maine.

The other story is that Doctor Hildreth's party camped one night beneath an oak tree standing in what is now the line of Columbia's Main

Street. A heavy rain fell during the night. The next day, while waiting for their blankets to dry, John Walker went prospecting. He found color in a gulch leading to the height now known as Kennebec Hill. Encouraged, the others joined him in the search and that day recovered an ounce of dust. The ounce persuaded them to remain there and pan, and, according to this story too, they called it Hildreth's Diggings. Subsequently the name was changed to American Camp and finally, in 1851, to Columbia. The accounts agree as to the date of the discovery: March 27, 1850.

The next day, hacking at the grass roots with knives and picks, they took 15 pounds of gold from the diggings, and the day after that another 15 pounds. News of the incredible bonanza spread to Sonora, a few miles to the south. From Sonora it traveled swiftly up and down the Lode and into the valleys. Within a week, miners by the thousand swarmed into the gulches that bordered the oaken glade. Additional thousands were on their way from valley hamlets and coastal cities. They were the wanderers and the misfits, the strong and the weak, the handful of saints and the army of sinners who had crossed the plains and doubled the Horn for California gold, and if it was beneath a field of wildflowers near a hill called Kennebec, that was where they were headed. That was the reason why they had said good-by to Ohio and Kentucky, New York and Rhode Island and Georgia. All through those soft spring nights their campfires twinkled along the valley trails that led to the foothills, and within a month 5,000 of them, they say, had pitched their tents where Hildreth made his strike, and the biggest, richest, wildest boom town of them all sprawled across these fair poppied meadows of El Dorado.

A winter passed and spring came again, and it was still growing, growing so rapidly, declared the *Sonora Herald,* it seemed *touched by a magic wand*. Strung along Main Street were forty saloons and gambling halls whose faro banks represented a combined capital of $2,000,000. There were seventeen general stores, eight hotels, three churches, three theaters, two fire companies, and four banks, one of which—the Gold Dust Exchange —was establishing an enduring foundation for the fortune of Darius Ogden Mills.

Daily into town thundered the riders of the Chain Lightning Express with fast mail and East Coast newspapers. Two companies operated eight stages a day between Columbia and Sonora, and all day long, above the uproar of the saloons and fandango houses, rose the jangle of freight bells from the white-topped wagons arriving with merchandise and supplies from the river ports of the San Joaquin Valley.

Miners whose six-shooters and bowie knives were as standard a feature of their equipment as their red shirts and rockers were making tall strikes at Saw Mill Flat, Gold Spring, and Yankee Hill on the outskirts of town, and from Columbia Gulch and Kennebec Gulch they were taking out twenty dollars apiece in pay dirt every day. Up and down the foothills they began calling Columbia the Gem of the Southern Mines.

With desperation and abandon they matched the prodigality of the Mother Lode with excesses of their own.

At Col. Thomas N. Cazeneau's Exchange, the town's first theater—unique in the foothills because a pine sapling grew through the stage floor—they roared themselves hoarse and sent buckskin pokes of gold dust and a rain of silver dollars across the candle footlights in tribute to the soaring soprano voice of Elisa Biscaccianti and the artistry of Catherine Sinclair, Alicia Mandeville, the Chapmans, Edwin Booth, and other players barnstorming the mines after their San Francisco triumphs.

On Sunday afternoons they flocked by the thousand to the ring outside of town for the weekly bull-and-bear fight. (It is said that it was from Horace Greeley's description of one of these contests at Columbia that Wall Street adopted the terms "bull" and "bear" for its own peculiar use.) When the fight was over they streamed back to Main Street for hurdygurdy house jigs and polkas, for French monte and lump-o'-gold poker in the gambling tents, and for their heart's content of scorching forty-rod.

In 1854, the year that Peter Ferguson opened "the largest and finest saloon east of San Francisco" at Main and Fulton Streets, next door to the Jenny Lind Restaurant, a correspondent signing himself " '51-er" wrote from Columbia to San Francisco's *Daily Alta California:*

*Drunken men were to be seen at noonday, as well as at midnight, making night and day hideous with their bacchanalian yells and pistol shots, many so beastly drunk that they make the sidewalks or the gutter their bed to sleep off the effects of the indulgence with King Alcohol.*

But there was a more sober element in the camp that was swift to administer frontier justice when it seemed called for. It seemed called for,

for example, one day when Big Annie, hefty overseer of a back street fandango parlor, lurched out of a saloon, bumped into the town schoolmistress, and forced her off the sidewalk. As the schoolmistress primly lifted her skirt clear of the dust, Big Annie slapped her plump thigh and whooped. "Who'd 'a thought it!" she cried. "The angel walks on two legs, just like Annie!"

That night the boys of Fire Engine Company No. 2 decided that Big Annie couldn't get away with it. Dropping their buffalo-hide engine hoses into the State Street cistern and furiously manning the hand pumps, they turned the stream into Big Annie's parlor, washed her out of bed and into the middle of the street, and thence out of Columbia.

They approached more drastic action one Monday in November, 1853, and this occasion indirectly brought to light Columbia's now legendary bid for State capitaldom. (Although it was never submitted to the ballot and although you can find at least one authority who declares it to have been a tongue-in-cheek bid and from nearby Pine Log Crossing at that, Columbia is still popularly referred to as "the town that came within two votes of being the capital of California.")

On this November Monday, at the end of a prolonged spree, Peter Nicholas of Saw Mill Flat picked a quarrel with John Parrot of Pine Log in a Columbia store and fatally stabbed Parrot with a bowie knife. Several hundred grim-faced miners seized Nicholas, took him to a gulch behind the Broadway Hotel, and were about to hoist him to eternity when the limb supporting the rope broke off and crashed to the ground.

They then carried Nicholas to Gold Hill a few hundred yards away and proceeded to try again. Before they could hang him, however, a group of citizens headed by James Coffroth argued for cooler measures. In the tumult that followed this move, Sheriff Perrin L. Solomon and his men charged through the mob, picked up the manacled Nicholas, and dashed away with him to Sonora. A few days later, Parrot died. Nicholas was convicted of murder, and sentenced to death.

While he awaited execution, his lawyer, Horace Bull, stole a petition which was about to be forwarded to the State Legislature, then in assembly at Benicia. The petition, whether drafted seriously or in fun, sought the establishment of the State capital at Columbia (or Pine Log, if your authority is Bancroft's *Popular Tribunals*). It bore 10,000 signatures. From the document Bull scissored the State capital petition, and substituted, over the names, a petition of his own—a plea for commutation of his client's death sentence. This plea he sent to Governor John Bigler. Impressed by the 10,000 signatures, Bigler hastily and without investigation reduced Nicholas' sentence from death to ten years in San Quentin.

Nicholas served four years and was then set free. He long outlived the attorney who had so ingeniously rescued him from the noose. The trick had been too bold and involved too many for it to remain a secret; and when Bull's ruse stood revealed, it was too late for the governor to withdraw his ruling. Everywhere Bull went, the Mother Lode miners heaped upon him scorn and bitter abuse. Bull stood it as long as he could, and then committed suicide.

In New England, you had a stream or a river, and on the stream or river you had a mill or factory, and around the mill or factory you had a town. The town was put there to stay, and the people settled there to stay—as long as the stream or river turned the wheels of the mill, which would undoubtedly be a long time. The life there would flow like the water that slid smoothly past the town, turning where the riverbanks turned, moving always toward the invisible destination that waited for it beyond the far green pastures; or, it would be like the tireless wheels or spindles of the mill: they accomplished so much yesterday, they would accomplish precisely so much today and, at the end of the day's work, they would stand ready to accomplish the same even task tomorrow, the next day, the next month, the next year.

Many of the men who went to California for gold were in reality rebelling against or breaking free from that slow rhythmic round of days and years, whether it was represented by the even turning of a mill wheel above a stream, or by the spring planting, the summer growth, the autumn reaping, the winter torpor of their farms in New Hampshire or Missouri. It was a drab life, they thought, and they longed for a quicker, bolder tempo. Gold was a better excuse than most. So they kissed their wives good-by, and headed for El Dorado.

It was inevitable that the communities they founded in the foothills

should express their expansiveness at their own liberation, their recklessness
—and, at the same time, their inner awareness of the essentially worldly
and impermanent nature of their mission.

A town materialized overnight because of the presence on its site of an
ounce of dust. Nobody was going to stay there forever; nobody was going
to stay there any longer than the gold dust lasted. And so these were tran-
sient, temporary towns whose ultimate desolation lay in the very activity
that gave them life. From the moment they began only the passage of
their numbered days stood between them and the tearing down of their
buildings for the gold dust beneath their foundations or in the very bricks
which had formed the walls of those buildings. Their existence was like
that of a fire, which, to survive, must consume the materials essential to its
life.

They say that in '55 and '56, when Columbia was riding the crest of its
golden wave, its sons boasted that San Francisco was the first city in
California, and their town was the second.

They claimed a population of from 15,000 to 30,000; and a Methodist
minister from nearby Sonora observed that in the broad and dusty streets
of Columbia *10,000 miners lounged, ate, drank, gambled and fought every
Lord's Day.*

To this brawling turmoil you can surely add the commotion of the arriving and departing stages; the clamor of the freight crews as they drove
their wagons into town from Stanislaus City, sending the red dust billowing across the gulches and ravines; the blare of music from half a hundred
gambling halls and fandango houses, and the shouts of the revelers; the
long chant of Auctioneer John Leary hawking Dresden figurines, Floren-
tine mirrors, and Irish linens from the front steps of J. H. Clark's Hotel;
and, as evening fell, the languid melody of a Spanish waltz drifting from
the open windows of Charlie Cardinell's Terpsichore Hall, and the stirring
concert music of Professor Harris's thirty-two-piece brass band, which
Columbians vowed was the greatest brass band in all California, if not in
all the world.

Amid the throng, shouldering through the confusion and the tumult,
strode some of the town's most sedate citizens: Conrad Gischel, whose
Boston Bakery made the delectable Jenny Lind crackers; Henry Dose,

the town's first soap manufacturer; Antone Bixel, the first brewer, and young Jim Coffroth, whose brilliant oratorical gifts had already won for him uncontested eminence as "the life and soul of Columbia."

And along the same streets and through the same crowds swaggered such Gold Rush toughs and criminals as Tim Kelly, whose lilting Irish tenor wrung the hearts of the boys in Jones's Corner Saloon; Billy Mulligan, the prize-fight promoter and petty crook who would one day barricade himself in San Francisco's Hotel St. Francis to shoot it out with police and die on his hotel room floor with a bullet in his head; Yankee Sullivan, one of Mulligan's fighters, who would cut his throat in his Fort Gunnybags jail cell in Sacramento Street, San Francisco, rather than face vigilante justice; Chris Lilley, another of Mulligan's boys, at whose shady resort in outer Mission Street William Walker—"the gray-eyed man of destiny"—and others met San Francisco dawns on the field of honor with dueling pistols in their hands.

Back in '54—and so swiftly did life move that the two years seemed to some a lifetime—a $500,000 fire had all but leveled Columbia's business district. But thirty new buildings were up and fit for occupancy before the setting of the next day's sun. Now the town, though just as flimsy and tindery as it had ever been, was an even bigger, more prosperous settlement. "The richest, rip-roaringest mining camp in the world," was what they were calling it from San Diego to the Siskiyous, and nobody in or out of California disagreed with what they said.

Gold dust streamed onto the high counter scales of the Wells, Fargo office at the rate of $100,000 worth a week. While most of it came from the pans and riffle boxes of miners who were making a steady ten to twenty dollars a day, some was virgin gold struck in pocket mines that would have justified a dozen rainbows.

In the spring of '53, for example, on the Knapp ranch east of town, prospectors had taken out some of the largest nuggets ever found in Tuolumne County, and before they were through 40 acres of this ranchland had yielded $40,000 each.

In that same summer a guitar-playing entertainer in Columbia's hurdy-gurdy houses was John A. Stone, composer of the Gold Rush song "Hangtown Gals" and author of the collection of early California songs known as *Put's Golden Songster*. One day Stone hit a pocket mine and from it dug a piece of quartz weighing 722 pounds. The gold it held brought him $15,-000. Stone, bound for brighter lights and broader streets, left for San Francisco on the same stage that was carrying his gold to the San Francisco Mint. A few years later, his money squandered, he was playing his guitar for drinks in the saloons of the Northern Mines. Eventually, alone and despondent, he committed suicide in his log cabin at Greenwood, El Dorado County.

Two years after Stone made his strike, Charles Jarvis discovered a 132-pound nugget in Columbia's Poverty Gulch. It was worth $28,000. For a year Jarvis lived the life of a pauper turned millionaire, and then was shot and killed in a barroom brawl.

All in all, '55 was quite a year for the Gem of the Southern Mines, even without the finding of the Jarvis nugget. Two other things happened which, civically speaking, ranked in importance with the great fire of the year before, and made it stand out in the memory of old-timers long after they had forgotten Stone, Jarvis, and the hosing-down of Big Annie.

The first of these took place that March, and the background of it was that Columbia, like many of the other diggings, had the gold dust but not the water necessary to separate it from the dirt and clay. Nearly every one of the 5,000 Forty-niners who had rushed to the scene of Hildreth's strike five years before had been forced to pack the earth into sacks, carry it to streams, and there wash it in their cradles. It was slow, laborious work, and wildly frustrating to the prospectors. That there was not enough water (or whisky) even for drinking purposes, let alone for panning or sluicing, is implied in the fact that one Charles Bassett disposed of large quantities of milk, peddling it through the tent and shanty settlement at "one dollar a whisky bottle full."

Soon, however, water was successfully brought from nearby Matelot Gulch in wooden pipes primitively made of pine poles through which holes had been augered lengthwise. They were bound together end to end by iron bands. By 1852, the Tuolumne Water Company was bringing water to Columbia from Five Mile Creek, but its rates instantly precipitated a bitter struggle.

For three years the miners endured the company's charges, and then, when it rejected their petition for a rate reduction, decided that they had

*The commotion of the arriving and departing stages*

had enough. Not only would they get along without the Tuolumne Water Company, they would pitch in and construct 44 miles of canals and flumes for the rival Columbia and Stanislaus River Water Company, which had promised them Stanislaus water at half the Tuolumne Company's price when and if the project was completed.

The swift capitulation of Tuolumne Water to their demands failed to impress them, and 200 Columbian volunteers, supplied with their own tools and provisions, broke ground for the Miners' Ditch on March 19, 1855, amid a spectacular display of community fervor and approval. Sonora and other neighboring settlements sympathetic to the cause sent delegations to Columbia to cheer as the diggers swung the first pick. From one end of Washington Street to the other plank-and-sawhorse tables sagged beneath free food and whisky for the heroes, and the town itself was wide open to all who cared to come and help with the celebrating. Restaurants, hotels, and saloons—from the wildest groggery to Ferguson's crystal and mahogany palace—flung open their doors and, according to one account, proceeded happily to *serve whoever might enter without money and without price.*

Defiance and enthusiasm were in the bracing Columbia air that spring day, and it was a day that Columbians told their grandchildren about in the years that followed, long after the gold dust was gone and the flumes had decayed away.

They would be a little less ready to recall the second event of civic importance that they wrote into the annals of '55, for it betrayed the undercurrents of violence and brutality that flowed beneath the surface of mining-camp life—violence and brutality that in turn revealed the tragic desperation of men who had bartered their trust and belief in law—any kind of law, eternal or temporal—for the promissory notes of Chance.

Not all Columbians had a hand in the matter; only a small percentage of the citizens, in fact, were involved, but out of it these few managed to create an epic of savagery. More than once in the preceding five years the mob had seethed down Broadway hell-bent for the high Gold Spring flume, in their grasp a screaming victim and a long rope to hang him with. Things had, in a general way, gone smoothly enough: this time, when they hanged John Barclay, the gambler, it was different.

On a chilly October evening in that year, John Huron Smith, a miner from Nickerbocker Flat, accidentally broke a pitcher in Martha's Saloon, which stood on the corner of Main and Jackson Streets. Martha, Barclay's wife and the proprietress of the tavern, turned on Smith in a fury. Smith laughed, and pushed Martha into a chair. At that moment Barclay broke through the swinging doors with six-shooters blazing and shot Smith dead. Barclay was arrested immediately and locked in jail.

A short while later, a yelling crowd of several hundred smashed its way through the jail doors with crowbars and axes, seized Barclay, and rushed him to the flume. A kangaroo court in session less than five minutes convicted Barclay of murder and sentenced him to death. When Sheriff Stewart attempted to rescue the prisoner, he was clubbed with a pistol butt and dragged away.

As a triumphal bonfire cast a lurid glow over the scene, a dozen men scaled the flume's trestle and from its highest point lowered a rope. It was made fast about Barclay's neck. Howling, the men on the flume pulled him 40 feet above the heads of the milling throng on the ground. The hangmen had failed to bind his arms, and Barclay grasped the rope above his head and clung to it to keep from strangling. The men on the flume tried to jar loose his grip by raising Barclay and dropping him. One of them leaned down from the flume and cried, "Let go, you damned fool! Let go!" At last Barclay's grasp weakened. His arms fell to his sides, his body hung limp at the rope's end.

*For an instant,* said an eyewitness, *an awful calm fell upon the mob; they seemed to realize the full extent of their horrible work, and men spoke in whispers as they gazed upward at the shape dangling between heaven and earth. Then the reaction came; the swinging body lost its interest, and the hoarse yells broke forth once more.*

They streamed back to Martha's Saloon and stoned all its windows. Then they capered drunkenly in the streets. Shortly after midnight, they reeled down the dark alleys and disappeared.

Out by the Gold Spring flume the bonfire burned low and Barclay's body swung gently in the soft night breeze, and all was quiet in Columbia.

By the next year Columbia was already in the late summer of its best life. Many of the itinerant miners had left for the scenes of later strikes. The lights in the gaming tents and fandango houses blazed not quite so brightly, and more and more of the town's leading citizens were joining the Sons of Temperance. Flouncing their red skirts saucily, the hurdy-gurdy girls boarded the stages for Frisco's Portsmouth Square, where a girl with a figure still had a future and the used-up men were few and far between.

The editor of the *Weekly Columbian* dipped his quill pen in his inkpot and started an editorial on the state of affairs in the Gem of the Southern Mines. It developed into an essay on serenity.

*. . . In truth, Columbia now presents as many attractive features as any mining town to be met with in the mines, either north or south. It is located in a valley, with ground in abundance not only for business lots but for family residences; and right well have some of these business lots been improved; neat residences have been erected; the gardens, horticultural and vegetable, in several, the peach, pear and apple tree may be seen growing very finely. . . .*

*The population of Columbia is estimated in the Tuolumne County directory, from which we draw most of our statistics, at about five thousand, including two hundred families. But we should think it an over-estimate. The town itself, cannot, in our estimation, number over twenty-five hundred to three thousand. It contains probably over one hundred businesses, houses, shops, saloons, stables, etc., and among them may be seen over thirty brick fireproof stores.*

*The first church organization was by the Methodists; they were soon followed by the Presbyterians, and both denominations now are in possession of comfortable houses of worship. In addition to the other churches, we may name the Catholic as numbering the most communicants, and they are erecting a large and imposing brick church on an eminence a short distance south of town. It is seventy feet by sixty on the ground, and the walls were up a month since.*

*The diggings around Columbia are deep, and from appearances, one would judge cannot be exhausted for years. Claims have been worked for years, and pay equally as rich now as when first opened. Some of them in Columbia Gulch have been sunk sixty and seventy feet without reaching bedrock, the dirt paying all the way down, and how much lower it will pay is not known.*

So the tempo was changing. It was no longer how many saloons and faro houses the town could boast, but how many churches, and most of the town,

Catholic or not, trooped proudly up Kennebec Hill the first Sunday in that November to hear Archbishop Joseph Sadoc Alemany himself, from San Francisco, dedicate to St. Anne the little brick church that looked out over the valley.

To them St. Anne's was (and it is today) a symbol of foothill faith and foothill unity. Three miners donated their claims for its site, and the gold dust of miners paid for the bricks that came from the kiln down by Sonora, for the timbers that came from Saw Mill Flat 2 miles out of town, for the mellow-toned $1,500 bell that came around the Horn from New York, for the altar paintings that had been done with great and loving care by James Fallon, whose father ran the Fallon Hotel, hard by Columbia Gulch.

The bell was scarcely hung in the newly completed belfry the next year, 1857, when, one hot August afternoon, it pealed ominously over the town. Sensing disaster, miners dropped their picks and pans, deserted their claims, and sprinted across the meadows. Even as the men reached Main Street, flames broke through the roof of a Chinese laundry. They twisted, flickered higher, bent before a freshening breeze, scorched the wooden wall of the warehouse next door.

Moments later, the hand-drawn pumpers of the town's two fire companies, Young America and Columbia No. 2, went into action. Cheers rose above the rhythmic clanking of the pumps as two heavy streams from the buffalo-hide hoses poured into the billowing smoke. Suddenly the streams grew weaker and fell back toward the nozzles.

"Man the pumps! Faster! Faster!" yelled the hosemen.

The toiling sweating men at the pumps quickened the beat. But already they knew it was useless: in the cisterns, midsummer-dry, the hoses were sucking half air, half water. Soon no more than a trickle flowed from the nozzles. The flames swept on.

All that night the fire blazed high. About midnight it reached a hardware store. Forty kegs of blasting powder tore loose in a mighty explosion that killed five men and sent blazing timbers high into the night sky. One after another, the interiors of sixteen brick homes, believed to be fireproof, went up in flames and, as they burned out, collapsed in rubble and ruins.

Although they fought it for nearly forty-eight hours with water transported by bucket brigades from the mining ditches, and even with barreled vinegar, the fire at length subsided only because there was nothing else to burn. Columbia's business district, worth $700,000, lay charred and smoking on the ground.

*Our people are gloomy and sad; all is confusion,* a Columbian wired the *Daily Alta California* in San Francisco. *Thousands are coming in from the adjoining camps, who deeply sympathize with us in the loss of life and property. . . . The families are being provided for by the people of the adjacent towns. Three thousand men, women and children have not had a morsel of food since yesterday. Thank God, they will be provided for in a few hours.*

But with that rebounding spirit that has always been Californians' reply to catastrophe, they set about rebuilding their town for the second time in three years. Fifty new frame houses were under construction in less than a month. New brick buildings went up along the main streets with heavier iron doors and shutters, thicker walls, and more thoroughly fireproofed roofing than before.

*The new brick buildings in their gradual rise,* reported the *Columbia Gazette* late in September, *are a distinctive and ornamental feature of Main Street. Washington Street and the lower part of Broadway are rapidly resuming their former appearance only with new and improved costume. State Street, between Main and Broadway, will be more improved by an additional number of buildings than any part of the town destroyed by fire. . . .*

A town's good times are no less a part of its life than the bad times and disasters, and it was toward the end of November of the next year that Columbians had their last best time of all.

It had been three and a half years since the spring day when Professor Harris's brass band struck up a lively tune and the 200 volunteers began the digging of the Miners' Ditch, and now at last it was finished. To Columbians, the day that Stanislaus River water flowed that full 44 miles through their own canals and flumes—that was their Independence Day. They could now defy the company whose exorbitant rates they had been forced to pay; they could run its directors out of town on a rail, if they wanted to, or tell them to jump off the Gold Spring flume. They had water of their own, and plenty of it, at rates that didn't take half the yield of a man's claim. Through them all surged a wonderful feeling of release and liberation, and they all believed and told each other that it was only the beginning for the Gem of the Southern Mines. Now she'd shine so in the foothill sun you could see her sparkle clear to San Francisco Bay. The *Tuolumne Courier* reported:

*Scarce had Aurora lit up the chambers of the east before hundreds of our population were awake, alive and doing. Thousands of the denizens of the neighboring towns soon came pouring in, dressed in their best go-to-meeting. Guns were firing and banners were flying. Sweet and powerful tones of music, in harmonious mingling, filled the ears.*

*Sonora and all the neighboring villages were soon depopulated, and everybody and everybody's relations and acquaintances, with all their wives, their daughters and their daughters' daughters, were here. Fourth of July, and all such common demonstrations was no circumstances to the display, the crowd, the jam, and the jollification of this day.*

*Our streets were full; our stores were full; our saloons were full and our houses were full.*

(The reporter could probably have added, without being in the least uncharitable, that everybody in town was full, too. What was a Gold Rush celebration without rivers of forty-rod and Old Monongahela?)

Out to the Gold Spring flume and back again moved the jubilant victory parade. The cool autumn sunlight glinted on the jaunty instruments of Columbia's brass band and Faxson's Sonora Band, on the shining muskets of the Saw Mill Flat Infantry and the horse-drawn cannon of the Springfield Artillery, and struck golden sparks from the gleaming brass of the apparatus and hose carriages of the Columbia and Sonora fire-engine companies. Falling leaves drifted down from the locust trees and were lost in the bright swirling banners of the mounted sheriff's posse, of the marching men who had dug the ditch, of the thousand cheering miners who followed, four abreast, the officials of the Miners' Union.

Back they came to the square before the Presbyterian Church to listen with bared heads to a prayer of thanksgiving by the Reverend Mr. Baker and stirring marches by the bands and a rousing speech by Jimmy Coffroth.

When Jimmy finished telling, in rounded and sonorous periods, the story of the Miners' Ditch, they whooped and sailed their hats in the air. He held them rapt as he unveiled for them Columbia's glittering destiny, the destiny to which their courage and strength would lead her, and whose blessings they themselves and their children after them would enjoy. While his ringing words died away, their cheers rolled out across the plaza and down the streets and over Maine and Columbia and Kennebec Gulches, where the spires and pinnacles of the limestone bedrock rose bare above the diggings.

Bright and late burned the lamps of Columbia that night. Down the streets floated laughter and the scuffle of dancing feet, the chants of the callers and the lively music of "Hangtown Gals" played by the fiddles and the harps. Glasses clinked in a thousand happy toasts, and Forty-niners roared again the songs they had sung by the wagon-train campfires and the lusty ballads that had shaken the rafters of Gold Rush saloons.

Out in the dark corrals the horses neighed nervously and stamped their hoofs. They could hear, beyond the distant music, the yelping of the coyotes coming from the hills, from the lone starlit canyons back in the hills.

It wasn't long, not more than a year or two, before Columbians began to realize that they were too late. On that bland November morning of the great water celebration Jimmy Coffroth had unfolded a dream for them, and they had set their hearts on it; but now they could see how their triumph and his eloquent words had carried them away.

It was true that they had the water they wanted so desperately; over 44 miles of rugged foothill country they had brought it to the very borders of their claims. But claims do not yield gold forever. The dust runs out. The earth gives what it has, and can give no more. What good was water when no gold was left, when it was gold you wanted?

So the numbered suns of even the world's richest mining camp dwindled away. The men who had exhausted her wealth packed their mules and left the buildings they had built and the trees they had planted, for other gulches, other hills. Some went to the Fraser River. Some went over the mountains in the stampede to the Washoe and the silver veins of the Comstock Lode. Still others just drifted down the valley trails, and were never seen again.

At least one came back to curse the day he ever heard of Columbia. Before joining the rush to the Fraser he buried all he had—$5,000 in gold dust —in a pine grove not far from town. Two years later he arrived back in Columbia broke and hungry. Borrowing a pick and shovel, he set out for his treasure in the pines. To his dismay, the pines were no longer there. Land-clearing farmers had cut them all down and uprooted their stumps. He threw the tools to the ground, turned his back on Columbia, and walked away.

Now, instead of the freight bells' jangle all day long you heard the far-away tinkle of the cowbell, and where once the natives were so used to the arrival of the six-horse Concords pulling in from Sonora and Angels and the valley that they never looked up from their monte games, now they left their drinks and walked to the barroom door to watch the carriage of the village doctor move sedately up the street.

Five short years after the cheering throng had milled in front of St. Andrew's a traveler visited Columbia and found it *a quiet little place* of pastoral charm.

*The gold has been mostly washed out,* he wrote; *many miners have left, so many houses are empty of inhabitants. Many of the houses are em-bowered with climbing roses, now in full bloom, and the place is lovely.*

Before the roses bloomed many more springs, the houses to which they clung were destroyed by miners eager to reach the gold in the earth be-neath them. When this was taken, the gaping cavities where the houses once stood and the naked limestone bedrock that now, like the very skeleton of the earth, lay exposed across the valley floor—these remained as a record of the decline and last days of the Gem of the Southern Mines.

It is strange to consider that there is so much to write and say concern-ing the first ten or fifteen years of a town's life, and then nothing at all to write or say about its next sixty years. Yet that is the position in which you are left by the phenomenon of the Gold Rush and the phenomenon of a Gold Rush town. When the gold petered out, there was no reason why men should stay, and so they left. The town's life was over. It happened to Columbia, and to a hundred other Sierra camps. On a day in '56, say, their streets are crowded, and alive with stir and purpose. On the same day ten years later, these same streets are empty. The buildings stand bleak and expressionless; they are like eyeless faces. Breezes whisper along the eaves. Grass grows through the puncheon floors. You peer through a cracked windowpane and see a barroom gray with cobwebs, a safe in the corner with its door ajar, a broken chair, perhaps, leaning against a dusty table.

The whole town is a graveyard of dead ambition, schemes, and hopes, and you think that a town once lived in cannot possibly be as devoid of life as this town seems. You understand why people, feeling the same way, have endowed it with an invisible life, a haunting spirit, and have called it a town of ghosts.

It is not true that Columbia was entirely abandoned. There is a sermon, perhaps, in the curious fact that it owed its survival not to the golden grains men wrested from its earth, but mainly to the enduring white stone of the marble quarries that lay largely neglected during all the years of the excitement, a little way out of town. A few Columbians and their families remained to take out the marble. Others stayed with their little orchards and their pastures. But the brick buildings that had gone up with such assurance after the last big fire stood shuttered and vacant. To walk past them was to commune with the dead, with the gone-forever, with a horde of ghostly memories.

The schoolhouse of which the pioneers had been so proud fell into disuse. Up on Kennebec Hill, stately St. Anne's stood silent and brooding upon virgin ground that even the greediest of miners had not dared to violate with their picks and shovels. It is said that once some miners dragged hydraulic monitors through the silent streets and took them up to Kennebec Hill to defy the curse that would befall them for plundering the church ground. The first stream feathered through the air, hit a ledge at the border of the churchyard cemetery, and washed a section of it away.

As this section fell to solider soil, it broke apart to reveal a leaden casket whose lid had been jarred loose by the fall. The awe-struck miners gathered around the coffin, lifted the lid, and saw inside the body of a perfectly preserved and richly dressed young woman. No identifying mark told who she was or who had prepared her so carefully for burial. Silently the miners fastened the lid in place, bore the casket back up the ledge to the cemetery and restored it to the earth of St. Anne's. A few moments later they rode away with their hoses and monitors, and never returned.

Travelers passing by Columbia late at night arrived wide-eyed and breathless in Sonora with reports that they had seen lights flickering behind the Gothic windows of the abandoned church. Some said they had heard the organ playing a wheezy tune.

Sonorans never scoffed at stories like these; their town, after all, was a

Gold Rush town, too, and was aware of the curious ways in which the surviving spirit of the Gold Rush days sometimes manifested itself. Prudent
ones would nod and say nothing, or say yes, they had heard the stories about
St. Anne's. The superstitious ventured an explanation: "It's the ghosts
of St. Anne's graveyard. Someone's a-fixin' to mine beneath the church, and
they're meetin' to lay on him the Miner's Curse."

It is the legend that this spooky band of guardians has never failed to
protect St. Anne's. To this day, they say, the rich claims on which it stands
have never been disturbed, and beneath it lies a fortune in gold.

Campers who have pitched their tents on the flats beside Kennebec Gulch
have reported that sometimes, late on summer nights, they have heard light
and airy music coming faintly from somewhere, and the natives they have
seen the next day have told them they heard it too, last night: it was the
ghosts of the Forty-niners gathering for a spectral polka in the moonlit
glades of their lost and forever bygone youth. The campers, looking about
them at the silent old buildings and the haunted houses, half believed what
they were told.

Years passed, and these campers and a few hunters, an occasional tourist
who ventured off the beaten highway, students of history on field trips,
a roving artist or two—these were the only interlopers to profane the stillness
of the deserted streets.

But as the Gold Rush and the institutions of the Gold Rush receded into
the past, some Californians feared that they might vanish without a trace.
Many of the mining camps had already disappeared, and historians quar-
reled over whether they had been located on this creek bank or that, on
this hillside or the one across the valley. In contrast, Columbia, the richest
camp of them all, was in a rare state of preservation. Twenty or thirty of
its main buildings dated from the '50s and were in conditions ranging
from fair to excellent. Some had been modified from their original design,
but they still had the Gold Rush feeling and atmosphere.

These qualities appealed to Frederick Law Olmstead, who in 1928 was
retained by the California State Park Commission to make a survey of the
areas to be included in a State park system. He recommended that Columbia be acquired by the State and restored, and preserved as an authentic
example of an early-day mining camp. Seventeen years later, the Legislature acted favorably upon this proposal.

Now, most of the property desired by the Park Commission has been bought, and the area is officially described as Columbia Historic State Park. Restoration of some of the buildings, complete reconstruction of others, landscaping, zoning, and other aspects of the project are proceeding in accordance with a master plan drafted by Dr. V. Aubrey Neasham, regional historian for the National Park Service in San Francisco. It is hoped that the work will be completed by 1959.

A few years ago, Columbia was the scene of California's major Gold Rush Centennial celebration. A ferris wheel turned its incessant round amid the tailings and raw bedrock of Columbia Gulch. Close by were a merry-go-round and the booths of a carnival midway. In a blazing summer sun a team of two brawny men, stripped to the waist—one was a timber faller and the other an electric company lineman—drove a steel bit 20 inches into a block of granite in ten minutes, swinging their massive double jack-hammers in a dramatic exhibition of mining-country skill and precision. On a platform at Main and State Streets costumed quadrille teams swung their partners with sprightly grace and promenaded to the outside ring against a backdrop of locust trees. Columbia's volunteer firemen unlimbered "Old Papeete," their antique but still serviceable pumping engine, and, spurred by the cheers of the spectators, pumped themselves to a frazzle sending a stream 130 feet down State Street. Foothill folk in jeans, plaid shirts, and broad-brimmed hats and in printed cotton dresses milled up and down the short, broad streets, buying souvenirs, eating hot dogs, staring at the historical exhibits in the Cavalier Memorial Museum and in the old Wells, Fargo building, drinking cokes and beer in the Pay Ore Saloon.

Old-time residents sat on a bench in front of the Stage Drivers' Retreat, in the shade of an old catalpa tree, and looked about in wonder at the movement and life. Johnny App, whose mother crossed the Sierra with the Donner Party in '46, cocked an ear to the strident notes of "Baby, It's Cold Outside" coming from the juke box in the bar behind him. He nudged his companion, Hubert Brady, bearded seventy-year-old son of Matt Brady, who arrived in Columbia from Taunton, Massachusetts, in 1854 and struck it rich in Corral Gulch east of town.

"If we could've heard that there tune at Cassidy's Saloon in Sonora fifty years ago," Johnny said, "wouldn't we have kicked up our heels, though?"

Brady's eyes brightened and his beard wagged as he shook his head in eager agreement.

The music stopped and another graybeard spoke up. "Folks all along the Lode call this a ghost town. I ain't a-sayin' they're right, and I ain't a-sayin' they're wrong. What I *am* a-sayin' is, there don't seem to be any ghosts hangin' around here today." He cackled, and pulled at the brim of his torn felt hat. "But ghosts've got plenty of time. They'll be back some day, to claim their own."

Brady and App nodded solemnly, as if these words were the echo of their own deepest thoughts. The three of them fell silent. Like the old brick buildings around them and the old catalpa tree above them, they seemed suddenly withdrawn and remote from the carnival crowd that passed them by.

# DONNER COUNTRY

# CHAPTER SIX

# Truckee

LEAVING THE Mother Lode town of Auburn and climbing the long grade of Highway 40 toward the Sierra divide, the car began to pass snow at the 4,000-foot level, or about at Baxter's Camp. It lay in patches beneath the pine trees where the sun couldn't reach it, and along the side of the road where the plows had pushed it after the storm a couple of days before.

It had been seven years since I had seen snow, and it was a lovely thing to see again. There were others who must have felt the same way. A pretty girl in slacks and a mackinaw and a knitted cap, brightly red, had stopped her car, got out, and scooped up a double handful, and when I passed her she was getting back into her car eating it. She was smiling.

Maybe she was just thirsty, but I do not think that people who live in the snow and see it every day for five or six months take a drink of water like that, and smile. You do that when you're seeing snow for the first time in a long while. You do it when you remember how you ate snow when you were a kid in Connecticut or Wisconsin, before you went to California to live in San Francisco or Santa Cruz or Sacramento or any one of a hundred other places where it never snows; and now that you come upon it once again after all that time, beneath mountain pines so far from home, wherever it was, you follow the impulse to do it again just to take yourself back for a moment to that other life. That is what I felt, anyway, when I saw the pretty girl with the slacks and the red cap and the smile on her face.

There must have been skiing on the mountain slopes higher up, above and away from the road, for many cars were parked in front of the Cisco Pines, the Big Bend Inn, the Donner Summit Lodge, and the other resort hotels. Riding with me were two hitchhikers, a discharged paratrooper named Tom and a young merchant seaman who never mentioned his name. They had been bound across the mountains alone and were trying to get home by Christmas, Tom to St. Louis and the seaman to some small town in Georgia. I had picked them up, one right after the other, on the outskirts of North Sacramento.

Three feet of snow lay over the Donner Summit—the winter was mild this year and not like that winter of 1846, a century ago—and as we drove through the pass and down the winding road on the eastern side of the divide, all around us were granite peaks and boulders. The Southern Pacific snowsheds, half buried in the drifts, sloped gently down the far canyonside to our right; and directly below and in front of us lay Donner Lake, 3 miles long, half a mile wide, cold-looking, gray, and ringed by the straight pines and the snow-covered peaks. Over by Reno, 40 miles to the east, Mount Rose and the Washoe Mountains loomed bleak and lonely against a gray monotone of winter sky.

Tom had never crossed the Sierra before, west to east. The landscape, he said, was something he never saw in St. Louis, or anywhere near St. Louis. "Isn't that terrific!" he exclaimed, pointing down at the lake. "There it is—the lake—all to its own." He stared ahead through the windshield. "Say, that is sweet." He put a lot into the word. The way he said it, it meant that everything—pines, snow, mountains, lake, solitude—harmonized. Nothing that he saw was inappropriate. Everything clicked.

The view was lost on the merchant seaman. He was sound asleep on the back seat. He had said he had not slept two consecutive hours in eight days.

We drove past the lake shore and down the Donner Creek meadows at the lake's eastern end. Off to the right was the immense Donner Party monument, standing where the cabin of "Uncle Patrick" Breen had been one hundred years before on that day, up to its eaves in snow. Beyond it and out of sight in the tamaracks would be the great boulder that marked the site of the Murphy cabin, where in that winter of 1846–1847 the big-eyed emigrant children had starved, frozen, and died.

Down the meandering stream half a mile toward Truckee was the white cross beside the highway. I knew that if you walked south from that cross, sixty-five paces along a stone-bordered path, you would come to the site of the Graves cabin, another shelter in the Donners' Camp of Death.

A little farther down the highway—three or four minutes by car—were the granite slab and the plaque reading: "The Emigrant Trail in the pioneer days of California came through the low pass to the north facing this monument. . . ." Across the road was a sign and a white post with an arrow on top of it. The arrow pointed to a notch in the pine-covered ridge beyond, and the sign said: "The Donner Party came through the pass at the north. Arrow points to pass. . . ."

A few miles over that pass would be where the Donner brothers, George and Jacob, died, 2,000 miles from the gentle waters of the Sangamon River they left behind them in Illinois.

I mentioned these landmarks to Tom as we went by and told him how the Donner Party, going overland in their ox-drawn canvastops, had been snowbound here and how almost half of them never got over the summit we had just crossed, but died there in that country, under those trees, in sight of that lake.

He spoke at last. "You never hear about those guys any more, and if you do you forget them, don't you? You breeze along in your car—and what happens? You get to California in a couple of hours or a couple of days, and it's been simple. Just sit at the wheel and breeze along and take in the scenery. You forget all about the first ones."

We rounded a turn in the road. Up ahead glowed the neons of the place where I was going to stop. I swung into the driveway. Tom woke the seaman and they got out quickly and thanked me, their minds already on the next lift. Then they walked rapidly down the highway toward Truckee, a mile away. This was Highway 40, transcontinental and all-year-round, and they'd probably get picked up before they were halfway there.

I watched their dark, hurrying figures grow vague in the cold winter dusk. A car rushed past, and then it was still with that incredible, dry, absolute mountain stillness. After a while, I heard the distant drumming of airplane motors, and looked up. High above, its riding lights burning like stars, an airliner flew west across the Sierra, toward the land the Donners never saw.

Truckee is a mountain railroad town of one main street, fronting the Southern Pacific tracks, and of 1,500 people. You know it if you've ever crossed the mountains on Highway 40, or spent some time at Lake Tahoe, ten miles or so to the southeast, or skied on the summit ski fields; otherwise, it could be that you have never heard of it.

Sometimes the westbound limiteds take on a helper engine there to get them up through the snowsheds and "over the hill," as the railroadmen say. While they are at rest, the passengers gaze with curiosity out of the pullman windows at the façades of the stores and bars and a hotel or two, and at their corrugated-tin sidewalk awnings. They read the name on the station signboard: Truckee.

"What a strange name for a town," some of them say to themselves, and for the first time, perhaps, note that they are in California.

Hills rise behind the town, to the north, and there are hills to the south, beyond the flats of the Truckee River, covered with straight-standing pine and fir trees. The town itself has a frontier look about it, as though it marked the beginning of a wilderness—or the end of one; and it sometimes draws a strange expression to the urbane faces of the travelers sitting in the pullman windows. The expression is a troubled one: they seem to be saying to themselves, "Are there such hills, and is there such a town? Is there such a life—so small, so candid, so free?"

But it had been on other visits to Truckee, when I had seen those limiteds come down the westbound tracks from Sparks and Reno; it had been mostly in the summertime, or in the autumn, when the poplars were golden flames by the riverbanks. Now it was December—and a hundred years from the day when Patrick Breen, snowbound in his cabin by the lake, opened his diary and, by firelight, scrawled, *Milton got back last night from Donner's camp. Sad news; Jacob Donner, Samuel Shoemaker, Rhine-*

*hart, and Smith are dead; the rest of them in a low situation; snowed all
night, with a strong northwest wind.*

Tonight, a hundred years later, Christmas-tree lights glowed in the
Truckee windows. Parked near the S. P. Hotel beside the little railroad
station were the big diesel tractor-trailers. Their drivers were warming up
in Tony's Coffee Shop, and fighting off fatigue with hot black coffee. After a
while they'd pick up their gloves, pay their checks, and go out into the
ten-above-zero night to start the trucks rolling west again toward the Donner Summit and the broad valley that lay beyond.

Down the short deserted street, at the California Café where you turned
sharp left to go to Reno, the boys from the helper engines that lifted the
freights and the limiteds over the hill were putting away their short stacks
and pork sausages, and when they had finished the wheatcakes they'd go
home to their wives and kids and Christmas trees, their hot baths and their
warm beds.

Up on Donner Summit, a mile and a half in the sky and 1,500 feet above
the dark still waters of Donner Lake, an airplane beacon gleamed to guide
the airliners on their night flights across the mountains. And higher still
hung the cold glittering stars.

Perhaps it would not have been far-fetched to think that a hundred years
ago that night the lost emigrants of the Donner Party raised their eyes to
those stars, above that summit, and asked for help. They were 50 miles from
safety, and now the big trucks would cover those 50 miles in two hours,
grinding up the winding grade to the top and then pounding down Highway 40 toward Norden, Soda Springs, Big Bend Camp, and Emigrant Gap.

But a century ago, those 50 miles might as well have been 50,000, and the
stars sent down no miracle.

At first, it had been almost like a picnic—the blazing campfires, the men
smoking and talking, the women laughing softly, the children sleeping in
the wagons, the watchdogs dozing, the banjo or the concertina playing, and
"Oh, Susanna!" sung under the prairie moon.

The whitetops had gathered at Independence, Missouri, and one May
day in 1846 had formed their lines and creaked west. There were two or
three hundred wagons in that train. As they rolled across the great sweep

of the Middle Western plains, lifting the dust in long rolling clouds, there
were two miles between the leaders and the stragglers at the caravan's end.
Two or three days out of Independence, they broke from the Santa Fe
Trail and turned their lumbering oxen to the northwest, along the road
to Oregon.

They had been on the move maybe three weeks when Tamsen Donner,
true and steadfast wife of George Donner, wrote a letter to a friend back
home in Illinois. At forty-five, she was going West with her three children
and her two stepchildren: she was collecting wildflowers along the Oregon
Trail, and in one of her husband's three wagons were cases of schoolbooks,
for she planned to start a girls' seminary in California.

*Our journey so far has been pleasant, the roads have been good, the food
plentiful. . . . We feel no fear of Indians, our cattle graze quietly around
our encampment unmolested. . . . Indeed, if I do not experience anything
far worse than I have yet done, I shall say the trouble is all in getting
started. . . .*

As she wrote, and a thousand miles to the west, the Sierra peaks among
which Tamsen was to die towered serene against the bright blue sky, and
the soft June wind whispered through the pines beside the lonely lake that
now bears her name. . . .

A wagon train was a fluid thing. Its units formed and reformed, grouped
and regrouped as the emigrants made new friends, or disagreements parted
them, or as the luck of the trail shifted their positions in the line. The final
split in this one came beyond Fort Laramie, by the willowed banks of the
Little Sandy. There the old, established trail to California and Oregon
veered northwest to Fort Hall, where it forked, one branch continuing
northwest to Oregon, the other turning southwest to the Humboldt River
and California.

But it was still another route that intrigued George and Jacob Donner,
the Reeds, the Eddys, the Murphys, the Breens, and the Kesebergs. By
cutting directly west and passing south of the Great Salt Lake instead of to
the north, they could save 400 miles. They knew that this was true, because they had read it in the *Emigrant's Guide* of Lansford W. Hastings.

Hastings was up ahead of them now, leading a train over his trail to Fort
Bridger. He had left word he would wait there for the emigrants that fol-

lowed him, and take them across to the Humboldt by his new route—a route which, in actual fact, he had never seen; he was a professional path-finder and promoter, and had recommended it in his guidebook simply because it looked good on the map.

Stubbornly, against the advice of Jim Clyman (who, this time the year before, was crossing the Sacramento Valley to Sutter's Fort with Marshall and the rest of the party from Oregon), and against the warning intuition of other leaders in the train who favored the old road, the Donners clung to their belief in the Hastings Cutoff. And on July 20, 1846, they and the others in their party set out. Westward rocked the twenty wagons on their high, iron-rimmed wheels. Across the sandy plains before them, beckoning them beyond the horizon, stretched the tracks of the Hastings train. The sun blazed down from a blank blue sky.

That July was coming to an end when the Donner Party reached Fort Bridger, the crude, two-cabin outpost in southwestern Wyoming.

You couldn't say that their arrival there was important. It wasn't, to anyone but them, for they were the merest chip on the empire's westward tide. Already the Yankees had scattered the Californians toward the Rio Grande and Baja California and had hoisted the Stars and Stripes over Monterey, Yerba Buena by the shore of San Francisco Bay, and Sonoma. In another day or so, Frémont would raise them over San Diego. America was moving west and wouldn't stop until her land of liberty reached from ocean to ocean, from the forty-ninth parallel to the Gulf of Mexico.

Some five hundred canvastops crossed the prairies and the mountains to Oregon and California that year, but they made it, and so you don't hear much about them. With the Donners, it was different.

A bad guess, but a bad guess that anyone might have made. A day's extra rest beside the trail, but one they needed and had to have. Harsh words, but words that had been uttered a thousand times and in a thousand ways under similar circumstances of stress. These things accumulated, and so delicate was destiny's timing, the Donners did not know what had happened until their position was hopeless, until it was too late for them to do anything but starve and wait and die in the Sierra snow, in the dark shadow of the Sierra escarpment.

The guidebooks to the Promised Land hadn't told them how to equip themselves for that. They had mentioned the supplies necessary for the overland journey (George and Jacob Donner started West with three wagons, $10,000 sewn into a quilt, and trinkets with which to pacify the Indians; the aristocratic James Reed also had three wagons—one of them fitted with two floors—a sheet-iron stove and a hired girl to cook the meals). They told you where to ford the rivers and the wildflowers you would find beside the trail; but they didn't tell you how to keep your children from dying when all you had to feed them was a boiled strip of rawhide. .

The *Emigrant's Guide* of Lansford W. Hastings hadn't mentioned that, but it had mentioned the cutoff that would save 400 miles, and it was along the beginnings of this route that the Donner train had moved to Fort Bridger. They had believed Hastings would be there waiting for them, to guide them across the Wasatch Mountains and the Great Salt Desert to the Humboldt. But the season was already growing late: at the head of his sixty-six-wagon caravan, Hastings had pushed on without them. The Donners rested briefly, repaired their wagons, and once more rolled westward. Between them and Sutter's Fort on the Sacramento, there was nothing now but wilderness.

Four days out of Fort Bridger the twenty wagons creaked to a halt beside the Red Fork of the Weber River. Hasty hands snatched a letter from a split stick beside the trail. It was a message left by Hastings. The Weber Canyon ahead of them, it said, was a difficult, dangerous passage. Hastings said he didn't know whether his own party could get through it. If they sent a messenger ahead to him, he would return and take them around it by a better way.

On the meadows at the canyon head, the emigrants went into camp. Three men rode on and overtook Hastings by the shore of Great Salt Lake. In spite of what he had said in the note, he refused to go back with them; his duty, he said, was with his train. He rode to the top of a ridge with one of the men and indicated vaguely the route that seemed to him preferable to the Weber Canyon passage that had caused his train so much trouble. Then he hurried back to his camp and prepared to move on. The Donner Party was on its own.

They avoided the canyon road, and instead, foot by foot, hacked their way over the Wasatch Mountains, fording streams, scaling canyon walls, double-teaming their wagons over the boulders and up the steep slopes,

making roads of tree trunks, raising the wagons over the ridges with rudely
fashioned windlasses, sliding them down the ridges with locked wheels,
cutting a road, a trail, a way through where wagons had never gone before.

They were plainsmen and farmers from Illinois and Iowa and Tennessee,
and the guidebooks hadn't told them about this, either. They had gone
West to sit in the sun and watch their cattle and their kids grow fat, and
take life easy, not to break their backs to get a wagon across a creek, not
to curse their lumbering stupid oxen, not to blister their hands with pick
and shovel. Here and there, little by little, the finish began to wear thin.
Some grumbled. Some shirked. The heroes among them set their jaws, said
nothing and plugged on.

Twenty-one bitter days it took them to cover the 36 miles between the
head of Weber Canyon and the Salt Lake Valley, and it was the end of
August when they reached Salt Lake. There they buried the first to die,
twenty-five-year-old Luke Halloran, an Irish wanderer who fought the con-
sumption as long as he could, and then died with his head in Tamsen
Donner's lap.

They were eighty-six now: twenty-eight adult men, fourteen adult
women, four adolescents, and forty children from fourteen to less than a year
in age.

They buried Halloran in a salt grave, in a coffin made of wagon boards.
The next day they moved on, out into the desert.

The words on the base of the Donner Party monument on Donner Lake's
eastern shore read, *Virile to risk and find; Kindly withal and a ready help.
Facing the brunt of fate; Indomitable, . . . unafraid.*

You can see the figures above the words as you go by on Highway 40:
a pioneer mother with a babe-in-arms, a brawny pioneer father, and their
little girl. They face west, to the lofty granite crags of Donner Summit.

There were some in the Donner Party to whom those words would ap-
ply; some of them were heroes. But when the going got tough in the rocky
Wasatch canyons and the salt slush of the Great Salt Desert, they were
facing the brunt of fate all right, but there was nothing kindly or readily
helpful or indomitable or unafraid about most of them. They were human
beings then, scared, worried, and desperate. They looked into each other's

eyes and saw there, as clearly as if it had been spoken, the blunt assertion that it was every man for himself.

*No water for your kids? That's too bad, mister; what I've got is for my kids and me. Try someone else. . . . Your baby's too young to walk and you're too weak to carry him, and you want me to take him in my wagon? Sorry, lady, my wagon's got all the load my oxen can pull. Try someone else. . . .*

That is what the look in their eyes said. And sometimes, when they had to, they put it into words. . . .

They had picked up the tracks of the Hastings Party again and another note left beside the trail told them that the long dry drive across the Salt Lake Desert was a 40-mile stretch and would take two days and nights. Hastings was wrong again: it turned out to be 80 miles, and disaster.

Scorched by the sun, choked by the dust, blinded by the dazzling glare of the salt, taunted by mirages and the cool blue mountains low in the west, they struggled for six days and nights before they reached Pilot Peak and water. Thiry-six of their oxen, half of them John Reed's, had died of thirst, or, maddened by the sun, had bolted into the white wastes.

They left four of their wagons on the desert, and there they left, too, the last shred of organization and teamwork. The bad breaks were wearing them down. The men's lips now were tight-set and grim, their eyes hard. They began to hoard their food, their water, their cattle, and, where they could, their strength. All of them were in the early stages of exhaustion, and they plodded along with fear ever and invisibly at their sides—fear that they would starve, fear of Indians, fear that their oxen or their wagons, brittle-dry from the desert sun, would collapse, fear that there would be snow on the mountains, and fear, undeniably, of what they themselves could and might do, if their spirits cracked.

Charlie Stanton (he had failed in business in Chicago and was on his way West to make a new start) and strapping Bill McCutchen from Missouri, who would leave a wife and a year-old baby with the wagons, volunteered to ride ahead to Sutter's Fort for food. It was September 18 that they disappeared up the trail. Would they make it? Would they get through? the others thought, as they watched them ride away. And if they did, would they come back?

The gaunt men and gaunter oxen, some now yoked with cows, pushed wearily onward, across Nevada, across the broad valleys and the sagebrush plains, south to the pass in the Ruby Mountains, through the pass to the Humboldt's north fork, then north again, along the foothills of the Diamond Mountains. At last, on the last day of September, they came to a river flowing west. It was the main Humboldt. They had reached the emigrant road to California.

Now they made 20 miles a day, but the days were growing shorter and the night chill was forcing them closer to the campfires. They were on short rations. The women and children toiled on foot beside rickety wagons loaded to the hindgates with household goods they had managed to save from the mountain and desert passages. They were all of them traveling on nerve, and the limit to which it would take them was almost in sight.

On October 5, double-teaming up a steep and sandy grade, Reed and John Snyder argued peevishly about the right of way up the hill. The words grew abusive. Snyder struck Reed on the head with the butt of his bullwhip. Reed unsheathed his hunting knife and plunged it into Snyder's chest. Snyder staggered back, turned, lurched a few steps up the hill, and fell to the ground. In fifteen minutes he was dead.

While Virginia, Reed's thirteen-year-old daughter, dressed her father's scalp wounds, other members of the party debated his punishment. Some were for lynching him there beside the trail, and even propped up a wagon tongue from which to hang him. Finally, however, they decided to banish him from the train. Bidding his wife and four children good-by, Reed started on the lonely wilderness trail to Sutter's Fort. With him rode Walter Herron, a teamster who had traveled with the Reeds from Illinois. They bore a letter from George Donner, the captain of the party, asking Sutter for all the aid that he could send.

Four days later, Hardcoop, sixty years old, sick, feeble, and traveling with the Kesebergs, fell behind the train. Those with the few remaining horses refused to return for the old man. He was left to die alone in the sagebrush.

Three nights after that, Indians stole eighteen oxen. The next night, their arrows killed twenty-one more. Wolfinger, a wealthy German member of the party, lingered along the trail to cache some possessions. Two of his countrymen, Reinhardt (the "Rhinehart" of Breen's diary) and Spitzer, stayed behind to help him. Later, these two rejoined the wagons. Where was Wolfinger? Indians had killed him, they said. No one believed them, but a little treachery, a little ugly work on the trail, didn't matter much now.

They came to the desolate hell of the Humboldt sink and plunged on. They were down to fifteen wagons now. In the rear, through the choking dust, plodded William Eddy and his wife, Eleanor. They carried 3 pounds of sugar, which was all the food they had left, and their three-year-old son and one-year-old daughter. The oxen were so far gone that no one would take the babies into a wagon. The next day, still on the waste land of the sink, Eddy was afraid the babies were dying of thirst. Breen, the Irish patriarch from Keokuk, Iowa, had a cask of water in his wagon. He refused to share it. Eddy told Breen he would kill him if he interfered, and took it.

At last they came to the cool swift waters of the Truckee River. They were toiling along the river toward the Truckee meadows when Stanton met them, back from Sutter's Fort with seven pack mules, two Indian guides—Luis and Salvador—and food. One of the heroes, with nothing to gain and a life to lose, Stanton had come back. Yes, he said, McCutchen had made it; he lay ill at Sutter's. Reed and Herron had nearly died of starvation, but they had got through, too.

They moved up to the meadows, where Reno is now, and there they stayed for five days, resting. There, too, they buried William Pike, killed by the accidental discharge of a pistol. He was the fifth to die. His dry-eyed widow and his two children, with falling snow in their tousled hair, turned away as the earth was shoveled into his grave.

It was October 25 when they broke camp and started for the summit of the Sierra divide, some fifty miles to the west. Exhausted, disorderly, bordering on panic, they left as they could, one section at a time. The two Donner brothers and their families brought up in the rear.

Ahead of them, already beneath 5 feet of snow, the granite peaks lay waiting.

Capt. John Charles Frémont of the United States Topographical Engineers, seeking the fabled Buenaventura River, had been through this country in the winter of '44. On St. Valentine's Day of that year, from a ridge to the south, he had discovered the sapphire-blue "Lake of the Sky," which he named Bonpland and which is now called Tahoe. And in that October, the Stevens-Townsend-Murphy Party, with which rode the brothers John and Daniel Murphy, hastened across those same meadows. They had been guided there by a friendly Paiute Indian whom they called "Truckey," or "Truckee," and for whom they named the river and the lake now known as Donner.

The party had there split into three groups. One crossed the divide to the north, to the headwaters of the Yuba. Another got through to the south, by Tahoe, to the American River. The third had gone straight ahead, over the divide where it rose above the lake. All but one of them had made it: too weak to climb the snow-covered summit, seventeen-year-old Moses Shallenberger had stayed in a pine-sapling cabin by the lake until he was rescued the next February.

Breen, now snowbound in Shallenberger's cabin by the lake with his wife and seven children, started a diary. The first entry said:

*Friday Nov. 20th 1846 Came to this place on the 31st of last month that it snowed we went on to the pass the snow so deep we were unable to find the road, when within 3 miles of the summit then turned back to this shanty on the Lake. Stanton came one day after we arrived here we again took our teams & waggons & made another unsuccessful attempt to cross in company with Stanton we returned to the shanty it continueing to snow all the time we were here*

*we now have killed most part of our cattle having to stay here untill next spring & live on poor beef without bread or salt   it snowed during the space of eight days with little intermission, after our arrival here. . . .*

Thus Breen recorded the heartbreaking attempts to scale the summit, the blizzards that swirled down from the peaks with blinding ferocity and choked the passes with 30 feet of snow, and the last crushing misfortune in a chain of misfortunes that began back in Sangamon County, Illinois, when the Donner brothers picked up Lansford Hastings' guidebook and believed what it said. Thus he recorded the simple catastrophe that unseasonal snow had beaten them to the bleak barrier that stood between them and the haven of the Sacramento Valley.

The other wagon trains had all made it and were all safely in, and their men were already building their ranch houses and cutting their winter wood. The Donners had saved their 400 miles, but in saving them they had seen their time dwindle and at last expire here in the desolation of the mountains and the snow.

Twenty-one days to cross the Wasatch. Six days to cross the Great Salt Desert. A precious five-day rest here. A priceless three-day delay there. Snows a month too soon on the Sierra. And now they were trapped. Now the situation was desperate.

Another storm struck from leaden skies. This one lasted eight days. The thin, bony cattle yet unslaughtered wandered off in the snow and perished, and so did the seven mules Stanton had brought back from Sutter's. The food he had packed in was gone. Firewood was almost impossible to obtain because the snow lay 20 feet deep all around them. Eddy had shot a bear and two or three ducks, but more than that was needed. There were eighty-one exhausted and famished persons in the Shallenberger cabin and two others they had been able to build by the lake, and in the two Donner shelters on Alder Creek.

They had no way of knowing that Reed and McCutchen had driven a thirty-horse pack train out of Sutter's Fort and had floundered through the snow to within 18 miles of the summit before they were forced to turn back; all they knew was that unless they were all to die, someone had to make it to the valley for help. "Uncle Billy" Graves, a Green Mountain man, fashioned crude snowshoes from split oxbows and rawhide. On December 16, the day after the first man died at the lake, five women and ten men (including the Indians Luis and Salvador) started for the snow-covered peaks. Four of them were fathers, three of them mothers, leaving children with those who stayed behind. With them gone, it would mean more hides for the children to eat, more bone gruel to drink. And, if they got through, it would mean aid from across the mountains.

These fifteen have become known in western legend as The Forlorn Hope. It was thirty-three days later that William Eddy, their leader, staggered to a ranch house on the rim of the Sacramento Valley, half dead with exhaustion and hunger. Rescuers, back-trailing Eddy's bloody footprints, found the others that night. There were six—the five women, and one man. The rest had died, and, after dying, all but one had been butchered and eaten by the starving, half-crazed survivors. That one had been Charles Stanton, who'd come back from Sutter's Fort with food. Soon after they had started from the lake, he had gone snow-blind. He grew weaker and weaker. On the morning of the sixth day out, they left him sitting in the snow by the campfire. He told them he'd be along in a little while, but they never saw him again. . . .

Late in the December that I remember, the hills of Sonoma were already turning green. I had seen them in the north, as the car left Black Point and crossed the bridge over Petaluma Creek. Along their slopes grazed fat, white-faced cattle, and wild ducks swam in the Napa River sloughs, rippling the still water with their spreading wakes. There was soft rain in Sacramento, and outside the city, beside the highways, plump sheep cropped the pastures. Orchards on the valley hillsides slept beneath gray skies, waiting for the spring sun to waken and warm them and hang their branches heavy with apricots, peaches, pears, and clusters of cherries. Everywhere in that land were peace and plenty, and the promise of plenty.

It was country like that for which the members of the Donner Party left Illinois and Tennessee. It was the peace and plenty of California that they sought, for a hundred years ago the Sonoma hills were as tenderly green, the Sacramento rain as gentle, the cattle of Sutter and Vallejo as fat and plump. The far illusion realized was all there, across the snow-covered Sierra divide that loomed high above their desolate cabins beside Donner Lake.

But now it was no longer the illusion or the mirage that sustained them: it was the instinct to stay alive. That and the flickering hope that someone would come to their rescue, before they died of starvation or lost their minds and ran raving into the white wastes that imprisoned them.

The death of one by the lake and the departure of The Forlorn Hope left sixty-five men, women, and children (seven of these were nursing infants) in the cabins and the two tents of the Donner brothers, five or six miles to the north.

Now above their rooftrees in snow, the crowded shelters were dark, evil-smelling, vermin-ridden dugouts filled with the wailing of famished babies, the moaning of the weak and the sick. Their slender reserves of beef were gone. They had eaten all but two of their dogs (and these would be in the kettle before long), and were now living on hides taken from the cabin roofs, or mice, or bones they had once thrown away.

They would cut the hides into strips, then singe off the hair. They would

drop the strips into boiling water and cook them until they became soft
and glutinous. When the mixture had cooled to a jellied mass, they would
pepper it and eat it. The bones were boiled until they crumbled in the
mouth. Hungry children in the Murphy cabin cut tiny pieces from a fur
hearth rug, toasted them over the coals, and ate them. Pretty soon, the hearth
rug was all gone.

Before Christmas came, the infirm and the aged were dying. Milton
Elliott, with the Reeds by the lake, struggled through the drifts to the
Donner tents. Eleven days later, Breen wrote in his diary how Milton
had come back with the news that Jacob Donner, Shoemaker, Reinhardt,
and Smith were dead and that the situation with the rest was low, and that
it had snowed all night and that the wind had blown strong from the southwest.

Two days after that, and two days before Christmas, Breen, a devout
Catholic, began reading aloud the Thirty Days' Prayer by the light of pine-
twig torches.

There was joy in the Reed cabin on Christmas Day. From places where
she had carefully hidden them, Mrs. Reed took a piece of tripe, a cup of
white beans, a half-cup of rice, a half-cup of dried apples, and a two-inch
square of bacon. While her children cried and danced with happiness, Mrs.
Reed cooked the morsels of food and served them, cautioning, as she must
have on other, happier Christmas Days, "Children, eat slowly. There is
plenty for all."

New Year's came and passed, and still they waited for help. Their lives
were now fixed in monotony and despair. Growing weaker, they lay helpless in their damp and rotting blankets, or crawled about on the floors of
their dark, filthy cabins. They gave up watching the heights for rescuers,
for it took all their strength to gather firewood. In a few more days, they
would barely be able to drag their dead up the cabin ramps to the surface of
the snow.

As the hides dwindled, the struggle for survival grew more savage. On
January 30, 1847, Breen wrote:

*The Graves seized on Mrs. Reids goods untill they would be paid  also
took the hides that she & family had to live on, she got two pieces of hides
from there & the ballance they have taken. . . .*

Baby Keseberg starved to death. William Eddy's baby died, and Mrs. Eddy. Baby McCutchen died, and Spitzer and Milt Elliott and fifteen-year-old Landrum Murphy, who babbled deliriously of feasts and then sank into a sleep from which he never wakened. His mother was spared the sight of his emaciated corpse; a month before he died, she had gone blind.

It was February 19, and beautiful thirteen-year-old Virginia Reed was dying, and the setting sun was sending long shafts of light across the snow-mantled meadows when a shout from the lake shore broke the vast winter silence. In answer, a bony ghost of a woman crawled from a hole in the snow. Gibbering wildly and waving her arms, she floundered through the drifts in the direction whence the sound had come. Her eyes made out the forms of seven men, dark and haggard in the fading light. With horror on their faces, they watched her approach.

She tottered forward, fell in the snow, crawled toward them on her hands and knees. In a high, cracked, heartbreaking voice, she cried out, "Are you men from California—or do you come from heaven?"

As she labored closer, she saw that their prayers had been answered. Relief had come.

That was February 19, 1847, when the first relief party reached Donner Lake, and you would think that from then on it was a simple process of gathering the stranded emigrants together and herding them over the Sierra divide and down the western slopes to the sanctuary of the Sacramento Valley. Instead, however, the story of the Donner Party now entered a prolonged and complicated phase that had best be treated here in generalities.

For one thing, the members, the movements, and the motives of the relief parties (there were four) are confusing and difficult to keep in their proper place. A week or more apart, they left the valley for Donner Lake, reached it and began a harrowing return trip with as many of the survivors as they could guide, assist, or carry. On the way back, they would meet the next relief party, proceeding in the opposite direction.

Sometimes the relief parties would split up, some members going ahead in search of food, the others following more slowly with the all but helpless emigrants. Sometimes they had to leave the weak and the dying in the snow while they pushed on for provisions and more help. The snow still lay 20 and 30 feet deep, the blizzards still broke in fury across the barren peaks, children had to be carried, and wild beasts stole the precious food cached on the rescue trail.

The rescuers were risking their lives to save the people by the lake, and they had their reasons for doing it. Some of them, like James Reed, William Eddy, Bill McCutchen, and William Foster had safely crossed the mountains and were now going back to learn the fate of the families they had left behind with the party, and to rescue them if it cost them life itself. Others, like Aquilla Glover, Sept Moultry, Joseph Sels, and John Starks wanted to help fellow humans in trouble. Still others were in it for the three dollars a day they were promised. And a few were vultures bent on looting the encampments of the dead and dying victims.

When the seven of the first relief party came upon the scene of death and desolation by the lake, the situation was this: of the eighty-seven original members of the Donner train, ten were safe across the mountains, twenty-five were dead, and fifty-two were dying there in the Sierra snow.

In the two months that followed, rescuers and rescued alike suffered more hardships than most of us now suffer in our lifetimes—hardships caused mainly by cold and an appalling hunger that drove many to eat human flesh in order to stay alive. In the time of their trial, some of these pioneers assumed, as the legend on the monument said, the stature of heroes; others showed the colors of cowardice and the basest depravity. Looking back, you cannot appraise their deeds morally, or say that this man was good and that man bad. They were human beings, and they did what they did, and that was all.

Of the fifty-two, they saved thirty-eight. Six died on the way across the mountains, and eight never left them. On April 25, when the last relief party reached the valley with the last survivor, the totals were: alive, forty-eight; dead, thirty-nine.

Of the living, remember the four who went back—Reed, Eddy, McCutchen, Foster.

Of the dead, remember Charlie Stanton, who also went back and died for it; who, snow-blind and helpless beside the trail, sent the others on because they could travel faster without him. Remember, too, Old Man Hardcoop, abandoned to die alone in the sage, 6,000 miles from his native Antwerp; and the murdered Wolfinger. And the children who starved to death and never played in the California sun.

*Ahead of them, already beneath 5 feet of snow, the granite peaks lay waiting*

Think of Tamsen, George Donner's third and truest wife. Her pupils in the country school back on Sugar Creek in Illinois had called her "little teacher," for she was only a wisp of a woman, five feet tall. *The prairie between the Blue and the Platte Rivers is beautiful beyond description. Never have I seen so varied a country, so suitable for cultivation,* she had written on her way across the plains.

Then had come the hell of the Hastings Cutoff, the desert of salt, the mountains, the brush-choked canyons, the lost cattle, the abandoned wagons, the dwindling supplies; October, and the early impassable snow on the summit; and the Camp of Death at Alder Creek, a few miles from Donner Lake.

She sent off the eldest two children with the first relief party in February. Although strong and still able to walk, she had refused to abandon her three other children or her husband, who was slowly dying of an infected hand. She tried to get the youngsters out with the second relief. She dressed them in their best and warmest clothes, tenderly combed their hair, and said good-by; but the men took them only as far as the lake cabins, and there abandoned them.

She was there with them when the third relief party arrived. They would take the children, they said. She was strong enough to make it; why didn't she come with them?

Tamsen thought of her husband, dying in the tent on Alder Creek. She made her decision. Kissing her children good-by once more, she set out alone on her way across the snow—toward the shelter beside the frozen brook.

She did not hurry or look back. There was still, she knew, a little time left between George and her, and the last, darkest divide of them all.

That time ran out, before the last relief arrived.

General Kearny, eastward bound after the conquest of California, came upon the cabins by the lake in the sharp clear Sierra sunlight of the next June. Even then and to this man of war it was a ghastly scene, a stage set for a ballet of ghouls.

Edwin Bryant, who had been a lieutenant in the California Battalion in the war against Mexico and an *alcalde* of San Francisco, was a member of the general's party. Of what they saw there and what they did, he wrote:

*A more revolting and appalling spectacle I never witnessed. The remains were, by order of General Kearny, collected and buried under the superintendence of Major Swords. They were interred in a pit which had been dug in the center of one of the cabins for a cache. These melancholy duties to the dead being performed, the cabins, by order of Major Swords, were fired, and with them everything connected with this horrid and melancholy tragedy were consumed.*

And so the story that one historian of the West has called California's *Iliad* and her *Odyssey* ended to the lifting of smoke and the annihilating flame of the funeral pyres. When the cabins were ashes, the party left the lake and pushed on down Donner Creek to where it joined the Truckee River. They passed the Rocking Stone that the God of the Wind had given to the Washoe Indians, on the hill above the site of Truckee, and rode east through the canyon, toward the Truckee meadows.

The Gold Rush wagon-train emigrants of '49 and the years that came after avoided, for the most part, the barrier at the end of the lake. They did not like its looks, and they did not like the look of the lake. What had happened beside its frozen shores a few years before had transformed it into a symbol of death and madness; in the shadow of the mountain tragedy, its tranquillity became ominous: its very solitude and peace seemed a sinister deception, an innocent invitation to doom.

So most of them shunned the lake and the pass over the granite heights that loomed 1,200 feet above it. Most of them, a few miles before they reached it, veered slightly to the north to Henness Pass, which took them to the Yuba, Downieville, and the Northern Mines. Or they turned south, skirted Tahoe on the east, and crossed by the Carson and other passes to the American River, Hangtown, and the mines of the southern Lode.

For many years the site of Truckee was a bleak and lonely place, there above the Truckee River, in the mountain basin that stretched for 20 miles between the Donner Summit in the west and the rocky Truckee River canyon in the east. No miners panned this river; no tent settlements materialized overnight on its banks. That was all going on across the mountains, west (as you would have seen it from the river) of the sunset.

The gold here would not be dug or picked or panned. Here the treasure had the color of evergreens and the smell of fir, and when men got around to it, it would come crashing to earth with a downward sweep that was like a cry of pain, and be plundered to the whine of the biting saws and the swift flashing arcs of ax blades.

Those diggings at Coloma and Murphys, Angels Camp and Columbia were petering out. It was the '60s in California: the Pony Express riders were pounding down the trail to Placerville and half the miners on the Mother Lode were hitting the same trail east to the new and glittering bonanza of the Comstock Lode, and to the West's newest and gaudiest boom town, the merry and by-no-means virgin queen of the Comstock's Mount Davidson, Virginia City. In the years that immediately followed, the six-horse Concords of the Pioneer Stage Company and the twenty- and thirty-horse freight wagons rolled day and night along this twisting mountain boulevard that was watered in the summertime to lay the dust, like a city street, all the way from Placerville to Carson City. Nearly all the freight and 75 per cent of the passenger traffic between Virginia City and the San Francisco Bay made this road a daily pandemonium of creaking wagons, toiling mules and horses, drivers' yells, and the echoing swish and crack of the blacksnake lashes.

*When the teamsters stopped at night or noon,* wrote Dan De Quille, *the stations at which they halted would be blockaded for a great distance, and it looked almost as though half the teams in California were crossing the Sierra in one grand caravan.*

The rest of the freight and passenger traffic out of Virginia City bore to the northwest, to Donner Lake. There it joined the old emigrant road that went over the Henness Pass to the towns of the Northern Mines, and thence to Marysville, on the Sacramento. The rimrock loomed high above the coaches, as they passed beneath it for the other easier pass; the lake lay lonely below the peaks, and the basin remained a wilderness.

What brought life that lasted to the basin was the challenge that steam and iron flung at the Sierra granite—the challenge that the granite could not meet and that ultimately took the rails up the foothill slopes to Emigrant Gap, and across the crest of the Sierra to the summit above the lake, through the long tunnel and then down the spur of the summit, past the lake to the basin floor, eastward to the canyon and then through the canyon, and farther eastward in the direction of the desert, the Rockies and the land beyond the Rockies.

The year that marked the beginning of the railroad, in fact, marked the beginning of Truckee. Historians will not pause for reflection before this coincidence, for it is of little significance in the broad vivid pattern of the Western past. But if you know it when you're there in Truckee, you'll understand why nothing but a long-drawn lonely freight whistle at night, or the streamliner's air horn as its diesel-electric engine leaves the summit and unwinds down the Stanford Curve—why no other music could express the town so well, or tell you better what it is thinking about as it sits there beside the east-and-westbound tracks.

The way it happened was that the railroad company decided to build a turnpike along its right of way, in advance of the tracks, to handle the forward construction camps and to draw transmountain traffic to the Central Pacific, even as its tracks were being laid. By 1863, when the first rail was put down in Sacramento, the turnpike had already gone over the Donner Summit and down into the basin, and Joe Gray had built a log stage station below the hill where the Washoe Rocking Stone trembled in the mountain wind. Joe Gray's cabin was Truckee's first building.

The following year California Company stages began moving over the road between Virginia City and the railhead then at Clipper Gap, not far from the Mother Lode mining town of Auburn. It was the start of the finish for the great Placerville Road, for the Henness Pass road, and, in truth, for all the transmountain stages. A few more years, and the rugged, romantic drivers would hang up their whips forever, the messengers would turn in their shotguns and forty-fives, and the graceful Concords would vanish from the mountain trails. Already the shrill whistles of the diamond-stacked woodburners were echoing down the canyons, and the rails reaching east toward Promontory Point and the day when East and West would meet over a Gold Spike and a tie of California laurel.

Truckee was a rowdy little town from the start. Before Gray's cabin had been up a year, J. McConnell built a shack not far away, and he got into a fight with someone named Owens, and Owens plugged him, and when his wound was healed McConnell sold his place to a man named Coburn and cleared out for good.

It took two years to bore the 1,659-foot summit tunnel through the granite ridge above the lake. While they were doing that the advance gangs were laying track down through the basin toward the Truckee River canyon and the Nevada state line. Some of the trackworkers built shingle shanties for themselves near Gray's and Coburn's, and for a time they called the place Coburn's Station.

At the same time, a few miles west, by the lake shore and at the foot of the pass, the two hotels, the general store, and the sawmill of Donner Lake City were struggling to keep alive on the proceeds of their business from the California stages. But when, in the spring of '68, the tunnel was finished and the tracks were down across the Sierra all the way from Sacramento to Reno, there was no longer use for the turnpike stages, nor any need for Donner Lake City. Its few residents gave up trying, left the lake, and moved to Coburn's.

Throughout its early years the place seemed always to be burning down. (The longest chapter in the history of almost all the Northern California towns would be the one devoted to its major fires.) The first fire was in July of '68, when Coburn's establishment and the few stores and saloons along Front Street all went up in smoke. But there were fourteen or fifteen lumber mills nearby, all taking the mountain fir and pine for the Central Pacific snowsheds and ties, and for the prodigious timbering of the Comstock drifts and winzes, and so the town was rebuilt. The autumn's first snow that year fell upon a new and bigger settlement, one that boasted nearly three hundred buildings, a Central Pacific roundhouse, a theater with a permanent stock company, and a new name—Truckee.

For all its newness and brashness, it was from the beginning an illegitimate child, the product of the self-interest of the Comstock Lode and the Central (later the Southern) Pacific. To both it was useful, yet neither cared formally to acknowledge it. And to both its physical position seemed in peculiar harmony with its social standing: it was, and always would be, on the wrong side of the tracks. The right side was solidly occupied by the genteel resorts and expensive pleasure pavilions of the Lake Tahoe coves and bays. Thus shunned and disowned by both its parents, Truckee went its own independent way, and promptly became a juvenile delinquent among the California mountain towns.

It was neither as raucous or as tough as Bodie, for instance, but it was trying hard for the same effect. The lights along Jibboom Street, a few steps from the main drag, were just as red as any that beckoned the swaggering, free-spending Bodie badmen. The nudes over the backbars of the Front Street saloons were just as lush as those you found in the plush-and-crystal bars along Virginia City's C Street. But Truckee worked too hard at the sawmills and on the railroad for anyone to take it seriously as a wicked and naughty town. It was a wage earner, a swinger of axes and sledges, a tender of mills and locomotives—not a happy-go-lucky miner that was broke one day and had banknotes to throw to the birds the next. It wasn't geared for excesses in any field, and sometimes even the violence of its early days seemed to achieve nothing more than a burlesque or, at best, a poor imitation, of the real thing.

Once—it was in the spring of '69—five masked desperadoes walked into Burckhalter's Store waving six-guns. At first, no one paid any attention to them. The cashier calmly went on counting the store's receipts, some $18,000 in cash. Hank Brown, in a chair beside the stove, scarcely looked up from his newspaper. The holdup men approached a clerk, and robbed him of his pocketbook.

"Boys," Brown observed from behind his newspaper, "you're a-layin' yourselves liable to get hurt."

One of the bandits, smarting under the casual reception he and his comrades were receiving, crossed to Brown, swept aside the newspaper, and pointed his gun at Brown's chest.

"By God," said Brown, "this means business." He rose to his feet, picked up the chair, and brought it down with a crash on the bandit's head. The badman sagged to the floor like a sack of barley. Brown stepped over him and charged his four confederates so furiously that they fled in panic through the door and into the street. The cashier continued his counting. Brown put his chair back by the stove, picked up his paper, and went on reading. When the man on the floor showed signs of revival, they sent for the town constable and turned him over to the law. That was the beginning and the end of the annual spring crime wave in Truckee.

The summer crime wave that year was a little more spectacular. Experience, if nothing else, had told the girls of Jibboom Street that a good man was hard to find, and the trouble developed when two of them, Belle

Butler and Carrie Smith (known familiarly as "The Spring Chicken"), gave the heart off their sleeves to the same one. It reached the point where the town was too small for the three of them. Carrie declared the third of July a personal Independence Day. Accompanied by her friend and pander,

George Prior, she invaded Belle's boudoir in Lotta Morton's Jibboom Street bawdyhouse. Face to face, they upbraided each other so loudly and so shrilly their squawks carried up from the riverbanks and across the tracks to the Front Street saloons. "Must be a fox in the hen coop," grinned the boys at the Virginia Bar, and called for another pre-holiday refresher.

Meanwhile, in answer to Belle's cry for reinforcements, John Whipley, the house pimp, charged into the room and the two couples attacked each other as if their objective were nothing short of total dismemberment. Havoc swept the boudoir. When it was completely dismantled, Carrie and Prior retired to the street, leaving Belle and Whipley to disentangle themselves from the wreckage.

The holiday sun was only a little higher than Mount Rose's summit when Whipley burst from the bawdyhouse determined to shoot Prior on sight. His intention had preceded him down the street, and as he pushed through the swinging doors of a Front Street barroom, the boys at the mahogany dissolved and Prior was left standing there by himself to confront his gun-toting enemy. Prior drew. They exchanged eight shots. The boys crawled out from under the poker tables to find Prior lying wounded on the floor.

At this point, Carrie appeared on the scene. She took one look at Prior and ran down Front Street for a doctor. A few doors from the bar, she encountered Lotta Morton on her way from Jibboom Street to learn the outcome of the duel. Next to meeting Belle Butler, it was all Carrie could hope for: halting in her tracks, she threw a haymaker at Lotta's jaw. They both went down swinging. As they kicked and clawed like wildcats in the Front Street dust, Belle Butler rounded a corner with six-gun blazing, aimed at Carrie, and hit her friend Lotta.

This turn of events put a stop to the fight. Before she could mow down any innocent bystanders, Belle was disarmed and arrested. Doctors got busy on Prior and Lotta and assured them both of recovery. Truckee picked up where it had left off before the shooting, and settled down to its old routine. And though they were pretty dazzling, the Fourth of July fireworks that night seemed pale indeed compared to the morning display along Front Street.

Later, Belle got eighteen months in jail for her shooting spree. And, for all anyone knows, she got the good man that had been hard to find as well. Carrie decided that, after all his trouble, the least she could do for Prior was to marry him. And, a few months later, that is what she did.

If it wasn't a fight or a shooting, it was a five-alarm fire. Truckee was a ramshackle lumber town, and with all that pine and fir around, Truckeeans saw little use in building with expensive bricks; it was cheaper to rebuild your house of wood four or five times than it was to bring bricks over the mountain and make it fireproof to start with. And when, in the wintertime, the snow covered the basin floor 8 or 10 feet deep, and the thermometer was well below zero and the fires were burning brightly in the cast-iron stoves, it was not at all difficult for a drunken timber faller or a careless housewife or an overheated chimney to set the whole town ablaze. (Photos show that most of the buildings in Truckee during this period had outside stairs from the street to the second floor, not only for

convenience during the heavy snows, but also for use as fire escapes.) Two
of these fires roared through Truckee with disastrous effect in the early
winter of '71. Scarcely had the snows melted and the town recovered,
when a third and even greater conflagration reduced Truckee once more
to ruins. As the story of this fire was pieced together, it emerged as the
most spectacular (and costly) climax to a domestic quarrel in the history
of the West.

One night that July, Louis Derr, the owner of a Front Street saloon, had
a violent squabble with his wife. He finally declared that he had had
enough. Announcing that he was going over the hill to San Francisco, he
packed his bag and stormed out of the house. "And I'm never coming
back!" he shouted as he slammed the front door.

"I'll say you're never coming back," Mrs. Derr retorted grimly, and set
fire to her husband's saloon. The saloon blazed merrily, and so did twenty
other shops and bars, a number of homes, a hotel, and the schoolhouse, all
together valued at more than $100,000. Headstrong Truckeeans were all
for seizing Mrs. Derr and stringing her up to a tall pine, and thus con-
ferring upon her the distinction of being the first woman lynched in California since the Downieville hanging of Juanita in '51. While they were
talking about it, Mrs. Derr prudently left town. She never came back, either.

*Truckee in 1873,* wrote Bancroft, the historian, *was one of the liveliest
towns in California. The new overland railway brought to it money, merchandise and activity; but it also brought the bad element common to new
prosperous localities.*

In that very year (and so closely does it still resemble a Hollywood set
for *West of the Pecos,* you can imagine it happening there today as you
look at Front Street from your pullman window) two representatives of
that element burst through the doors of a Front Street saloon, with Navy
revolvers in their hands, and shot it out in the street.

They were Jack White and Andy Fugate, and the cause of it all was a
woman. White, riddled with bullets, reeled back and fell in the dust. But
as Fugate continued firing, he pulled himself to his elbow and emptied
his gun at Fugate. Fugate, hit and bleeding, staggered forward a few steps
and crumpled to the road. For a few moments the street was utterly still.
Then there was the scuffle of hurrying feet as men appeared from their

hiding places in bars and stores. They ran to the gunfighters lying in the road. Someone said they ought to get a doctor, and someone else said a doctor wouldn't do either of them any good, and he was the one that was right. Both White and Fugate were dead.

For a while, the boys and girls of Jibboom Street quieted down, but by the end of the next year they were getting rough and out of hand again, and the upright and upstanding citizens of the town decided they would have to do something drastic. As a result of this decision they organized a Vigilance Committee they called the 601. A few days later, small red ribbons fluttered a sinister warning from the Front Street awning posts; the 601 had given the boys and girls their ticket-of-leave.

Most of them, remembering how Virginia City's 601 had given short shrift and a long rope to two undesirables who refused to get off the Comstock only two years before, left quietly. A rebellious pair, however, defied the Truckee vigilantes: Carrie Prior, the "Spring Chicken," and a desperado named Bob Mellon, whose favorite story in the Jibboom Street ginmills was of the time in San Francisco he had fought and won a Spanish duel, in which his and his antagonist's left arms had been bound together, and the weapons were razor-sharp bowie knives.

Carrie scoffed at the red ribbons. "Come and get me," she jeered. "I'll be at Hayward's place in the alley. With me will be forty men, every one of them ready to blow your brains out."

As for Mellon, he told them to come after him, too. They'd never get him alive, and when he went out, he'd take a dozen vigilantes with him.

The 601 met at midnight. There were about twenty-five of them, ranging in prominence from D. B. Frink, editor of the *Truckee Republican,* to the owners of small Front Street shops and restaurants. All of them were armed, and all wore black masks that covered their heads and shoulders. To frustrate identification further, their coats were turned inside out.

After carefully laying plans for their assault, they left their hall and stole silently through the night to Hayward's back-street establishment. Four of them separated from the group to stand guard at the back door. The others boldly entered the front door. Hayward quailed before their masks and drawn pistols.

The leader spoke with muffled voice.

"Take us through the house. Open every door as you go."

Hayward, trembling with fear, did as he was told. The masked men were tense. At any moment, from any dark room or corner, they might be ambushed.

The first-floor rooms were deserted. Hayward, holding aloft a lantern, preceded them down the narrow hallway to the stairs that led to the second story. Suddenly he stopped short. The vigilantes, in a file behind him, halted. He pointed a quivering finger at the back door at the end of the hallway. Sticking through a break in its panel, covering the entire line of men, was a gleaming pistol barrel.

There was no time for conjecture: this was the resistance Carrie and Mellon had promised. The vigilantes started shooting. Caught in the line of fire, Hayward spun around and pitched to the hall floor, fatally wounded. A shrill cry arose in the blackness outside. The shooting ceased. A dozen vigilantes rushed upstairs and in a matter of seconds returned, herding before them Carrie, Mellon, and several quaking hoodlums. The others went to the back door, flung it open, and beheld a horrifying sight. Three men, in the black masks of the 601, bent over a fourth man, also masked, who lay still on the ground.

"It—it was all a mistake," one of them stammered. "He thought you were Carrie's men."

The leader stood over them, holding the lantern Hayward had dropped. "Who is it?" he asked slowly.

Someone reached down and ripped off the dead man's mask. The pallid rays of the lantern fell upon the face of D. B. Frink.

It was a long time before the town recovered from the results of this night's work. As Bancroft said, it *sent a thrill of horror through the community, never to be forgotten*. But a few days later, the red ribbons went up for a desperado named Spencer. He left town all right, but came back again and on Christmas Day stood at a Front Street bar having a drink with his father. Eight masked members of the 601 pushed grimly through the door. This time there was no wild firing. Spencer fell in a hail of buckshot. He was taken over the mountains to Nevada City, where he recovered. For the rest of his life, Spencer avoided Truckee.

After this, they say, no badman was brave enough, or rash enough, to defy the red ribbons. It must be true, because they appeared on the awning posts quite a few times in the years that followed. Those for whom they were meant must have drifted away quickly and quietly, for after that Christmas Day no one ever again saw in Truckee the guns and black masks of the 601.

That was Truckee—still a frontier town of red warning ribbons and vigilantes twenty years after San Francisco, Columbia, and the Gold Rush camps had grown beyond the need of organized citizen vigilance. San Francisco, in fact, was now a metropolis of elegance; she was crowning herself with a crown of Comstock silver, calling herself the Pacific Paris, and doing her best to forget the reckless, roistering days of her Gold Rush youth. As for the Gem of the Southern Mines, and most of the other towns that had had nothing but their gold to make them great, their gold was gone and their life already over. Time had only to reduce them to ruins for them to fulfill their destiny.

And now, in the '70s, the second and last bonanza was running out. Pretty soon the Comstock drifts and crosscuts that lay under Virginia City would have no more silver and gold to yield, and that town, too, would fall silent and deserted. The famous mountain zephyrs—the relentless winds that blew down Mount Davidson's barren slopes—would whistle eerily through the shafthead timbers and the abandoned stamp mills, and the lustiest, liveliest boom town of its time would become a mountain rookery and a bleak haven for the desert rats.

Such a fate might have confronted Truckee, had she been nothing more than a timber town. Men in those days took timber the way they took gold and silver, and slaughtered entire forests of pine and fir in an orgy of greed; and any town that these men built was doomed, as the Mother Lode towns were doomed, by the fact that rapacity sets its own limits when it selects its area of operation. After it has snatched everything this area has to give, it must cease, or go its predatory way, leaving behind it a waste land.

Truckee had its stake in the Comstock: its humming sawmills were still cutting millions of feet in lumber for the mines under Virginia City, and no doubt the blue smoke of its sawdust burners lay hazy over the town and the basin many evenings for many years; its kilns produced tons of charcoal for the Virginia City stoves and furnaces. That was one life of Truckee that would die with the mines and the timber. But her best and longest life was represented by the rails of steel that lay east and west, through the center of town. Let the veins peter out, let men denude the mountain slopes of the tall evergreens; as long as the rails was there, Truckee would be there, and the rails would stay for a long time.

So it lived in its ramshackle houses on the wrong side of these tracks, on its one main street, and confidently did its work. If the picnic basket and the parasol symbolized the life of the fashionable summer resorts of nearby Tahoe, then the life of Truckee was represented by the lunch pail and a pair of coveralls. And that was all right with Truckee.

Further encouragement to independence came from another source: its isolation. As it was cut off socially from the world of Tahoe, so it was cut off physically from almost any other kind of world it could imagine. A bare five miles to the west rose the Sierra barrier, and to the east stretched the desert of Nevada. Truckee sensed that, except for the railroad, it was on its own in every possible way.

Toward the end of the '70s, when its population had reached 3,000 (including 1,000 Chinese), and its sawmills and kilns and Central Pacific roundhouse filled the keen mountain air with smoke and dust, the scream of saws, and the panting of engines, C. F. McGlashan, the editor of the *Truckee Republican,* discovered for Truckee something that it had always wanted—a past.

For its first ten years the town had had gunplay and sawmills, Jibboom Street and locomotives on its mind and hadn't given much thought to Donner Lake; but by the time those ten years had passed Donner Lake was exerting an appealing charm over thousands of summer and winter visitors. Thoughtfully McGlashan looked at the lake and listened to the laughter that rang from its tamarack groves and over its calm and reflective surface.

*Tourists and picnic parties annually flock to its shore,* he wrote, *and Bierstadt has made it the subject of one of his finest, grandest paintings. . . . In winter it is almost as popular a pleasure resort as during the summer. The jingling of sleighbells, and the shouts . . . of skating parties, can be heard almost constantly. The lake forms the grandest skating park on the Pacific Coast.*

It seemed passing strange to him that a brief thirty years ago—before the Comstock boom, before, even, the great Gold Rush—Donner Lake had been celebrated from the Pacific to the Atlantic as the wilderness setting of the most dramatic event in the annals of all the overland trails. The very name of the lake had been synonymous with catastrophe, and its story had contributed an entire pageant of despair and death to the history of the West.

As McGlashan said, *It is a tale that has been repeated in many a miner's cabin, by many a hunter's campfire, and in many a frontiersman's home, and everywhere it has been listened to with bated breath.*

Surveying the happy throngs that came to the lake in the late '70s, and considering this paradox—considering also the circulation of his newspaper—McGlashan decided to revive the story of the Donner Party and run it in serial form in the *Republican*. It would make good reading for the tourists and give a background to the resort and, for that matter, to Truckee and all the rest of the basin country. The other side of the mountains was welcome to its Mother Lode and its ghost towns; in Truckee's past was The California Tragedy.

He began his serial in 1878, working from the varying accounts that had been written years before by several survivors of the party. As he picked up and passed along their discrepancies and errors of memory, he received numerous letters of protest from members of the party who were still alive. His interest quickened. And what had started out as a commercial running feature of historical hack work soon developed into a research project to which he was devoting nearly all of his time and energy. Confronted on every hand by conflicting stories, fragments of reports, hearsay, gossip, patent distortions, and an almost hopeless tangle of factual detail, McGlashan became obsessed with a desire to know and write the truth about the Donner Party. He found the survivors ready and willing to help.

McGlashan's *History of the Donner Party* ran until late in 1879. In its final form it was drawn, he wrote, . . . *from all the works heretofore published, from over one thousand letters received from the survivors, from ample manuscript, and from personal interviews with the most important actors in the tragedy. . . . Neither time, pains or expense have been spared in ferreting out the truth.*

Not long after the last installment had appeared, McGlashan revised his narrative and published it as a book. Its warm and wide reception by historians and the general public convinced him that he had accomplished all he had hoped for and more: not only had he written the definitive story of the Donners, but he had, in writing it, brought clearly into focus the dramatic, pre-Gold Rush past of the Truckee Basin.

Donner Lake, the region east of it to Truckee and west of it to the pass, and the pass itself, were established once and for all as a natural monument to the ordeal of the pioneers in their quest for their land of promise, their land of dreams.

A ten minutes' walk from the Truckee railroad station, on the slope of a hill northwest of town stood the Rocking Stone, said to be one of twenty-four in all the world.

There was, on this hillside, an immense flat-topped granite boulder about thirty feet high and slightly more than thirty feet in diameter. Exactly centered on the top of this boulder was a smaller stone. It was about six feet high, its maximum diameter was also about six feet and it tapered at the base. So delicately poised was this stone that it could be rocked back and forth with a push of the hand. Both boulders were granite.

The Rocking Stone was a work of nature that defied explanation. McGlashan was an amateur dabbler in science. Years before the United States Coast and Geodetic Survey got around to it, he sounded Lake Tahoe with a rope and a bottle of champagne and announced that its maximum depth was 1,645 feet, a figure later verified to the inch by the government scientists. He was both intrigued and baffled by the curious boulder. He had his friend John Muir, the noted naturalist, examine it. Muir's analysis was that the arrangement had been created by glacial action. McGlashan, apparently, was willing to take Muir's word for it, but aged braves of the Washoe Indians, who had hunted along the Truckee meadows before the time of Frémont, told him another story, an ancient tribal legend. (Several years ago, this legend was contributed to the permanent records of the Nevada County Historical Society by Mrs. Nonette V. Hennessy of San Francisco, McGlashan's daughter.)

Many moons before the coming of the white man, these braves said, the Washoes pitched their wigwams about the great granite boulder. No prowling animal could scale the sides of this rock, and so they would put their meat upon its shelflike top, to dry for winter use. But one day, while the young braves were hunting and fishing, and old men and women and children tended the wigwam fires, a large flock of birds swooped down on the rock and flew away with all the meat.

Time and again this happened. At length, the Washoes, faced with winter starvation, prayed to their gods for help. The Wind God took pity on them and caused a great storm to darken the sun. In the dawning light that followed the storm, the watchful Indians gave a cry of thanksgiving, for, balanced atop the massive boulder, was another smaller stone, "as like the great rock as a youth is like his father."

When the birds came again for the drying meat, the Wind God breathed upon the new stone. It rocked like a treetop in the wind and frightened the birds away. "And as long as the Washoes lived in this place," the legend concluded, "they had an abundance of dried fish and meat for the winter."

A few years after completing his Donner Party history, McGlashan bought the Truckee hillside of the Rocking Stone. Near the stone he built a house, and around the stone itself, on the flat top of the large boulder, he constructed a small fourteen-sided tower. He used this odd structure as a private museum in which he exhibited the many rusty utensils, wagon irons, and other relics that he had excavated during his research at the Donner Party cabin sites, and also a large collection of mounted butterflies and moths. Atop a flagpole on the roof of his tower McGlashan hung a newfangled electric arc light, which he turned on every night and which bathed the building and the hillside in an eerie glow.

In their book, *Sierra-Nevada Lakes,* Dr. and Mrs. George Hinkle, both natives of Truckee (Mrs. Hinkle is also a daughter of McGlashan), told of the weird night scene and its startling effect upon anyone seeing it for the first time:

*Not infrequently wild-eyed train passengers, wakened from a deep sleep to catch a glimpse of the glowing, wraith-like edifice, would wonder querulously what in God's name that thing was up on the hill.*

But in another moment, the strange scene and the other lights of Truckee would flash past. Another engine out of the roundhouse would have been coupled onto the train, and the train, its long whistle fading into the night, would pull away toward the conquest of the dark summit, 5 miles west. The awakened passengers would compose themselves again for sleep. The red marker lights on its observation car would recede into the darkness, down the straight westbound track: the click of the wheels would grow faint in the distance and die away. McGlashan's light on the hillside would gleam fitfully over the Rocking Stone of the Wind God, and over the little town that the train had left behind.

Now it was more than half a century later, and a hundred years from the night that Patrick Breen had written in his diary of Milton's return from the Donners' camp with the sad news about Jacob Donner and the others.

As I emerged from the café and stood for a moment in Front Street I heard the sound of another train—the faraway rumble of a freight coming down off the divide. I took the crosswalk through the high snowbanks that lined the street, and stood on the station platform in the dim half-light of the station lights and waited for her to come through.

Orion rode high over Truckee, glittering brightly in the night sky; but no light shone above McGlashan's tower, which was still there above the Rocking Stone. The tower was dark, the Donner Hotel was dark, and so were the Donner Theater and the Donner Garage, down at the end of the street, and most of the town's 400 homes, except for the colored Christmas-tree lights in the windows.

McGlashan was dead and his house had burned down years before. A large Quonset hut, converted into a Veterans' Auditorium, now stood upon its site. The Ice Palace and the toboggan slide that he had built in the '90s to promote Truckee as a winter-sports center were gone, too. But had he come back to Front Street on this December night, his first impression might have been that no time at all had passed since he had left it. It was still a frontier town, a like-me-the-way-I-am-or-the-hell-with-you kind of town, and, at night, a lonesome town.

That afternoon, Walter Barrett, publisher of Truckee's weekly newspaper, the *Sierra Sun,* had told me that native Truckeeans felt as though they lived in No Man's Land—a remote region legally part of California, yet separated from it physically and in nearly every other way by the Sierra barrier.

"Up until ten years ago," he said, "the nearest law enforcement officer was the sheriff in Nevada City, 53 miles away. The closest thing to the

law around here was the game warden—and nobody wanted him within
a hundred miles of Truckee."

Sometimes, he said, Truckeeans wish the Nevada state line were west of
them, instead of 21 miles to the east.

"The way most of them look at it is this: Our deer herd in Nevada; the
fish swim down the Truckee River into Nevada; we trade in Reno, so
most of our money goes to Nevada. Even Donner Lake water goes to
Nevada. So they figure that California might as well give the land to
Nevada."

The development of the automobile and the construction of the transcontinental highway through the town did not mean a great deal to
Truckee; the cars just kept going through. If they came from the east, they
were on their way to Tahoe or San Francisco, and if they came over the
mountains they were bound for Reno or points beyond.

When, about 1930, the State made 40 an all-year highway, the winter
sports area developed, not at Truckee, as McGlashan had once hoped, but
westward on the Donner Summit. And now, on a winter Sunday, as many
as 40,000 skiers swarmed to the summit slopes and lodges, making a winter
playland of the desolate wastes that, a century ago, were a white and
frozen hell to the half-crazed emigrants of The Forlorn Hope.

But Barrett, who had been a metropolitan newspaperman, told me that
he wouldn't live anywhere in the world but Truckee. It was a good,
friendly little town, he said, to live and work in. The air was fresh and
sharp, and when you looked out of your office window you saw mountains
and pines, the green meadows in the summer, and in the winter the splendor of the snow and the summit peaks, that had loomed like that against
the sky for sixty million years. . . .

The rumble of the freight grew louder. Its air horn blew a crossing
signal, and the proud blasts came down through the night like sword
thrusts. Its great headlight suddenly appeared as it came into the straightaway. The locomotive, a cab-ahead mountain engine, came working
smoothly down the eastbound tracks, its half-mile of cars a dark line behind it.

The night agent appeared at the door of the station. We waved to the
fireman in the cab window and watched the locomotive charge past as if
we were waiting to hear it shout, above the rush of the exhaust and the

pounding of the drivers, some word, some iron cry of triumph to us as it went by.

The earth trembled beneath our feet as it thundered on toward the Truckee canyon and the destination that lay somewhere in the dark, to the east.

# SHASTA COUNTRY

# CHAPTER SEVEN

# Shasta–I

ABOUT NOON on October 3, 1843, thirteen men, each with a riding horse and a pack mule, turned their backs on the Snake River and the high adobe walls of Fort Boisé and headed west for the Malheur, and when, about four o'clock that afternoon, they reached the grassy banks and the brush willows of this river, they pitched their camp for the night.

Although the 15 miles they traveled had not tired them very much, they turned in early that autumn evening by the Malheur's swift-rushing waters. They had something on their minds, something there wasn't much use talking about. Not what lay behind them—nearly four months had passed since they left Westport Landing on the broad Missouri—not all that wilderness, but the wilderness that lay ahead of them.

Francis Payette, the Hudson's Bay Company factor at Fort Boisé, had told them they would have rough going ahead of them. The mountains were high and rugged. There were no trails. The Indians were treacherous. It might be wiser to strike northwest across the Blue Mountains to the Columbia and Fort Vancouver, winter there, and move south next spring, with the melting of the snows. . . .

But the thought of the long California Valley had led them like a mirage of Paradise across the wilderness behind them, and they could not dispel it now if they wished. Joe Chiles, their guide and leader, had been to California in '41; he had told them he thought he could get them through. Thirty-five days, it might take them, but they'd make it.

So with all the food Payette had been able to spare—a meal a day for each man for two weeks—they had said good-by to Boisé. No one from the East had ever gone into California this way before, Payette had said; but here they were, under the stars of Oregon, beside a stream the French-Canadian trappers had named the Misfortune, with the long valley of the Sacramento sleeping beneath the same night sky, far to the south-west.

And in that direction they struggled on, over the ridges and the cut-rock highlands. Sixteen, and twenty-two, and twenty-five miles a day. On the evening of October 8, as they camped near a mountain covered with stunted cedars, an Indian approached their fire. They gave him a little food and some presents. When they awoke the next morning he was gone, and with him one of their best rifles.

Two days farther on, as they were breaking camp, many Indians appeared and crowded about their horses and pack mules. Payette had warned them of this country. Trappers had vanished out here. They saddled their horses silently, enduring the derisive and truculent gestures of the Indians, and pushed on.

They reached the country of the old fire mountains, and crossed pumice fields that were like expanses of white encrusted foam.

Their food was running out. At dusk on the 16th, they killed some ducks, and that evening by the campfire, twenty-six-year-old Pierson Barton Reading wrote in his journal:

*. . . They were most welcome in our starving camp. Our provisions are nearly exhausted, we have been living for the past three days on a pint of weak soup for each man twice a day, not knowing the distance we may have to travel before finding game. Leaves us in a most unpleasant uncertainty.*

But on the 18th they stalked an antelope, killed it, and ate it all. They

*They traveled along ledges that dropped a sheer 1,200 feet*

built their campfire high that night. As they turned in, it commenced to snow.

They made their way down the west shore of Goose Lake, that was walled in by high mountains (crossing the forty-second parallel that now marks the boundary between Oregon and California), still bearing southwest toward the California Valley, and on the 22d, Reading said, they saw *a very high point of a high mountain covered with snow and running up in the shape of a sugar loaf.* He did not say in what direction it lay, but it could have been, and undoubtedly was, Mount Shasta, 14,000 feet high and some eighty miles westward.

After leaving the lake, they struck a winding creek flowing to the southwest. It was the home of many beaver, and it took them across as desolate and hellish a land as they had ever seen or imagined; but still in their minds was the magic mirage of the Valley in the Sun, and this land was what they had to cross to get there, and so they followed the creek because it led them where they wished to go.

On the 23d, they came to many pitfalls, eight or nine feet deep, whose mouths were concealed beneath twigs and grass. The Indians inhabiting the region through which this creek flowed had dug them to trap game. That morning, Milton McGee, breaking a trail ahead of the party, tumbled into one of them, but climbed out uninjured. (Later, because of the traps, Californians called the stream the Pit River; the Indians who dug them became the Pit River Indians.)

Three days later they traveled along ledges that dropped a sheer 1,200 feet to their guiding stream. Day and night they were haunted by Indians who lurked warily behind them on the trail. Once more their food was exhausted, and the barren volcanic reaches of the country yielded no game, nor even berries. On this night, a Thursday, Reading wrote:

*We are certainly able to speak as regards the resources of this country in the way of edibles, having eaten nothing since Tuesday morning. In this condition we suffer very much, not only from the pain of starvation but from the fatigue of walking as we begin to grow weak, and walk we must, the mountains being so steep that our horses can scarcely climb them alone. Have traveled hard all day and only made 20 miles southwest.*

The next evening, ten minutes after they had pitched camp, a band of yelling, paint-streaked Indians broke from the underbush and attacked with bows and arrows. Rifle fire drove them away. All that night the vigilant guards stared nervously into the darkness beyond the firelight and the picketed animals, but the Indians did not attack again. In the morning they left the river and struck more directly south.

They awoke on the morning of the 30th to find that seven of their horses and mules had been arrow-slain during the night. Swearing vengeance, they determined to shoot on sight, for the next two days, every Indian that they saw. The animals they butchered and of the meat thus obtained ate what they could; the rest was packed for the trail. Then they burned the superfluous saddles and broke camp about noon. On this day they traveled 7 miles, and began to see oak trees.

It was on the last day of October that they left the highlands. And as they came to the crest of another hill, they looked to the west—and saw the valley they had come so far to find.

*Never were a set of poor worn out travelers more gratified than we were, after so much toil and travel, to have the Eldorado in view,* Reading wrote that night. *No one can imagine our feelings. . . . Thanks to the great Giver of all Good for our success!*

The next day, as they pressed on toward their destination, they killed two deer and two grizzly bears. The day after that, the 2d of November, some Indians, naked and timid, offered them pieces of acorn bread as a token of friendship.

It was cloudy and raining as they raised camp on the 3d. They followed a westward-flowing stream that was cut with many canyons. After riding 8 miles, they came to a high rocky ridge. Of all the ridges they had crossed this was the last.

*[We] descended from there into a beautiful valley, very large, being the main valley of California. No hills and the appearance of an immense prairie, the streams winding through it with a considerable growth of timber. . . . The climate is most delightful, the grass and trees are as green and fresh as in the latitude of Philadelphia in the month of May! Saw plenty of deer, elk and bear.*

*. . . The valley today presents a more beautiful appearance than any we have passed through. Should suppose its width to be about 60 miles, length ranges north and south. In the last direction appears the same beautiful country as far as the eye can reach.*

As far as the eye could reach was the long valley of California, mirage and enchantment no longer, but a Paradise gained and true.

For Reading, as for thousands of the emigrants, California held out the promise not only of a new way of life, but of a new life. A member of a prominent family of New Jersey pioneers, he had, as a twenty-one-year-old cotton broker in Vicksburg, Mississippi, gone bankrupt in the panic of 1837. No sooner had he recovered than the dishonesty of a partner again brought his firm into bankruptcy, and left him $60,000 in debt. About the same time he suffered another blow in the death of his young wife. Reading wrote an I.O.U. for the $60,000 and cleared out for Westport Landing on the Missouri, and an emigrant train west.

Now, at Sutter's Fort, impressed by Captain Sutter, his 172,000-acre kingdom, his 10,000 cattle, the fort itself with its massive walls and embastioned cannon and armed guard of sixty Indians—his imagination stirred by this frontier barony and the valley itself, which he always associated in his mind with the Indian heaven, the Happy Hunting Ground —Reading determined almost at once that he would seek no farther. However appealing and filled with charm might be the old mission vineyards and fields to the south, the palms and pepper trees and red-roofed adobes of Monterey, the village seaport of Yerba Buena on San Francisco Bay and the pueblos warm in the sun—this green valley, he felt, was his country, the native land to which he had at last come home.

It was Sam Hensley, one of his trailmates on the journey from Boisé, who told Reading about the northern end of the valley. While Reading had stayed at the fort as a clerk and chief trapper for Sutter, Hensley had gone north on a trip of exploration. He returned with glowing words for an expanse of land he had seen as he had returned down the Sacramento. On the west bank of the river it was, slightly to the north of where they had struck the valley on their way from Boisé. Reading listened eagerly, his eyes alight at the memory of what he had glimpsed that November morning as they stood upon the ridge, at the valley's rim.

A few weeks later—early in '44—he rode north with Hensley and John Bidwell to see that land again. In February he was in Monterey with letters of introduction from Captain Sutter, and a favor to ask of Manuel Micheltorena, the cultured, courteous governor of Alta California. Anxious to secure his far northern frontier against the Indians and a growing tide of settlers from the east and north, Micheltorena yielded at once to Reading's request. That month Reading wrote to his brother in the East:

*I have received from the government a large tract of land as a grant. The title is good and secures the land to me forever. The tract is in length five leagues, on the bank of the river, and one league deep. . . . A more beautiful tract of land I never saw.*

But it was two and a half years before Reading permanently achieved this ultimate end of the quest and adventure that he had begun at Westport Landing, on the banks of the Missouri.

In the autumn of '45, a few months after a trapping expedition into the Trinity Mountains and along the Klamath and Shasta Rivers, he built a small house on his ranch and stocked his land with cattle and left a man there to take care of them. The next spring marauding Indians set fire to the house and destroyed it, and ran his cattle into the wilderness. In June of '46 he took part in the Bear Flag Revolt, and the next month sailed south with Frémont's California Battalion for the closing phases of the Mexican War in California.

James Marshall, you may remember, took this trip, too; and it is strange indeed to detach these two pioneers from the roster of this motley army and reflect for a moment on the varying fortunes of two lives interwoven by their common desire, by time, place, and the dynamics of history.

Both were born in New Jersey, not so many miles apart, yet the circumstances of birth gave Reading everything (his great-grandfather had been a governor of New Jersey and a trustee of Princeton University), and Marshall nothing. Reading was tall, erect, and gentle; Marshall was tall, shambling, and crude. Reading was a man of decision and action, Marshall a neurotic and a dreamer. Reading was liked and respected; Marshall was shunned and distrusted.

As disparate as they were, something in both of them responded to the California promise, and they headed west.

They must have known each other for several years around Sutter's Fort. On the *Cyane,* which took the Battalion to San Diego, they must have seen each other daily. When they met upon the *Cyane's* decks, what did they find to say to each other? Perhaps they did not speak at all. Already Reading was rising to his natural level: his leadership in the June rebellion at Sonoma had earned him appointment as a lieutenant, and soon he would be named paymaster of all the United States troops in California, with the rank of major. Marshall, who also participated in the revolt, remained nothing more than a gunbearer.

The nature of the campaign that followed gave no one an opportunity to distinguish himself for gallantry. Reading, however, made the most of what came along. At the campaign's end, he was one of the three United States peace commissioners who drafted the Treaty of Cahuenga, which ended the war in California. To Marshall the campaign seemed to have been arranged only for his personal inconvenience. He did what was expected of him and no more, and vented his irritation in grumbling and an occasional spree in the *cantinas* of the southern pueblos.

When the war was over, one more odd coincidence of interest would send both of them hastening northward to their ranches at the far end of the valley. There Marshall would find disaster and defeat, and would give up his brief struggle for independence and return embittered to Sutter's Fort. Reading, on whom the same misfortune had fallen a few months before, would start anew and ultimately, with Bidwell, would become one of the two great ranchers of the northern valley.

Reading would be asked several times to accept the nomination for the office of governor of California. He would die respected and loved by all who knew him. The writers of his obituaries would be hard-pressed for adjectives with which to describe this pioneer to the satisfaction of his friends and contemporaries, and for newspaper space extensive enough to permit mention of his many contributions to the early history of the north.

Among those inevitably noted would be the fact that Reading, during his trapping expedition in '45, had named the Trinity River, which in turn gave its name to the Trinity Mountains and Trinity County. His land grant was the northernmost given by the Mexican colonial government. When he occupied it, he became the first permanent white settler within the limits of what was later Shasta County, and the first between Bidwell's *Rancho Chico* and the Oregon line. He was the first to discover gold in the far north, and one of his discoveries led to the founding of Reading's Springs, which subsequently became Shasta, the Queen City of the North. He inaugurated navigation on the upper Sacramento River, served as Special Indian Agent for the Federal government, and planted the first cotton in the State, the first olives in Northern California, and the first grapevines north of Sacramento. As a civilian surveyor and engineer, he laid out several of the largest cities north of San Francisco.

Against this record, there is almost nothing to oppose in behalf of Marshall. He made some wagons, fashioned a few household implements, built a sawmill, and died in poverty, a shattered and disillusioned wreck. But because on a raw January day in 1848 he picked a gold flake from the mill-race, because of this, and only because of this, it is Marshall whom the world remembers—Marshall the artisan, the unhappy, haunted carpenter.

Reading, the wellborn, the pathfinder, the builder of the commonwealth, stands in history's shadows, his accomplishments familiar now but to a few. If there is a public monument to him, I do not know where it is. If a town, mountain, or hill in California bears his name, I cannot find it on the map.

Yet, in spite of it all, who is to say upon which man fell the smile of fortune?

In April, then, of 1847, when they were mustered out of the Battalion, the two turned northward. Marshall, as we have seen, found his cattle stolen or slaughtered, and, cursing his luck, went back to working for Sutter, who wanted a sawmill built somewhere on the American River. Reading, on his 5 leagues of the most beautiful land he ever saw, that stretched north for 15 miles from Cottonwood Creek along the Sacramento's west bank, began building his big adobe ranch house.

Already he had selected a name for his *rancho,* one as suggestive of the mystery and promise of the West as Gran Quivira, the Seven Cities of Cibola, and El Dorado. This name was *El Rancho Buenaventura*—The Ranch of Good Fortune.

West of the Sacramento, the creek called Cottonwood formed the southern boundary of the Shasta country. Beyond it lay the farthest corner of the California Valley, walled to the west, north, and east by a vast uncharted wilderness of swift and lonely highland streams, evergreen forests, and bleak towering ranges, that, to the whistling swans and the snow geese flying high and flying north in the springtime, must have appeared a limitless sea of mountains.

Rising from a 3,000-foot plateau in the center of this country, visible for a hundred miles and more and lifting its snowy crest higher by far than the swans would fly, was the fire mountain Shasta.

In Tertiary times, sixty million years ago, it was a gigantic volcano, splitting the heavens with its flames and thunder and pouring forth rivers of smoking lava. Now the flames had withdrawn into its depths. In place of the thunder was a brooding, majestic silence. Snowfields mantled its two craters and its mighty shoulders. Five living glaciers, like sculptors of eternity, shaped and carved its wind-swept slopes. Springs gushing clear and frigid from the side of the mountain formed two rivers which became one—the Sacramento, slowly flowing south to make the valley grass green for the black-tailed deer and the wild oats taller, mile after mile, than the antlers of the stately elk that came down from the north to graze by the alders and the spreading willows.

Tribes of Indians inhabited this country: the Klamaths north on the Klamath River; the Rogues also north, on the Rogue; the Pits and Modocs to the northeast; the Shastans, at the mountain's base; the Wintuns in the south, along Cottonwood Creek; the Yuroks and the Karoks to the northwest, along the middle reaches of the Klamath.

Like the Indians of the plains, the men were tall and muscular, with intelligent faces and bright, keen eyes. The women were small, with delicate hands and feet and smooth, hazel skins.

Both men and women pierced the dividing cartilage in the nose and in it wore a goose quill or a string of shells. Both were tattooed, the men on the arms and chest, and the women on the face, with three blue lines reaching from lower lip to chin.

The men wore belts of ornamented deerskins, and in the wintertime rabbitskin mantles, and sometimes deerskin robes on which were sewn, in patterns, the scalps of bright-plumaged ducks. The women wore aprons, front and back, of deerskin or braided grass, with shells along the fringe; and basketwork caps, painted or interwoven with woodpecker or quail feathers. Sometimes, instead, they wore oak leaves in their thick black hair.

Their winter homes were earthen huts. In the summer they built for themselves shelters of woven swamp flags. The braves hunted deer and antelope with their flat-backed yew and cedar bows and obsidian-tipped arrows, and along the rivers trapped salmon in willow weirs or speared them by torchlight. The women wove their baskets, and ground acorns to flour, and gathered *camas* root and manzanita berries, and cooked the meals, broiling the meat on hot stones or boiling it in their watertight baskets.

The money they exchanged was white shells, the scalps of redheaded woodpeckers, and the all but priceless skin of a white deer.

Within their tribal memory, the volcanic fires of Shasta had again been active. A thousand snows ago, their forefathers had watched the mountain in awe as it shot forth flames by night and a pillar of smoke by day. And now they still believed that it was the part of the earth that the Great Spirit created first of all, and that he was still living far below the crater, within the mountain's depths. To them it was the Creator's home, the Wigwam of the Great Spirit.

For ages, for these thousand snows and many more, the mountain, the dark forests, and the northern valley belonged to the Indians. It is not known precisely when the white intruder first saw or reached the borders of their lonely fastness.

Spanish explorers, venturing north from the Bay of San Francisco in 1817, may have glimpsed the snows of Shasta, low like a white cloud on the northern horizon; it is not certain. The expedition was led by Captain Luis Argüello, and its boats may have ascended the Sacramento River as far as the three buttes that have come to be known as the Marysville Buttes, at the union of the Feather and the Sacramento.

There, or roughly there, on May 20, Fray Narciso Duran, in his diary of the expedition, speculated upon the existence of a pass through the Sierra Nevada, which they discerned far in the northeast. Once this pass through, or around, the mountains were discovered, they would know whether the Indians had been telling the truth . . . *that on the other side of the Sierra Nevada there are people like our soldiers.*

Then he continued:

*At about ten leagues to the northwest of this place we saw the very high hill called by the soldiers that went near its slope Jesus Maria. It is entirely covered with snow. They say that a great river of the same name runs near it and that it enters the Sacramento River, and they conjecture that it may be some branch of the Columbia. This I have heard from some soldier; let the truth be what it may.*

The ambiguities in the entry, the element of hearsay injected, render it all but impossible to interpret the padre's words intelligently. They were approximately one hundred and fifty miles, as the snow goose would fly, from Shasta, and it is perhaps possible that on the clearest of days, from a particular point, through a particular notch in the range of hills to the north, they could have seen the distant peak. But if they did, how did they arrive at the estimate that it was only 10 leagues—about thirty miles—away? And to the northwest?

It is the simple fact that there was no *very high hill,* snow-covered in May, that was visible thirty or even a hundred miles to the northwest of the Marysville Buttes. Perhaps Duran meant that from a point ten leagues to the northwest *we,* in the sense of "our advance scouts," saw the hill in the distance, in some other direction. If this was what he was saying, it could have been Shasta; or it could have been the mountain that came to be known as Lassen Peak, 10,400 feet high, and 70 miles to the southeast of Shasta. So the identity and location of Duran's *very high hill* remains unknown, and a mystery.

On the same day that he mentioned it in his journal, they carved a cross on an oak tree along the riverbank to mark the farthest point of ascent, and blessed it; then turned their boats downstream, traveling southward with great swiftness, because the river was swollen with the melted Sierra snows. . . .

Fours years later, at a time when Governor Pablo Vicente de Sola was asking of the central government in Mexico City 200 infantrymen, four field pieces, and an armed cruiser for the protection of the seacoast and frontiers of Alta California, Argüello was sent on a second expedition to find and challenge some strange people, said now by the Indians to be roving the valley forty or fifty leagues north of San Francisco Bay.

With a force of more than fifty soldiers, Argüello left the Bay late that October and proceeded north for nine days. They saw Indians that approached with hostile attitude and gesture, and fired a round of shot over their heads to send them fleeing in panic. But they came upon no strangers, or trace of any, and somewhere near the valley's end they turned west into mountains of the Coast Range, and then south; and on November 12 reached San Rafael, 20 miles north of San Francisco and the outpost of their northern frontier.

On the last day of their northern advance, and the day before they turned west, Padre Blas Ordaz, the expedition's chaplain and diarist, noted that they had reached a point whence had been seen *two mountains called "Los Cuates"—the Twins.*

Were these twin peaks Shasta and its companion crater Shastina? Were they Shasta and Lassen? Were they Lassen and its prominent neighbor Broke-off Mountain? Because Ordaz failed to include in his notes the length of the days' marches, interpretations of the northern limit of the journey vary from the present site of Chico to the present site of Redding, some sixty miles northwest of Chico. Again, it is not known what peaks the explorers saw, or which ones, to them, were *Los Cuates.*

This expedition has gone down in California history as "Argüello's Expedition to the Columbia"—all the unknown region of the north country was called by the Spaniards Columbia—and it was the last ever undertaken by the Spanish pathfinders, and their leather-jacketed soldiers, and the brown-robed Franciscan priests, who would have converted the very valley oaks, had they ears to hear and souls to save.

These wild and rocky highlands demanded more than the Spaniards had to give, or were willing to give. No one can underrate the performance of the early explorers—Coronado and Portolá and Anza—who had strug-

gled across blazing deserts and hacked their way across the mountains of
the south more than half a century before; but that was in the days of
Spanish pomp and might, and these were the days of the empire's decline
and fall, and the sons of Spain no longer plunged into uncharted desolation
for the glory of Castile, to flash their Spanish blades on every peak from
Darien to the Frozen Sea. And so the diaries tell of turning west, or turning back.

*At four o'clock in the afternoon we began to go down the river, and at
sunset stopped on the western bank. . . . Course south and southeast.*

From the north, from the banks of the Columbia, from the shadow of
Mount St. Helens and Mount Hood, from the Vancouver fort of Dr. John
McLoughlin ("the White Eagle," chief factor of the Hudson's Bay Com-
pany in the Northwest) came a gayer, tougher band of men.

The fur brigades bound for the inland mountains left Vancouver in the
fall of the year, in the flame of the maple and the poplar. Their departure
was a scene from a forest pageant, something wonderful, something brave
and lovely and something that you and I will never see.

Under the high picketed walls of Vancouver the brigade assembled:
Indian hunters and packers, with eagle feathers in their black hair—Ojib-
way from the Lake Superior country, Iroquois from the faraway St.
Lawrence, Sioux and Assiniboin and Cree from the prairies; hardy, husky,
swarthy French-Canadians in buckskins, with bright sashes round their
waists and their straight black hair bound with scarlet handkerchiefs, wearing brightly beaded pouches for their Brazilian trail-rope tobacco, and
leggings trimmed with hawks' bills. Beside them were their Indian wives
in deerskins, wearing quail or duck feathers in their broad-brimmed hats
and little tinkling bells on the fringes of their sleeves. In moss-lined baskets
hanging from their saddle straps were the round-eyed half-breed children.

The tall, imperious Doctor McLoughlin, his black cape furling and
his white shoulder-length locks stirring in the fresh September breeze,
shook each man's hand to wish him happy hunting and Godspeed. They
mounted their Cayuse ponies. The 200 pack horses, laden with provisions
and traps and trade goods for bartering, were pulled into line. The bright
blue, white, and yellow ribbons that decked their packs fluttered in the

wind. There was in the clear air the smell of smoke, borne from the mountain meadows miles away where the Indians were burning pasture lands
for elk and deer.

The chief trader—who would be Alex McLeod, if the brigade were bound
for the Willamette Valley and the Umpqua; or plump, jovial Peter Skene
Ogden if it were bound south and east for the Blue Mountains and the
headwaters of the Snake—raised his arm in signal. A bugle sounded
quick notes, clean and high. The caravan began to move. Laughter, shouts,
farewells, singing, and the skirl of the brigade bagpiper rose with the dust
of the stockade ground. And the White Eagle, waving, watched them go
down the river trail, down into the pines, until the last man and the last
streaming ribbon vanished from sight, and the sound of their singing
faded into the forest.

It must have been like that in the autumn of 1826, when Ogden took the
brigade out of Vancouver, not for the beaver swamps of the Snake, but
for the unexplored regions to the south, beyond the divide that lay between southern Oregon and California.

The beaver runs of the headwater uplands had yielded seventy skins to
a hundred traps; perhaps to the south there would be the same good yield,
or even a greater one.

In the minds of these trappers and mountain men, from the days of Joliet,
were beaver pelts, rich and soft; but in their hearts, as they roved the prairies
and mountains and deserts, was the longing for a glimpse of a mythical
river—swift, beautiful, and clear beyond compare. They had heard it said
that it was born in the waters of a lovely lake somewhere east of the shining
Sierra Nevada, and that it flowed through these mountains to the western
sea. They called this river the Buenaventura. They plodded across the
barren reaches of a dozen deserts to find it, and strained their eyes from
a hundred mountain peaks to catch a tell-tale line of distant cottonwoods,
or the flash of reflected sunlight from its smooth and tranquil waters. If
they ever found it, they knew that it would take their canoes to heaven
on earth, for it flowed through Paradise. Somewhere, they knew, there was
this broad, winding, gleaming, peaceful river flowing through the mountains to the sea, and so they sought it, and so it eluded them, withdrawing
across the next range or beyond the far drifting horizon of sand, all their
lives. . . .

Danger and peril beset the brigade from the beginning. On the evening that they left the Columbia, near The Dalles and an easy one week's travel east of Vancouver, Ogden wrote in his beaver-hide journal . . . *Many horses are wild and throw their loads. Indians are moving in all directions. Strict watch is kept day and night.*

As they moved south into the Snake and Malheur Lake country, it began to snow. Snow would cover the trail signs they had carefully left behind for expressmen who were to overtake them from Vancouver with fresh supplies; and to make matters worse, the trappers, branching out from the main brigade under Tom McKay and Gervais and Sylvaille, could find few beaver. The traps remained in camp. *Truly, gloomy are our prospects,* wrote Ogden, early in November.

In the middle of the month, with a catch of only 500 skins and their provisions so low they had been limited to six meals in the last ten days, Ogden's party headed south and west for the Klamath Lakes, the Klamath River, and California. As they crossed the mile-high alkali plains of southern Oregon they scooped snow from crevices along the cut-rock trail and melted it and drank it. Two thirst-crazed horses dropped dead. The famished trappers tore them apart and ate them raw.

On December 2, Ogden noted, they found the expressmen from Vancouver.

*One of the trappers hunting lost horses discovered them; otherwise they would never have reached camp. They could no longer walk and were crawling. For fourteen days they had been without food; for nine days without quenching thirst. Their horses were stolen by the Snakes. On entering my lodge, the poor man fell from weakness and could not rise. I immediately sent back for the other man. About midnight he was brought in, thank God, safe!*

They spent Christmas on the rim of the alkali plains.

*Did not raise camp. We are reduced to one meal a day. Discontent prevails. We have yet three months of winter travel. God grant them well over and that our horses escape the kettle. I am the most unfortunate man on earth, but God's will be done.*

They push southwest to the lava beds of the Modoc country and to the Pit River. Aroused by the mistreatment of trappers at the hands of Indians, Ogden enters in his journal the bitter conviction that leniency toward the savages breeds only contempt in their minds for the white man. He advocates the summary execution of twelve members of each new tribe as it is encountered.

*It would be the means of preserving many lives. Had this plan been adopted with the Snakes, they would not have been so daring and murdered forty men. The same is the case with all Indians.*

This was written on February 10, 1827, and here, in this entry, is the first known reference in writing to the northern tribe whose name (later modified by usage to Shasta) Ogden gave to the lofty peak at the head of the great California Valley.

*Here we are,* he wrote, *among the Sastice. Course this day west.*

With all the hardship and suffering and in spite of the discouraging beaver catch—but perhaps because of these things, and with a wistful hope that it lies on the other side of this desolation—Ogden seeks word of the Buenaventura, River of Good Fortune.

*The stream we are on has no connection with the Clammitte (Klamath) River; it flows south then west to a large river.* Does the large river then —as the Buenaventura must—flow into the sea? The natives shrug, shake their heads. *These Indians know nothing of the ocean.*

They come at last to a sagebrush plain limited on the southeast by bold and surging crags of lava. A little river flows through this valley to the north; above it, directly to the south, looms a mighty, snow-covered peak.

It is another St. Valentine's Day, seventeen years before the day when Frémont would climb Stevens Peak in the Sierra and discover the Lake of the Sky. The wind whistles shrill through the leather tents that are rotting from so much snow and sleet and cloudy winter skies. There are forty beaver skins for the women to dress and clean. Ogden decides against raising camp. In his journal he notes that yesterday one of the trappers saw a domestic cat that had gone wild. It must, he thinks, have come from the coast. Nothing more on the Buenaventura. *All the Indians persist in saying they know nothing of the sea.*

Then he adds, *I have named this river Sastice River. There is a mountain equal in height to Mount Hood or Vancouver, I have named Sastice. I have given these names from the tribes of Indians. . . .*

They remained there, with the trappers out along the Shasta, the Rogue, and the Sacramento, until the middle of March. The sun grew warmer.

Frogs croaked along the meadows in the evening. High on the mountain, just above the timberline but still far from the towering summit, the snows were beginning to melt.

It became time to raise camp and move on. They packed their animals and started east and slightly northward. The course would take them, Ogden knew, to the Snake, and, at last, to the lush green pastures of the Walla Walla rendezvous.

For days, as they sat around their supper fires, they could look to the west and see the evening sky alight with the rose and golden alpenglow of the lonely mountain that they had discovered and that Ogden had named Sastice and that those who followed him came to call Shasta.

Three centuries before, the first white-winged, high-decked caravels had crossed half a world of oceans from the East to lean in the trade winds off the rocky coast of California, bearing men seeking misty landfalls and good ports. Now the year and the month had come when other men, also from the East but on horseback and dressed in skins and in quest of the thick-furred beaver, gazed upon the long inland ridges, the limitless expanse of mountain and forest, and the snows of Shasta. The frontiers of California's north country—20,000 square miles of evergreens and rivers, canyons and lava deserts, gulches and lost meadows—had been broken. The years, the centuries of solitude were ended.

Twelve months after Ogden left the Shasta Valley the indomitable Jedediah Smith, who had been the first American to blaze a trail overland to California and the first to cross the Sierra, led an expedition up the Sacramento Valley, and believed, when he came upon its river, that he was looking upon the river that the trappers of the Rockies and the Great Basin called the Buenaventura.

So he named it, and called the valley Buenaventura Valley, and forded his 100 horses and 150 mules across below Cottonwood Creek. Then, in an incredible display of daring and trailcraft, he broke across the Trinity Mountain wilderness to the coast and headed north through the redwoods and the coastal swamps and fogs toward the Columbia.

But while he was attempting to cross the Umpqua River, Indians launched a savage attack against his camp. They killed fifteen of his eighteen men, scattered his horses and pack mules, and seized $20,000 worth of

furs. Smith and three other survivors (one of whom slew four of the at-
tackers with a blazing poplar pole) made their way on foot to Vancouver.

There Doctor McLoughlin heard the story of the disaster and at once
sent a small brigade under Alex McLeod to the Umpqua to recover Smith's
equipment and stolen furs. Three months later McLeod was back with
both. Smith took advantage of Doctor McLoughlin's offer to buy the furs
at the market price, rested, and moved on down the mountain and desert
trails that would bring him finally, in less than two years, to the sandy banks
of the Cimarron River—face-down and dying with a Comanche lance in
his back.

In January, 1829, the month after he had returned to Vancouver with
Smith's horses and beaver pelts, McLeod was sent south once more, this
time to explore and trap the valley of the Buenaventura that Smith said lay
southward in the sun.

McLeod reached the valley in the springtime, when the smell of honey-
suckle and wild grapes was in the air, saw it shimmering green as far to
the south as he and his men could see, and thought that it was indeed the
fabled reach of the fabled river. He continued south to the delta sloughs of
San Francisco Bay, then turned back.

It was December when he reached the northern mountains. As he attempted the crossing, a blizzard swirled across the uplands and stalled him
and his brigade in a furious snowstorm on the banks of a river a few miles
south of Shasta. They lost their horses, and were forced to cache their furs
and push ahead on snowshoes. (The river bears the trapper's name today,
though it is spelled "McCloud.")

They arrived at Vancouver the next February, and that was the end of
the first Hudson's Bay Company expedition across the Cascades and the
north country and into Central California. For the next ten years and more
the brigades returned every winter to the beaver runs of the valley swamps
and rivers, ranging as far to the south as Tulare Lake. And as they came
and went, their leaders—Big Mike LaFramboise, John Work, Tom McKay,
Francis Ermatinger—brought a touch of the mountains and the Great
Northwest to the sleepy pueblos of Yerba Buena and San Jose and Monterey, and at the same time blazed a crisscross of trails over the vague and
forbidding territory that the Spaniards had turned from, whenever they
confronted it, with fear in their hearts.

A brief ten years after Ogden's South Brigade struggled over the Siskiyou Mountain divide between Oregon and California, P. L. Edwards and Ewing Young, a Tennessee cabinetmaker turned Taos trader and trapper, drove 600 head of cattle from San Francisco Bay up the Sacramento Valley, over the wild and rugged Devil's Backbone at the valley's head, past Shasta, across the Siskiyous to the rich pastures of the Willamette Valley settlers.

Navy Lt. Charles Wilkes, arrogant and inquisitive commander of a five-year United States Exploring Expedition, was curious about the region that stretched south from the Columbia to San Francisco Bay, and in 1841 when his ships reached the northwest coast he detached eighteen men and sent them overland over the now well-worn trail to California. With them went six trappers and twenty emigrants and settlers.

The howling of wolves followed them up the winding trail of the Elk Mountains, and as they reached the Umpquas they saw Indian smoke signals rising in the early autumn air, and did not know whether they meant peace or war. But on September 29 they stood on the highest ridge of the Siskiyous, which they called the Boundary Range, and looked down into the Klamath Valley, and beyond it to the south.

*Mount Shaste, a high snowy peak, of a sugar-loaf form, which rose through the distant haze,* wrote Lieutenant Wilkes in his report, *bore southward, forty-five miles distant.*

They crossed the Klamath River and a plain strewn with lava blocks, and on October 3 passed beneath Mount Shasta, which, that day, emerged steeply from a sea of mist that enveloped its base. A few nights later they were awakened by a mountain storm that came from the west. At the height of the gale, in the depths of the forest about them, they heard tall pines crashing to earth before the wind.

On October 10 they left the mountains, and nine days later, after an easy journey down the Sacramento River, gained Sutter's Fort. And on the 18th, Lt. George F. Emmons, the company's commander, was in Yerba Buena reporting to Lieutenant Wilkes, who had made the trip from the Columbia by sea. The Shasta country was at last on official United States maps in detail. Wilkes could note with satisfaction in his report:

*Although this journey from the Columbia to the Sacramento was attended with much fatigue, yet the labour and the suffering were more than compensated by the information it furnished. . . .*

The myth of the Buenaventura lingers; it is an illusion too ardently wished-for to die easily. On his map of Upper California Wilkes gives the rivers their old names—Sacramento, San Joaquin. But down the long central basin west of the Sierra he letters *Buenaventura Valley*. . . .

Two years later, Captain Frémont of the United States Army Topographical Engineers, leaving Oregon with twenty-five men and a hundred horses and mules, heads south to explore the Klamath Lake region, whence he plans to push southeast *to a reported lake called Mary's, at some days' journey in the great basin, and thence still on southeast to the reputed Buenaventura River . . . flowing from the Rocky Mountains to the Bay of San Francisco*. Like a will-o'-the-wisp the magic name lures him across the bleak Nevada deserts. He finds Pyramid Lake and Tahoe, but not Mary's, and the Truckee River, but not the Buenaventura. And late in January, when his men are famished and frostbitten and his horses leave bloody footprints in the snow, Frémont abandons the quest and turns west for the Sierra crossing.

It was strange that it hadn't been there, flowing westward somewhere in the desert latitudes between 42° and 39° North, because if it wasn't there it wasn't anywhere. The Buenaventura mirage began to blur, to blend with the western haze and fade away. . . .

As they always had, the emigrants, a few at a time, followed the trails of the pathfinders. Lansford W. Hastings, who had yet to create his famous *Emigrant's Guide,* led a party of fifty-three men, women, and children out of the Willamette Valley in '43. A camp or two beyond the Rogue River ford, at the northern base of the Siskiyous, they met Joseph Gale's northbound cattle drive, an awe-inspiring project involving 1,250 head of cattle, 600 horses and mules, 3,000 sheep, and forty-two herders. When they learned that Gale was bound for the Willamette, the emigrants who had just left it eyed Gale's vast flocks and wondered if they hadn't made a mistake; perhaps Oregon had a future, after all.

They stayed in camp several days talking it over. At the discussion's end, a third of the party turned around and went back. The others remained firm, and continued south down the California-Oregon Trail to the waiting valley. The sycamores and the tall poplars stood perfectly still in the heat haze of summer as they made their way along the banks of the Sacramento to Sutter's Fort.

Four months later, Pierson Reading rode his weary horse to the crest of the last rocky ridge and gazed westward, and thanked the great Giver of All Good for bringing him and his companions safe to El Dorado.

# CHAPTER EIGHT

# Shasta–II

SPRING CAME soon that year; the daisies were blooming on the upland meadows and the valley lay fresh and green below the adobe ranch house at Buenaventura, when word reached Reading that James Marshall had discovered gold on the American River.

It was early, still. Charlie Bennett had blurted the secret to the yokels in the general store at Benicia; Mrs. Weimer had put the smart-aleck teamster in his place for trying to make her boy out to be a fool over the gold; and the Mormons building the Brighton flour mill were wondering if it was true, what Henry Bigler had said in his letter about the gleaming sand in the Coloma millrace. The secret was no longer a secret, but it was sifting out slowly. It would be another month or two before the Rush began.

On February 21, 1848, Marshall and Bigler harrowed 3 acres of ground across the river from the mill and planted it with peas; and it was perhaps late that afternoon when Reading arrived in Coloma.

The next day, Washington's Birthday, a light snow fell on the foothills. Because of the weather, Marshall was unable to raise into place the heavy mill frame, as he had planned. While he fumed over the delay and railed again against his luck, he may well have accompanied Reading to the race and showed him where, a few weeks before, he had seen the first gold.

But whether Marshall went along or not, Reading walked to the channel and carefully studied its raw red banks. He strolled up the river a few hundred yards past the mill, noting the gravel of its bed and shore, the rocky outcroppings. Were there any like them, he wondered, along the north-country streams?

All at once he stopped. He remembered a swift river that tumbled through the evergreen forests northwest of his ranch at Buenaventura. He had found it in '45, on the trapping expedition that winter, and, because his map showed it crossing the Coast Range and meeting the sea at Trinidad Bay, had named it Trinity. The earth back from its banks was the same red as Coloma earth. Beside its course were the same cracked and creviced ledges. The same gravelly stones paved its bed.

"If there is gold here," he said to himself, "there is gold up there, on the other side of Buenaventura."

He returned to where the cabins were, beneath some pines on the hillside, a half mile from the mill and the river. Marshall had given the men the day off because of the snow, and they lay around laughing and talking.

"Well, did you find a gold mine, Major?" they asked good-naturedly.

Reading smiled. "This is your claim, boys—yours and Marshall's and Sutter's. Like General Vallejo, I say, 'As the water flows through the millrace out there, may the gold flow into your purse.' "

He left them and went outside and saddled his horse. Swiftly down the foothills he rode to Sutter's Fort. The next day he started north for Buenaventura.

Before he reached the Trinity he discovered gold on a long sandbar that bordered a stream called Clear Creek. The creek rose in the hills above the valley and flowed south and east into the Sacramento, and the place where he made the strike, the first in the north country, was about twenty miles northwest of Buenaventura. He named it Reading's Bar.

He moved on to the Trinity, crossing the ridge at the headwaters of Middle Cottonwood Creek, and broke a trail along the riverbanks until he came to a gravelly bend where bars reached along and above the outside bank, and ledges rose back from the river like those he had seen on the American. With a pocketknife he dug bits of gold from the ledges. The sand yielded flakes and dust when he washed it in an Indian basket.

He remained there two days, returned to Buenaventura, and was back two weeks later with two white helpers, sixty-two Indians, and more than a hundred head of cattle, for food. They pitched camp by the river bend and in six weeks had taken out $80,000 in gold. Toward the middle of July a party of Oregon emigrants rode into Reading's camp off the Coast and Trinity Trail of Jedediah Smith and the Hudson's Bay trappers. They eyed Reading's Indians with hatred, and Reading himself with suspicion. Where they came from, they said, white men didn't hire Indians to work for them. White men didn't have anything to do with the thieving, sneaking rascals, unless it was to shoot them on sight.

"These are good Indians, from the Sacramento Valley," replied Reading. "They have harmed no one."

The leader of the emigrants stared at Reading coldly. "Oregonians think the only good Indian is a dead Indian."

Reading noted the smooth-bore muskets of the riders, held now in readiness, the pistols in their belts, and the knives. His party was equipped for prospecting, not for war; there was nothing to do but yield. That afternoon he ordered the raising of camp, and led his train and his Indians out of the diggings and back over the trail to the valley.

Actually, he didn't care very much. His heart was in the broad rolling acres of Buenaventura, and he had all the gold he wanted—$20,000 more, in fact, than he needed to settle the debt he had left behind him in Vicksburg. This debt, he would pay, with interest, in Trinity River gold, on a trip to the East in 1850.

As for the Oregonians, perhaps Reading, in his way, was grateful to them for cutting short his career as a prospector and a gold seeker. Looking back ten years later he remembered them and the incident without bitterness or regret.

*I left the stream,* he recalled, *and returned to my home where I have since remained in the enjoyment of the tranquil life of a farmer.*

The valley grew green once more, and the news was around the world. The Gold Rush ships were standing through the Golden Gate, and they swung at their anchors in the Bay by the hundreds. The Gold Rush white-tops rolled West, bound for the Sierra passes and the land of promise. The villages of the California Valley and the coast stood deserted through the April suns. Mustard grew wild, high and yellow across the fertile fields, and the bells of the missions hung silent in the late afternoons, at the hour when the Angelus used to ring.

The people and all those who had come by ship and wagon train were off to the diggings to dig gold dust by the barrel. Their teams and wagons choked the river fords along the trails to the foothills. The towns like Angels Camp and Sonora and Murphys Diggings, the settlements like Rattlesnake Gulch, Murderer's Bar, Lousy Level, and Chicken Thief Flat were where they were going to pitch their tents, stake out their claims, and make their fortunes.

There was another way that the Forty-niners could get to the diggings. That was from the north. The secret had reached Oregon in '48, even as Reading and his Indians panned the Trinity, by the English brig *Mary Dare,* which had cleared away from Honolulu with mainland dispatches in early July. So stirred were Oregonians, they nailed up their pretty farmhouses and deserted their Willamette Valley orchards and pastures by the thousand, and before the end of the year the *Oregon Spectator* reported that *almost the entire male and a part of the female population of Oregon has gone gold-digging in California.*

Nearly all of them that year by-passed the Siskiyou Mountain crossing and the Devil's Backbone and the diggings that Reading had discovered, and headed east of Shasta, straight for the Mother Lode. But by the time of the green valley grass in '49, they were using the trappers' trails and were fanning out along the north-country creeks and ravines that the brigades had found and trapped a dozen years before.

Three or four hundred tents were on the hillsides above Reading's Bar at the end of that October, and the diggings were spreading fast along the gulches of neighboring creeks named Middle, Rock, and Salt. Six miles northeast and across Mule Mountain from his bar, Reading had found some perpetual springs. Forty-niners from Oregon had camped beside them on their way down in April and May. They had found there both wood and water; the place was only a few miles off the trail, in case they failed to strike it rich and wanted to pull up stakes and head south for the Lode; and it was as good a place as any, and better than most, to call home while they panned the nearby bars.

So here in October, at Reading's Springs, scattered down a flat grassy meadow and under the spreading oaks on a hill west of the meadow, were twice as many tents as there were at Reading's Bar, and it looked as though the camp were there to stay a while because Milton McGee—just six years after he had tumbled into the deer trap on the Pit River, on the trail from Fort Boisé—was building a log cabin and allowing as how, when the spring pack trains came through, he'd buy some red calico curtains and hang them in his windows to give the Springs a Frisco air and a touch of class.

When spring came around again in '50, McGee's calico curtains helped, but the miners looked less to them for the Frisco air and the touch of class than they did to Jim Mackley's St. Charles Hotel and W. S. Bonnifield's Trinity House that were going up on Main Street. The lumber to build them had come around the Horn to Sacramento and on wagons up the valley road to the Springs; and some was local timber that Jonathan Otis's whipsaw mill was turning out for them at a dollar a board foot.

The diggings spread fast that year. Before the wild lilac bloomed in the canyons, there were new strikes at Muletown and Piety Hill, Roaring River and Sheet-Iron Gulch, and someone had hit a quartz ledge at Spring Creek 3 miles north of camp. Anyone could tell by McGee's log cabin and the two frame hotels and just by the way the camp was flourishing there by the wood and water of the Springs that this town was going to be the Queen of the North.

For a town with such a future, the miners thought, "Reading's Springs" was a little rough and undignified, and so that June they had a mass meeting in front of R. J. Walsh's store on Main Street. There, gathered in their gray hickory shirts and their clay-streaked boots, they debated the new name for the camp.

"It owes its existence to the limpid waters of the springs. Therefore, I respectfully submit, gentlemen, for your consideration, the name 'Fountania,'" said an earnest young Harvard graduate from Boston.

"'Fountania!'" snorted a graybeard from Mad Mule Canyon. "You call it 'Fountania,' and I'll call it damned nonsense. Take a look up there." He pointed to the snow-covered mountain that loomed low on the horizon, sixty miles to the north. "What's the matter with 'Shasta?'"

The cheers of the crowd said nothing was the matter with "Shasta," and Shasta it became; and in September, when California was made a State, one of the twenty-seven original counties was Shasta County, bordered on the south by Bank Creek, below Red Bluff, and the Butte County line; on the west by the Coast Range; on the north by the Oregon line, and on the east by the Nevada Desert. Buenaventura was named the county seat.

The only public official the district had had was an *alcalde,* a position held by the Forty-niner Dr. Benjamin Shurtleff. In the same September, he resigned, and Shastans went to the polls in their first election. They chose him as county treasurer, W. R. Harrison as county judge, Dr. Jess Robinson as county clerk, and A. Z. McCandless as their representative in the General Assembly.

Years later, when anyone asked them what Shasta was like in the fall of '50, the Forty-niners told him about A. Z. McCandless. . . .

A few weeks before the election, Jim Mackley, Bonnifield, the boys from Otis's whipsaw mill and Roach's brick kiln and Carter's steam grist mill and some others who were going to keep the town on the straight and narrow—all of them met one night at the St. Charles, and when the meeting was over proudly announced their candidate for the Assembly: Mr. Watson, who worked at the Riddle, Weber & Co. store.

"Mr. Watson," they declared, "is an intelligent, temperate man. He is a model Christian, who brought his Christianity to California and always keeps it with him. He is a righteous, upstanding citizen. He deserves the support of all righteous, upstanding Shastans."

If the miners, talking it over in their tents and shanties, couldn't find anything to say for Watson, neither could they find anything to say against him, and so they let it slide. The choice could have been worse.

A few days later, however, a lean, stoop-shouldered young man rode into town on a small mule. Hitching his hungry-looking mount to the awning post of a Main Street saloon, the newcomer confronted the gathering of miners who had pushed through the swinging doors for a look at the lanky stranger.

The stranger shoved back his hat, put his hands on his hips, and deliber-

ately scanned their faces. "Understand," he drawled, "you had a meetin'
in town t'other night, and nominated a candidate for the Assembly."

"That's right," said the miners. "Mr. Watson was nominated."

The stranger grinned, and shut one eye in a broad wink. "Boys, I'm a
candidate for the Assembly myself. A. Z. McCandless is my name, and
whisky is my platform, and whisky is a-goin' to win this fight. Let's all
go in and take a drink."

When the campaign and the election were over, the righteous Mr. Watson was back behind the counter of the Riddle, Weber store, and A. Z. Mc-
Candless was preparing to ride his mule south to the State capital as the
assemblyman from Shasta. He and whisky had won, hands down.

The county seat didn't stay long at Buenaventura. In February of '51,
Judge Harrison, the other county officers, and a quorum of justices of the
peace rode on horseback to the ranch, organized a Court of Sessions and
voted to move the county government to Shasta. That was fine with Reading, who wanted no county courthouse and jail within miles of his ranch,
and so Harrison and the rest rode back to Shasta that night and proclaimed
the town the new county seat.

By summertime the camp was jammed with a permanent population of
2,000, and as many more had pitched their tents for the season on the flat
north of Main Street. On a hill overlooking the settlement, workmen were
installing a mahogany banister, French windows, and Franklin stoves in
the elegant, two-story mansion that Doc Shurtleff was having built of
hand-hewn timbers and lumber from around the Horn.

Stores and saloons were strung along Main Street, and every day the
170- and 200-mule pack trains were arriving in town from Sacramento with
supplies for the Shasta miners, and for those at the diggings along the
creeks, the Trinity River, and the Scott River to the north.

They really were calling Shasta the Queen City of the North by now.
The first stage from the south had rolled down Main Street that April,
with Michael Cummings at the reins and whip, and a few weeks later the
mail riders galloped in for the first time, with the first scheduled mail
delivery in the whole north country. So almost from the beginning the
town had more than the diggings to keep it alive and growing. Stages
and the freight wagons could get to Shasta, but now could go no farther.

They called it the "head of 'whoa' navigation," and there transferred their flour sacks and provisions and supplies to mules, and packed them on mules over the network of mountain trails that led up the canyons and over the ridges to the mountain camps.

With the miners and the muleteers and the drivers of the long jerkline bluff teams in town, there was as much hell a-popping every Saturday night in the Main Street saloons and hotel bars as there ever was in Sonora or Columbia or Angels; but the play wasn't quite so rough. Not many of the Sydney thieves and cutthroats or the waterfront harlots banished from San Francisco by the vigilantes headed for the north country. It was too far away, for one thing, and for another it was too cold in the wintertime, and for still another, the Lode was bigger: if one camp there got too hot, you could take your pick of a hundred others.

They didn't even have a jail in Shasta until '54. They had a Vigilance Committee that sentenced a man to the lash if he stole some dust or a horse, and that would string a man up for murder if it had to.

It didn't come to that very often, but for Jake Grose's sake the vigilantes almost wished it had late in '51, after Grose, thirty-three years old and from Georgia, got into an argument with a Whiskeytown miner named Frederick Oberman and picked up a pistol while Oberman was panning gold and went up behind Oberman and shot him dead.

After doing that Grose walked down the bar a way to his tent and got a butcher knife and attempted to cut his throat. It was too dull, and in a while he gave it up and tried to hang himself with a grapevine. Weak from loss of blood from the wounds in his throat, he couldn't manage this, either. He crawled back to his tent on his hands and knees. There he got a pistol, aimed it shakily at his forehead and fired. The ball glanced off his skull and buried itself in his blanket roll. He was found, still alive, on the floor of his tent.

On the morning of October 24, in a tiny, second-floor room of a Main Street building, Grose was convicted of murder and sentenced to be hanged on November 14. He was then hustled to a cabin at the west end of town. There fetters were riveted to his ankles. When this was done, he asked the sheriff to take him to an outhouse a few yards away. The sheriff complied with his request.

Twenty minutes later, Main Street was in an uproar. From the hotels, bars, and stores patrons ran into the street and headed in a noisy throng for the cabin. The sheriff, they had heard, was having trouble with Grose. They arrived in time to see a gruesome sight. The sheriff had pulled Grose from the outhouse. He lay on the ground with a bloody razor in his hand. His throat was cut from ear to ear. This time, he was quite dead.

Some said it was a good thing. Some said it was bad; such a terrible tragedy would never have happened in the fair city of Shasta if there had been a jail, where Grose could have been preserved intact for the hangman, and by God they'd have to start building one before the week was out. Everyone agreed that this, at least, was the truth.

Before the week was out, however, Grose, and even the jail, were forgotten. In Shasta the dead buried the dead, and yesterday, and the resolves of yesterday. The reality was today.

The placers yielded fifteen, fifty, and sometimes a hundred dollars a day to any man who took the trouble to pan or lay a hand to his rocker. They were striking quartz ledges up and down every creek within twenty miles of Shasta, and at nearby Middletown the miners were already tearing down their cabins to wash the earth they stood on. In the winter of '52 the boys at Weatherblow's Woodcock Bar were boasting as how the very snow that fell on Shasta was paying ten dollars to the pan. Gold-dust shipments to the south climbed closer and closer to $100,000 a week.

Some of those who had reached Reading's Bar and One Horsetown, French Gulch and the Springs in '49 were drifting away to the new diggings north on the Scott River and the Klamath. But for every one that left two came in from the East over the new road through Noble's Pass, that branched off the Applegate Trail above Honey Lake Valley, or down from Oregon over the old trail that the cattle drivers and the trappers had blazed west of Mount Shasta.

Seven hotels rose along Main Street. Sam Dosh was publishing the north country's first paper, the *Shasta Courier*. Rev. John B. Hill, the Methodist preacher, who reached town in April and won the town's heart at his first open-air prayer meeting by throwing a drunken heckler off a hotel balcony into the street, was building a town church. The business directory listed half a hundred thriving establishments, not including saloons and gambling halls, and they ranged from Doc Shurtleff's Drug Store, Schloss's Clothing

Emporium, and Anton Roman's Book and Musical Instrument Shop, to Loag's Horse Market, Goodwin & York's Bowling Alley and Billiard Hall, and Stephen Lane's City Bath House.

Hall and Crandall stages were spinning into town every day from Sacramento and Marysville; the Baxter stages pulled smartly away from the St. Charles Hotel every morning and vanished in the billowing dust of the valley trail with mail pouches for the river boat that it would meet at Colusa; and before the end of September Rhodes and Lusk's Shasta Express would take your letters and your orders south to Sacramento, turn them over there to Wells, Fargo and thus speed them on their way to San Francisco, around the Horn to New York and Boston, or even to London and Paris, if that was where you wanted them to go.

Doc Shurtleff and his cronies were never more serious in their life than when, gathered around his cider press in the cool, stone-walled cellar of his mansion on the hill, they raised their mugs in pure and fervent toasts to . San Francisco, to Sacramento, and finally, in a warm, ringing climax, to "Shasta—third city on the Pacific shore—and the fairest of them all!"

These were the years of Shasta's youth, and if it wasted no time on yesterday, it had less time than that for tomorrow; its life would last forever. And indeed, if you had been there in those golden years, you would have believed it, and wanted it to be true.

The summer sun rose early in Shasta, for the manzanita-grown hills to the east were low and sloping to the valley. It slanted down through the pines and the oaks, through the blue smoke that already drifted from the breakfast fires before the tents north of the flat, and from the chimneys of the cottages on the flat itself, and along High Street and Trinity Alley.

Main Street itself, rebuilt after the big fire of '53 and boasting the longest line of brick buildings in the State, was already alive and bustling. Merchants—bluff, genial Alpheus Bull of Bull & Baker's mercantile establishment, who not long ago had sold a $3,000 bill of goods before he sat down to the breakfast table; Anton Roman, bewhiskered and square-set, who bartered everything at his Shasta bookstore from Shakespeare to guitar strings and flageolets (and who, some ten years later, in San Francisco, would found the famous *Overland Monthly*); Dan Callaghan (who would become president of San Francisco's First National Bank, and grandfather of the heroic Admiral Dan Callaghan, who lost his life on the cruiser *San Francisco* in the World War II Battle of Subic Bay); George Grotefend; Adolph Dobrowsky, the jeweler—all of them and a score of others no less enterprising were sweeping or watering down the plank sidewalks and arranging their merchandise for the day's trade.

Jimmie Keene (who in his day, as a Wall Street financier, would become as famous as any of them) had already delivered the milk to the new jail on the hill above the east end of Main Street, remembering, perhaps, as he peered through the iron-barred doors into the two sheet-iron cells, the last big excitement at the jail.

That had been a couple of years ago, in '55, the year after the jail had been built. A seventy-five-man guard marched to the jail, took E. A. Higgins, the Horsetown murderer, from one of the cells and hauled him in a wagon to the gallows a mile outside of town. Higgins didn't seem to care very much. In fact, he seemed to be having much the best time of anybody there. Dressed in a white shroud set off by a gaily colored neckerchief, he waved jovial greetings to the throng that trooped along beside his cart and cracked jokes about how they had to walk in the hot sun while he, the doomed, rode in style. At the site of the execution, he called for a bottle of brandy, and, between nips, harangued the crowd for more than an hour on topics of general interest. At last, when the bottle was dry, he wished them all a long and merry life, asked their blessing, and told the sheriff he was ready to swing. An hour later he was deep in his grave in the Shasta cemetery.

Jimmie may have remembered this and thought about it again, as he left the milk at the jailer's door, and got back in his wagon and continued his morning round. . . .

In a little while, the clamor of the town began. Everybody and everything going to or coming from the Trinity and Siskiyou mining camps, and even those in southern Oregon, had to pass through Shasta; and from the time the four-horse Shasta mail-express stage tooled down Mail Street, harness glistening, its rocking body gleaming red and gold, and its wheels spinning circles of light in the early morning sunshine—from then until the sun went down and the storekeepers hung out their evening door lamps Main Street was a noisy dusty uproar of mules, horses, stages, freight wagons, and men.

The wagon and stage roads weren't open yet to Weaverville in the west, or over Trinity and Scott Mountains to Yreka in the north, or up the Sacramento Canyon and over the Devil's Backbone. So the northbound people and the northbound freight rolled into Shasta on stages and the ten- and twenty-horse freight wagons, and there were transferred to mules that plodded slowly and patiently up the winding canyon and mountain trails. Passengers and southbound freight reached Shasta from the north by mule train, and continued down the valley in the Marysville or Sacramento stages, or the stages that met the river boats at Colusa, and in the freight wagons that were returning to the river points below.

So the mule trains formed there in Main Street all day long. Even before the schoolbell rang out over the flat Greathouse, Slicer's train of thirty mules, each carrying 40 pounds of baggage, a canteen of water, and a passenger, was away from the St. Charles and moving north over the trail to Yreka via French Gulch, Callaghan's, and Scott's Bar.

Three of these passenger trains that connected with the California-Oregon Stage lines reached Shasta from the north each day, and as they and the valley stages pulled into town they found Main Street choked with the braying milling mules of the forming pack trains, and the air above Main Street filled with swirling clouds of red dust and the shouts of the mule packers and the crack of the long-lashed blacksnake whips. As the morning wore on, the brawling chaos resolved itself into order. The pack saddles were put on, and the sacks of flour and sugar were laced into the *parflêches* and made fast to the saddles. The mules themselves, three or four hundred of them, were hauled, kicked, and prodded into line, and then, to the yells of the muleteers and the slow tinkling bells of the leaders, they were off up the trail to Weaver' or the Trinity Mountain.

Unconcerned through the tumult the crowds moved slowly up and down the sidewalks of the Queen City, a Gold Rush passing show that somehow had more in common with Montgomery Street's "Ambrosial Path" in San Francisco than it did with the roistering main drags of the Mother Lode towns. Holding dainty parasols and lifting their dust ruffles clear of the street, ladies in velvet jackets and long full skirts of deep-toned taffeta, or dark dresses of imported delaine, made their way across Main Street on the arms of frock-coated escorts to mingle on the crowded sidewalks with an

incongruous throng: sunburned and bearded miners from Whiskeytown
and Mad Mule Canyon, French Gulch and Salt Pork Ridge; swaggering
freight-wagon drivers from the valley and calk-booted lumbermen on a
final fling before the log drives down the mountain rivers; bland-faced Chinese—there were 1,000 of them in "Hong Kong," Shasta's Chinatown—in
their blue linen suits and broad hats of lacquered rushes and black cloth sandals; Indians, black-haired and stolid, with feathers in their hair and sometimes wearing fringed deerskins, followed by impassive squaws bearing
papooses on their backs; traveling players—if one of these was tall and black-
haired and as graceful as a young birch, riding into town on a tasseled mule
and beating a drum, with a laughing mite of a girl with red hair and twinkling feet and sparkling eyes running alongside, then that was Matt Taylor,
the troubadour of Rabbit Creek, and the kid was Lotta Crabtree, whose ballads and Irish reels were the toast of the Mother Lode—bareback riders from
Rowe's Olympic Circus, making the summer circuit of the Northern
Mines; gamblers in shining top boots, fur vests, yellow gauntlets, and scarlet
sashes, wearing diamonds in their shirt fronts; raucous-voiced fruit peddlers hawking Willamette Valley peaches and apples for a dollar each;
Cow Creek refugees from the Indian raids; and lean, smartly uniformed
dragoons from Fort Reading down the river, or Fort Jones on the mountain trail to Yreka.

Here and there, stepping through the pageant of movement and life and
the uproar of the mule trains and ox teams, the jerkline bluff teams, the
arriving and departing stages, were the men of the town's affairs: smiling
Doc Shurtleff; Postmaster Isaac Roop, who had been president of the
Whig convention in '51, the year they'd nominated Reading for governor,
and who even now had on his mind Honey Lake Valley and the State of
Nataqua that he would organize with Peter Lassen; Major Reading himself, and Mrs. Reading—the former Fannie Wallace Washington of Washington, D.C.—up from Buenaventura on a shopping trip, perhaps, to look
at furnishings and imported draperies for their new adobe mansion; silk-
hatted W. P. Daingerfield, the district judge of the Northern Circuit of
California; State Senator Royal T. Sprague, who would become chief
justice of the State Supreme Court; Rev. James Rogers, who, in '53, had
succeeded Preacher Hill; Father Raphael Rinaldo, the Catholic priest, who

dreamed of one day building a Gothic cathedral amid the mountains and pines for his north country flock; Capt. Phil Sheridan, a year or two out of West Point and in town to requisition supplies for his men at Fort Reading; Levi Tower, who had built the famous log Tower House on the trail to Weaverville and Shasta's Globe Hotel (the only hotel in the north whose barroom safe was set in solid rock); and John Ball, proprietor of the new Charter Oak Hotel.

Almost imperceptibly, as the sun dropped lower over the Trinity Mountains to the west and the shadows lengthened along the flat, the tempo and the tumult diminished: the mule trains were away; the freight wagons due in that day were in, and their drivers were clearing their throats of the valley dust with long gin and forty-rod refreshers in the cool barrooms; the late stages had left for Marysville; the miners had weighed in their dust and were drifting off to their tents and shanties and their dutch-oven bean suppers; promenades and shopping over, the women were going home, and the shopkeepers were sweeping their floors clean of the red dust that the trampling hoofs had been raising all day and that had drifted through their open doors. Smoke from the supper fires, the cottage chimneys, and the hotel kitchen chimneys rose lazily upward, and the smell of burning oak twigs and logs mingled with the faint fragrance of the pines.

Evening came on to the tinkling of cow bells. Lamplight glowed in the cottage windows and in the shops that stayed open for the evening trade. The sidewalks began to fill again: Western Star No. 2, the second oldest Masonic Lodge in California, whose charter Peter Lassen had brought across the plains in '48, was holding, perhaps, its monthly meeting tonight; the Ethiopian Serenaders, who had come up on the river boat from San Francisco, were giving a minstrel show at Armory Hall; there was a prayer meeting at the Methodist Church, and an exhibition of "startling skill with the cue and ball" by Professor Thayer, fresh from a triumphant tour of the European capitals, at Mr. and Mrs. Gavand's Billiard Saloon. The music of the barroom fiddles—you heard them in every mining camp, everywhere you went—already floated through the open doors of the Main Street bars, luring within, with their promise of gaiety and warmth and good fellowship, the miners and the muleteers. There was a ball tonight at the Charter Oak. Even if it wasn't by the tuning up of the fiddles and the harps, you'd know this, standing in Main Street, by the warm glow of the tall colored-glass windows, lighted from within by the ballroom chandeliers.

Toward midnight, when they stopped for the intermission, the ladies would go quickly home and change into fresher, crisper gowns, and return cool and ready to dance until dawn. And dance till dawn they would, for you would hear the music of the lancers and the quadrilles, laughter and the sound of dancing feet until the stars began to go out, and the eastern sky grew pale, and the early shouts of the sleepy mule drivers came across the flat from the dark corrals by the edge of the wood.

It was hard to understand how the end of everything could have come to Shasta as quietly and deceptively as it did. Only as they gathered under the Shasta locust trees for the Home-coming Days of their later years, could the old-timers see how it had happened.

The thing was, their dads and mothers, and they themselves as youngsters —attending the school that had been made of the jail on the hill (after the new county courthouse was built on Main Street next to the Empire Hotel) or the Shasta Union Seminary that Professor Godfrey had opened in the spring of '60—they all believed with all their hearts that it would never happen to Shasta. She always had been the Queen City of the North, and Queen City of the North she'd be forever. Eventually, the placers would peter out, the way they had down on the Mother Lode; their dads and mothers admitted that. But what if they did? The stages had to go through, didn't they? And the mule trains had to move the freight, didn't they?

There was the railroad they were building north (the tracks, by '69, were up the valley, beyond Marysville), but how could they lay the rails north to the Siskiyous unless they laid them through old Shasta? When they reached the town, and it became the rail center for all Shasta County and for Trinity County to the west, the town would boom higher than ever, higher, even, than in the '50s. The bonanza days would be here all over again. They'd start to cut timber on a big scale all along the Pit and the McCloud, the river salmon fisheries would thrive, and all the timber and all the fish, all the grain and livestock from the southern part of the county, down by Cottonwood—all of it had to be shipped by rail all over the country. And where would the shipping point be?—Shasta. Why, the railroads would bring new industries, new money, new stores, new people, new everything. The Queen City would flourish and grow, and everybody'd be as happy as a bear in a beegum grove.

Some folks were saying as how the surveyors favored putting the road over east of Shasta, closer to the river, on Diestelhorst's ranch lands, and driving up through the Sacramento Canyon. They'd be fools to do it, when they could come right up the ridge to Shasta and follow the stage road north to Callaghan's and Yreka; but supposing they did—supposing they were just plain damned fools and did? Shasta was still the county seat of Shasta County, wasn't she? And you didn't go moving the county courthouse all over the county, just because they put the railroad tracks someplace else, did you now? . . .

The old-timers, looking back, remembered the long-lost words and voices. And as they remembered, they could see how quietly and deceptively it had all started, and how, little by little, it had all happened.

It was a sunny afternoon in June, and they were gathered there on a vacant lot next to the brick ruins of the county courthouse. Until a few years ago, other ruins had stood on the vacant lot—the ruins of John V. Scott's Empire Hotel that had been built in the '50s. Workmen had cleared these ruins away and had carted the bricks to Redding and put them into the Hill Building at California and Tehama Streets. So now there wasn't anything there, and they sat in rows across the lot—a hundred of them and more—on folding wooden chairs and on the ground itself, waiting with a quiet, curiously profound expectancy for the Home-coming Day address of Charles Shurtleff, who had come up from "down below," from San Francisco, to be with them in Shasta on this day.

The speaker was a dignified, rather portly white-haired man in his seventies whom the listeners had known all their lives as "Doc Shurtleff's boy Charlie." He stood on a small, low, bunting-draped platform. The sheets of paper in his hands trembled slightly as he smiled at the officers of the Shasta County Historical Society on the platform behind him, then, still smiling, faced the old Shastans, and began his address.

*Mr. President and Friends:*

*As I look into your faces I see many whom I have known all my life. Standing, as some of us are, in the shadows of the homes wherein we were*

*born, the deep emotions which rise "thick and fast" are best expressed in
the opening lines of the "Old Oaken Bucket,"*

> *How dear to this heart are the scenes of my childhood,*
> *When fond recollection presents them to view*
> *The orchard, the meadow, the deep tangled wildwood,*
> *And every loved spot which my infancy knew.*

*We are indeed upon hallowed ground* . . . Charlie was a lawyer, and
his voice was low, sonorous, and deliberate. His listeners sat forward, their
eyes intent upon his face, some with their hands cupped behind their ears
to catch every syllable, every inflection. . . . *It was here that many of us
had our birth; it was here that we spent our happy childhood days and
received the first rudiments of our education; it was here that we formed
friendships which to this day have endured in all the freshness and enthusiasm of their making. . . . It was here, under the tutorship and direction of beloved teachers, some of whom through the beneficence of Providence are still with us, that our characters were molded and the foundation laid upon which we were to build our future lives, but, as we look
about us, behold, how changed! The same heavens are indeed over our
heads; the mountains and hills resting against the horizon form the identical eternal skyline of long ago; the streets we knew so well, and upon which
we played remain intact . . . but all else, how changed!*

*Most of the buildings we knew and remember have fallen, victims of one
or the other of those monarchs of destruction—fire and decay—and only
live in memory. The parents of most of us who resided here in the early
days long ago passed into the bright Beyond, and in other ways our family
circles have been broken. But, notwithstanding these pathetic changes,
which deeply touch us and mean Shasta's physical and material decline,
our presence here upon this Sabbath day is living, eternal proof that it
matters not what vicissitudes may assail or misfortunes befall her, our affection for and fidelity to the old Town shall abide forever. . . .*

The old-timers, shielding their eyes from the sun with their programs,
listened, nodding. Behind them, down the vacant Main Street, now a section of State Highway 299 leading west to Weaverville and across the
Trinities to Arcata and the coast, stood a row of crumbling brick shells that
were all that remained of the buildings that had been built after the great
fire of '53.

*Until about 1861, most of the merchandise and freight bound for points north of Shasta, was, because of poor roads, transported by pack trains. North, toward the Tower House, some twelve miles from here, the roads remained in bad condition until the late Charles Camden, who landed in South America in 1847 and in Shasta in 1849, constructed a wagon road in 1861 from Shasta to the Tower House. . . .*

The old-timers could remember Charlie Camden's toll road. The year before, Williamson Lyncoya Smith had driven the California Stage Company's first mail stage over Scott Mountain, when the company had begun its daily mail run from Sacramento to Portland. Then had come the Camden road, and the stages could travel to Weaverville, and the first thing you knew the stages weren't stopping at Shasta the way they used to; they were going right on through, and the same was true of the freight wagons—they didn't need the mule trains much after the wagon roads were built—and as time went by Shasta wasn't the end of the trail any more. It was just another stop on the way. The Concords and the wagons were going on through, headed for someplace else.

*Immense political gatherings were held here in former days, and especially during a period following the Civil War. People came from miles around —distance was leveled by the devotion to the cause of the party holding the meeting. Some of the political processions consisted of a double line of vehicles for the full length of Main Street. At night huge bonfires illuminated the streets and enthusiasm ran high. . . .*

Sharply back to the old-timers came the acrid smell of gunpowder. It hung in the air all morning on the Fourth of July, when they used to fire "Old Teddy," the town cannon, thirty or forty times for the holiday sunrise salute. They remembered the parades, all right: the Shasta Home Guards, the Lyon Light Infantry, and the California Trumen Rifles from French Gulch stepping down Main Street to the music of Jim Lentz's Brass Band; the painted Wintun braves chanting and dancing on the flat; the throng of gold miners in from Clear Creek and Horsetown; the red glare and smoke of the torchlights in the evening and the crackling bonfires; and the Fourth of July balls at the Charter Oak. When Sumter had fallen they had fired Old Teddy fifty-two times in as many minutes, and when news of Lee's surrender came through, the town had gone wild. The fires had blazed on the hilltops all night that happy night.

*A. Z. McCandless is the name*

*Major Reading died at his ranch on May 29, 1868, at the age of fifty-one*
*years, six months and three days, and when you recall that he was about*
*twenty-seven years old when he came to the coast, and contemplate what*
*he accomplished between that time and his death, you marvel that he com-*
*passed so much in the space of twenty-five years. Although quite young—*
the speaker lifted his eyes and gazed out over his listeners, a soft look of
pride lighting his face—*I was present at the funeral of Major Reading. . . .*
*I often wonder, if, aside from the members of his family, I am not one of*
*the few now living who took part in the last earthly and solemn tribute to*
*this noted man of history. Major Reading is buried upon his ranch on a*
*slight elevation overlooking the Sacramento River and the valley he so*
*deeply loved, and how fitting it is that there, where many of the exciting*
*incidents of his wonderful and useful life occurred, his labors o'er, his*
*memory forever safely enbalmed in the history of this great state he helped*
*to found and build, he should rest in peace. . . .*

That was right, they were thinking. That was the fitting place for the
Major to be. They had all heard about Major Reading as far back as they
could remember: how he had found the gold on Clear Creek and the
Trinity, and here at the Springs; how he'd been the first white settler in the
whole county; and how, as soon as he could after he'd got started at Buenaventura, he'd gone back East and made good a debt he'd left behind him
when he came West in '43—$60,000 cash on the barrelhead, people said it
was, and he'd gone all the way back there to Mississippi and had paid up
like a man. He was a man California could be proud of, all right—one of
the old Californians. Kept a lamp burning all night in a tower on his
ranch house, to guide travelers who might be lost at night to a safe bed;
and he'd send them on their way the next morning with a smile, and a good
breakfast under their belts. Courageous, too, and a man to stand up for the
right. When the Indians had massacred Mrs. Dersch beside her soap kettles
over near Shingletown, and the posse had ridden hell-for-leather to Buenaventura and demanded Reading's Indians, because they thought some of
them had been with the raiders, hadn't Reading stood up to them with his
rifle and told them straight that his Indians were innocent, and not a hand
would be laid on them unless it was over his dead body? One man against
fifty, and there he stood. "Over my dead body," he said, just like that.
That was Reading for you, that was a real pioneer, gentle as a lamb most

of the time, but half cat and all wild when standing up for the right.

. . . *The flourishing, golden period of Shasta*—the breeze off Shurtleff Hill, where his father's mansion still stood, lifted Charlie Shurtleff's white hair, and played through the white papers in his hand—*is generally conceded to have been the years between 1851 and 1857, both included. It was then that she was in the zenith of her splendor. It was about 1858 that the Town began to give evidence that she was slipping, but her decline was slow and it was not until late in the '60s that her loyal and devoted sons and daughters began to see that the shadows were gathering and her star setting. . . .*

*Her star setting.* . . . The lined faces of the old-timers, men and women both, were tranquil as they thought back: manzanita blooming on the hillsides in February; Drury Harrill's rose garden that all the children of Shasta could play in, if they knew how to find the secret path through the apple orchard to the hole in the garden fence, and Old Man Harrill—he had owned the town soda factory, in the early days—sitting there among the roses and in the shade of the weeping willow, beside the rock fountain, laughing as he watched the children play hide-and-seek; the popping of firecrackers in "Hong Kong" at Chinese New Year's; the wailing of the Indian women when they buried their men at the old burial ground on the other side of Shurtleff Hill; the jangling of the freight bells, the pealing of the old bell in the tower of Union Church, and the high, glad blast of the bugle when the stage was nearing town and the driver was letting the station hostlers know that he was coming in for a change of horses; the grosgrain ribbons that the girls wore at their soft throats, the rustle of their satin hoopskirts, the golden earrings they wore, and the heavy chains of gold. There were hay rides on those summer evenings, and parties in the wintertime that lasted two and three days, with people coming to them in buckboards from many miles around, from as far, sometimes, as Fall River Mills, up on the Pit; berrying-time, when you hung empty kerosene cans to the sides of your horse, who filled them for you as you led him down the raspberry lanes, brushing the vines as he went, and sweeping the blackcap raspberries off the vines; Tom Thumb and his troupe of midgets coming to town; or Lee and Ryland's New York Circus, with the trained buffalo, and the circus parades down Main Street through the smiling, cheering throngs that came to welcome them. But they weren't for long, those days, with the railroad, the California and Oregon, the "C. & O.," reaching Chico in '70 and Red Bluff in '71, and the next year the surveyors of the road saying the road wasn't going through Shasta after all, but up the canyon by the site of Kennett, the copper town; and over there, 6 miles east on Poverty Flat, near Diestelhorst's ranch lands, had grown the city that Shasta should have been: Redding, named for the railroad official B. B. Redding. "Ridge too high," they said; "we're going to the end of the valley and up through the canyon." That was when the star of Shasta commenced to fall.

*Gathered as we are*—Charlie was leaving the best, happiest days behind—*in this quiet, friendly little valley, it is difficult to visualize the exciting experiences that have transpired here. . . . One Sunday afternoon in the early '70s, the exact year I do not remember, but prior to 1874, about five o'clock, Shasta was the seat of an exciting jail break. There were confined in the jail at that time four desperate criminals who had been arrested for robbing Wells, Fargo & Company's express box carried by one of the Oregon and California stages, the robbery having been committed in the vicinity of Cottonwood.*

*I recall that the name of one of the criminals was Shorty Hayes, and that Thompson was the name of another. On that Sunday afternoon the prisoners had accomplished their release from their cells, gone upstairs to the sheriff's office and fully armed themselves. When the cook from the Empire Hotel arrived at the jail with the prisoners' evening meal, they seized him and locked him in one of the cells and hastily proceeded to make their escape. In a moment the alarm was given and the Town was in a high state of excitement. A hot pursuit followed. Some of the escaped men ran through the Dunn Corral and, notwithstanding their pursuers were shooting at them, they did not slacken their speed until they reached the hills east of town. Thompson was overtaken and captured.*

*Shorty Hayes was more cunning than the others and made his way into the cemetery just north of town. Many of you will remember that in those days it was, and perhaps still is, the custom of the Chinese to ship the bones of their dead to China. They frequently failed to fill in the empty grave after the removal of the body, and Shorty slipped into one of these and quietly remained there that night, and until he felt that the excitement had abated. He then arose and made his way south. It was in the winter and his*

*feet froze, with the result that he was apprehended somewhere near Marys-*
*ville. All were recaptured and returned to the jail, but thereafter ordinary*
*handcuffs were not used, but a blacksmith was employed to make a special*
*handcuff consisting of straight bars of iron with a place just large enough to*
*fit the wrists, and these were riveted on the prisoner. The officers took no*
*further chances. All were convicted and punished. . . .*

There were a couple more, later on, that Charlie could have mentioned, mused the listening old-timers. Black Bart himself robbed the stages five or six times in '79 and the early '80s, and, in fact, once after stopping the Weaverville-Redding stage near the Last Chance Mine, he'd gone south on foot to a cabin on Eagle Creek, near the town of Ono, and cool as a cucumber had asked for his breakfast, and the fellow at the cabin had cooked it for him, and on top of that gave him a lunch to take with him and waved good-by to him as he went on down the trail toward Cotton-wood Creek and Tehama County. And that was nothing to the excitement in the county over the Ruggles boys' holdup in '92 on the Middle Creek Road, just a few miles east. George Albro would remember all about that; he tended the boys when they were in the Redding jail, before the night riders broke it open and hustled them out and lynched them both there by the railroad tracks in Redding.

*The fire of 1878 was crushing in its destruction; it reduced to ashes the*
*equivalent of two large blocks comprising many business houses and a*
*number of residences. It was indeed a disheartening blow, for the then status*
*of the Town did not warrant rebuilding. . . .*

The flames had done their work and that had been the finish. It had never been the same, and could never hope to be the same. The people never bothered to clear away the ruins, even, but moved over to Redding, "the fastest growing city in California and the Imperial City of the North," they called her. All the gold was gone; all the freight was gone because there weren't any diggings left for it to go to; Redding had become the terminal point for the stages; and now half the town that was left burned down and the other half was just hanging on. Then, in '87, up in Ashland, Oregon, they drove the Gold Spike that finished the line through from San Francisco to Portland. The same day they did that, the last stage was driven over the Siskiyous; and the next year the county seat was moved to Redding. The folks were sure done to a turn over that. Mrs. Scott, John V.'s wife, was so all-fired mad she wouldn't even take a drink of water in Redding for years after. But that was the way it had gone. That had been the end.

Remembering, on this Home-coming Day, the old-timers could see how it all happened. They could listen to Charlie Shurtleff up there on the platform, and as his words brought back memories they could look down the long road and see how it turned and climbed and descended, and how it had brought both them and the old Town to this sunny afternoon, in this late year of all their lives, sitting there and listening and remembering, as the shadows lengthened across the flat.

*The pleasures and enjoyment of this glorious home-coming*—Old Charlie's voice was tiring, as he reached his last page, and neared the end—*will abide with us always. In moments of meditation it will come to us enriched by time and laden with precious memories of a perfect day. It is well that we have gathered in this old Town of history, not alone to renew former associations and friendships, but to reaffirm our ever present obligation for the priceless heritage transmitted to us by the Pioneers—the frontiersmen of California. . . .*

*Do not weary, do not falter, do not let your enthusiasm abate, or your devotion lapse into indifference, but rather, let these pilgrimages to the hearths of your ancestors be oft repeated, and may you now, upon this very spot where long ago many of them dwelt, inspired by the past and the marvelous story of the Argonauts, unite in a solemn pledge, to the fulfillment of which you plight your sacred honor, that their deeds shall live "until time is o'er and worlds have passed away"; that the trails of the Forty-niners shall not grow dim or become effaced, nor their builders forgotten. With this accomplished, as it inevitably will be, the living, and the generations yet unborn, with one accord, their hearts filled to overflowing with gratitude, will call you blessed.*

The last ringing phrases rose and fell, and died away. They had brought tears to the eyes of some, and these sat still in their wooden chairs, watching the speaker as he stepped back and took his seat in the row on the platform reserved for the honored guests of the day. The others applauded, laying aside their programs to clap their hands, and smiled at each other and shook their heads with affection and approval.

The chairman of the day, an official of the County Historical Society, stepped to the front of the stand. Gradually the applause ceased. The old-timers settled once more in their chairs.

"Thank you, Mr. Shurtleff," he began, smiling, "for that inspired message of Home-coming Day. I know that I am speaking for all of us when I say, 'Thank you, from the bottom of our hearts.' "

He paused, bowed to Charlie, and turned back to the audience. "And now, it is my pleasure to announce the next feature on our program. . . ."

His cheerful, resonant voice carried out over the heads of the old-timers and down Main Street, where the cracked and crumbling façades of the old brick buildings stood under the locust trees, their doors and windows gone, their roofs fallen in, and open to the sky. The chairman talked on, but neither the buildings, nor the old-timers who had shared the days of their youth, were listening.

Now nearly a quarter of a century has passed since that day in June, and should you be going to Shasta, you first drive to Redding, a prosperous and busy community of a blazing summer sun and the earth-shaking crash and pounding of the mountain Mallet engines of the Southern Pacific, hauling valley freight north to the Siskiyous and Oregon. A few blocks north of the center of the business district, you come to a California State Highway marker reading "299" and a sign saying, "Shasta—Six Miles."

The road makes a left turn and takes you west over a railroad bridge from which you can see the spot where the Ruggles boys were lynched in '92, on past the Mormon church and the grounds of the new Shasta Junior College, and out into the country.

This is the road to Shasta, and also to Weaverville and the Trinity Alps and the coast. To the right as you drive along are the Sacramento River (here only a few miles below Shasta Lake and the massive Shasta Dam), and the northernmost corner of the long valley that the Spaniards and the trappers called Buenaventura. If the day is clear, a distant glimpse of a white peak tells you that Mount Shasta is up there to the north, some sixty miles away, beyond the valley's end.

It was in the early evening, a few days after the Shasta County Centennial celebration and the dedication of Shasta Dam, that I drove out this road to Shasta and parked the car in front of the old county courthouse, and got out to look around.

The Main Street of the Gold Rush is a 1-mile straightaway of Highway

299, and here, as the highway passes through the little settlement, it is bordered with tall locust and China trees that give both shade and a mining-country air to the courthouse, the gasoline station at one end of the street, Litsch's gasoline-station-general-store-and-pioneer-museum at the other end of the street, the roadside café called Old Shasta Lodge, and the stuccoed, two-story home of Western Star No. 2.

These are the only buildings left on Main Street that serve the purposes of the living. Curiously, it is they, and not the crumbling brick shells of the Gold Rush buildings lining the street's south side, that seem somehow out of place and out of time. The two gasoline stations and the café seem somehow to have wandered into the past and to have been marooned there. Now no one hears their mute calls for help, their silent signals of distress. Castaways on this island of the past, they sit beside the road with the old locust trees and the haunted ruins.

But Main Street is misleading. Shasta today is a community of several hundred. It is down on the flat, north of and below the highway, that the neat white cottages stand, concealed by groves of trees—on Back Road, High Street, and Trinity Alley—where the miners pitched their tents and sat beside their evening campfires.

An old man came limping along beside the highway, bound, perhaps, for the bench by the wall of the gasoline station, a few yards west of the courthouse. It was growing cooler, the shadows were deepening, and that would be a place to sit and watch the cars and lumber trucks go by, if any came down the road at all this late in the day. A lean and spotted cur with one ear erect and another that fell rakishly across one eye roused itself from the courthouse dust at his approach and circled him warily, ready to cringe away at a show of unfriendliness or drop fawningly at his feet at a kind word. The old man ignored the dog. The dog stood still, watching him pass, a study in indecision and insecurity. At length it turned and trotted swiftly across the highway to disappear among the ruins.

A hill rises prominently above the highway at that end of town, and I asked the old man its name. He paused and thought.

"Ain't got any," he said at last. "There's a hill down at the other end of town, Shurtleff Hill. That's the only hill I know of around here that's got a name."

I asked him if the residents commuted to Redding to work.

There was another long pause as he surveyed the deserted Main Street. "Well, I'd put it about that way. Most Shastans work in Redding. Some of them drive the logging trucks. There's one fellow here that goes all the way to Eureka, a hundred forty miles west, to pick up his lumber truck."

He limped on to the gasoline-station bench, lowered himself to it slowly and sat gazing down the empty road. I crossed the highway to a raised and newly graded piece of ground on which was a large boulder with a plaque fastened to its face.

Lettering on the plaque said that it had been erected by the California Centennials Commission, on a base furnished by the Shasta County Centennial Committee, and that it had been dedicated June 12, 1950, during the recent celebration. A small sign nearby, fixed to a low post, announced that this ground had once been the site of the Charter Oak Hotel. The text of the tablet offered, in telegraphic style, some of the facts about Shasta: that it had been founded in '49 as Reading's Springs, that it had been the county seat and the beginning, until '61, of the Oregon pack trail.

Down the street, under a pair of leaning locusts and between the courthouse and the ninety-seven-year-old Masonic Hall was another boulder with another plaque. This marker honored the brave Concords, their drivers, and Williamson Lyncoya Smith, who for many years was division manager of the California Stage Company. Erected by Mae Hélène Bacon Boggs (Smith's niece, Shasta County historian, and author of *My Playhouse Was a Concord Coach*), the plaque carried in miniature relief a six-horse stage rounding a turn on a mountain trail. Beside it, also in relief, was Smith's likeness. Underneath were the names of some hundred and fifty stage drivers, and the words, *In loving memory to these pioneers who "held the ribbons" but have turned the bend in this road*.

I left it and walked to the courthouse. A few years before, trees were growing within its roofless walls, but now it stood restored, with a new porch and a new roof, and its nine iron doors freshly painted green and black under their nine brick arches. Because it was so late in the day, the doors were closed and bolted.

Upon its facade was another plaque, which, like the ones on the boulders, had been dedicated June 12, 1950. This building, it said, had been built two years after the big fire of '53 by James Loag. It had been converted into the county courthouse in 1862. The McCloud Parlor of the Native Sons of the Golden West had bought it in 1922, and in 1937 had deeded it to the State, whose Division of Beaches and Parks had restored it.

Confronting this building from the other side of the highway was all that was left of the Gold Rush stores. The walls of most of them were intact, and their iron doors, like those of the courthouse, had been recently painted black and green; but their roofs and floors were gone. They stood beside the road defying time, as a man condemned to die might defy his executioners.

In front of each one was a small new sign relating each doorway to a name and a year that belonged to the old Shasta:

*Callaghan, 3 stores,* 1855; *J. A. Downey, store,* 1855; *Hullub and Isaacs,* 1853; *A. Grotefend, warehouse,* 1854; *A. Dobrowsky, jewelry,* 1854; *Quiside Building,* 1855; *Bull, Baker Store,* 1853; *Tomlinson and Wood,* 1854; *Dr. Benjamin Shurtleff,* 1853; *W. S. Wills Building,* 1854; *Young Building,* 1855; *Lewis Building,* 1855.

As I read them, it seemed to me that the leaning locust trees, these ruins, and the mellow and lovely bricks of the courthouse across the street said far more about Shasta than the words and dates of the plaques; they were the survivors, and in them you discerned dead men's hopes and disappointments, crowds, commerce, growth, life, death, change, decay, rain, and the procession of a century of suns.

I went back to the car and got in. A blond young man in white shirt emerged from the Old Shasta Café that stood beside the ruins, and sat down on the café veranda. A lumber truck and trailer loaded with five pine logs rolled swiftly down the grade from the west, roared past the courthouse, and disappeared around the curve at the far end of the street.

In the wake of stillness that followed after, and in the early dusk, there rose the distant cries of children playing ball on the flat beyond the courthouse. Among the leaves of the courthouse locust trees the sparrows resumed their twittering. Down the quiet air came drifting a faint fragrance that was a blend of oakwood smoke and the smell of mountain pines.

The next day, Mrs. Boggs, her friend Mrs. Edna Behrens Eaton, who is a member of a pioneer Shasta family and a resident of Redding, and I visited the museum now housed in several rooms of the restored courthouse.

Mrs. Boggs, small, pert, animate, led us through the iron doors and into two rooms that had once been used by county officials. "Come in," she said brightly, "and look around. Everybody laughs at me because I'm such a sentimental old dame, but in here are some of the things I've saved and given to the museum."

It was indeed an extraordinary collection. Several hundred volumes of Californiana stood in glass-paneled bookcases. On the walls were Liberty Loan posters from World War I. A suffragette pennant demanding "Votes for Women" hung over the door. On the walls of the room were thirty or forty oil paintings and various photographs and maps relating to Shasta County history. There was also an American flag, which, Mrs. Boggs said, was raised over the ruins of her house in Washington Street, San Francisco, after the earthquake and fire of 1906.

"It was," she said, "the first flag flown in the burned district after the disaster."

The second room was hung with seventy additional oil paintings from Mrs. Boggs's collection. These were dominated by a large portrait of her uncle, with whom she lived after her arrival in California from Missouri in 1871. Of the paintings, which were mainly regional in subject and treatment, one stood out sharply from the rest. It depicted a scene that was unmistakably Parisian: on a bench in a little park, a dapper young Frenchman bent ardently toward a prim French girl, who stared straight ahead, stonily unimpressed by his words of love. Behind them, its massive base concealed in the trees beyond the park, but unmistakable, rose the Statue of Liberty. It was enclosed in scaffolding.

I could not help wondering what chance or caprice had brought this painting to this town in the manzanita-covered foothills of Northern California.

"This," Mrs. Boggs explained, "was painted in 1884, two years before France presented the statue to the United States. Here we see it as it must have appeared when it was being assembled.

"I looked at it in an art dealer's shop several times before I understood why it belonged in Shasta. New York, I thought, now has its Statue of Liberty, on one side of the continent. This picture of it should be on the other side. And what more appropriate place could you find for it than Shasta, on the highway to Eureka, which is the name of the westernmost city in the United States, and the key word on the Great Seal of California?"

The logic of it all, her happy smile said, was childishly simple—and irresistible.

We passed through the room that held pioneer, Chinese, and Indian relics gathered by the members of the McCloud Parlor, and entered the old courtroom.

Its restoration had been faithful and painstaking. An old-fashioned clock ticked away on the wall. A kerosene lamp stood ready to repel the afternoon shadows, and down on the room and its curved, spectators' benches, from his framed portrait near the clock, fell the shrewd, appraising glance of Judge Edward Sweeney, who, after a term on the Shasta County Superior Bench, had become superintendent of the United States Mint at San Francisco.

The room, apart from a self-conscious tidiness, gave the impression that it was in reality in suspension: court was in recess; at any moment the bailiff would summon the lawyers and the courtroom crowd from the corridor; a frock-coated judge would appear from his chambers, step sedately to the tiny bench that resembled a schoolmaster's desk, and hear a case involving the theft of a gold-dust poke from a Forty-niner of Mad Mule Canyon.

In still another room was an exhibit representing frontier law in a grimmer aspect. Glass cases held a Torquemada's collection of leg irons, shackles, Oregon boots, fetters, and a ball-and-chain. Most of them had been donated to the museum by George Albro, Shasta's venerable jailer. Here also were two souvenirs of the county's most famous crime, the holdup of the Weaverville-Redding stage by the Ruggles boys: a bandanna that one of them had worn as a mask, and the safe that the night riders had blown open for the key to their jail cells, the night of the lynching.

In the courthouse basement were the immense cages that had served as cells, and a common room where the prisoners had taken their meals. A door led from this room into a fenced exercise area at the back of the courthouse. Above this area rose the gallows. Standing upon the gallows, you could look roughly north upon the same landscape that, for a number of unfortunate men, was the last they ever saw of this earth: hills rolling away to the horizon, trees, and a cloudless sky.

A few moments later we were on our way back to Redding. To leave

the courthouse and the brick ruins of Shasta was, for me, to depart from
another century and another California; but for Mrs. Boggs, whose playhouse had been a Concord coach, it was only to bid a temporary farewell
to the lineaments of a living past.

As we parted in front of Redding's Golden Eagle Hotel, she said, "To
me, Shasta is today what she always has been—the Queen City of the
North." The ringing pride with which she invested her words hung in the
air as she smiled, turned, and disappeared into the hotel.

One more thing remained. . . .

I found the old house on Court Street in Redding and walked down past
the oleanders to the back door.

"George? Mr. Albro?" I called.

A small, slightly stooped, elderly man appeared at the screen door. He
was wearing a blue shirt, a black, unbuttoned vest, jeans, and a dark felt
hat.

"This is George," he grinned, and held the door open.

The kitchen proclaimed the fact that George was a bachelor; its pleasant
disorder stated clearly that it neither had, nor cared to have, the feminine
touch. Amid the confusion several things clamored for notice: a wood-
burning stove; a large sign reading, "Consulting Engineer"; an ancient,
cantankerous-looking Remington-Smith Premier typewriter with two key
boards—one for upper-case and one for lower-case letters—and a large,
square, copper can that had once been part of a moonshiner's still. This sat
on the floor before an armchair, and George used it for a footstool.

The one that told the most about George was the sign. He assured me
proudly that it was indeed his: he had been the consulting engineer on the
restoration of the old Shasta courthouse.

"And," he added with a smile, "they couldn't have found a better one.
I was on speaking terms with every brick in that building."

George went to work at the courthouse as an eleven-year-old chore boy
in 1873. He stayed there until the county seat was moved to Redding, and
when that took place he went along with it to the new county courthouse.
He ended seventy-five years of county service in 1948, and in that year
retired as courthouse custodian. Two years before his retirement, George
was appointed a Superior Judge, Emeritus, of Shasta County for life, with

authority to preside over the court whenever he wished and to perform all the duties of judge except to officiate at weddings or to grant divorces and annulments of marriage. This distinction, unique in California history, was conferred upon him by Superior Judge Albert F. Ross of Redding, who, as a boy and the son of the sheriff of Shasta County, tagged after George as he went about his duties as jailer. George received the appointment on his eighty-fourth birthday—his annual birthday party is a civic event in Redding—for his services to the county and the court, for "his exemplary character as a good and upright man," and for his kind heart and ready smile.

The day I called on him was warm and bright. He had nothing to do, and suggested that we drive out the Middle Creek road to the bend and the cut where the Ruggles boys held up the stage.

As we passed over the railroad bridge on the way out of Redding, George pointed down the tracks to Roy Brown's furniture store.

"Right there near that furniture store building," he said, "there used to be two pine trees. They were later killed by the smelter smoke from Kennett and Copper City up in the canyon, and had to be cut down. On those two trees is where they strung up the Ruggles boys."

We turned off Highway 299 to a rough dirt road that followed the south shore of the Sacramento River. On our right was the river and on our left was a high bank of sand. George said that sometimes the river rose over the road and seven or eight feet up the bank.

Here, off the paved road, it was north country, all right. Still and hot, not a living thing in sight, the dust heavy on the leaves of the wild-grape and the blackberry vines, the slow-flowing river, the tawny river bars, and, to the north, the bare brown hills.

George pointed to a desolate area of sand beside some railroad tracks. "Middle Creek railroad station used to sit there years ago." He indicated the tracks. "Used to be the main line to Portland. And back in '85, this used to be the main road to Weaverville."

We bumped across the tracks and came to a dilapidated shack faced with cast-off newspaper mats.

"Who lives there?" I asked.

George shrugged. "Prospectors, maybe. Used to be the site of the Middle Creek Hotel. After the Ruggleses held up the stage and after all the shootin', the horses broke and ran wild, clear down to here, and here they took off the driver and the dead man, and got the doctors to wait on them."

A mile or so farther on—the road had left the Sacramento and was now taking us along the course of Middle Creek—George touched my arm. "Stop the car and I'll tell you a story," he said. I stopped the car.

"See that flat over there?" He pointed across the creek to a bench of sand above the creek bank. "Over on that flat once lived a miner in a shack. One day he went down the river in a boat, and the boat hit a rock, and he drowned. That was in the '50s.

"Years later, when they were building the railroad through here, some of the Chinese laborers went over there and tore down the shack. They were taking the chimney apart for bricks when they struck a cavity over the fireplace—" George paused for dramatic effect.

"Don't stop now," I said.

"—and out poured a cascade of gold pieces, $15,000 or $20,000 that the drowned miner had cached away in his chimney. Well, the superintendent of the gang happened to be there at the time. He jumped in, hitting China-men left and right, and grabbed two handfuls of the gold pieces and ran. He told me that story himself, and said he got a couple of hundred dollars out of that strike. I guess it was the only gold strike in California history made by Chinese railroad workers in an abandoned chimney."

He pointed higher up the bank to a low bluff above the flat. "Up there used to be the Bunker Hill Mine. Two companies claimed that mine, and were fixin' for a claim war. Filled all their sluice boxes with rocks, got behind them with their Winchesters, and were just about to start shootin' when a man named Mr. Harold appeared on the scene and talked them out of the war and settled the whole matter."

George laughed, poked me in the side with his elbow, and said, "Know what happened a week later?"

"No," I said. "What happened?"

"Mine petered out."

Finally, in our drive along the dusty road, we reached a point where steep banks rose on each side of the dirt highway. It was perhaps three miles west of Redding, in rough country, and half a mile beyond the Iron Mountain turnoff.

"A blue porphyry dike runs along here, and this is called Blue Cut," George said. "Some people call it the Ruggles Boys Cut, but they're wrong. I'll show you where that is in a minute or two."

A half mile farther on, we came to a second cut. The bank on the right was perhaps twelve feet high—higher, certainly, than a stagecoach. On the left the bank was lower, and where the bank ended and sloped down, an indistinct path led through the manzanita and along the side of a canyon to the dry and stony bed of Middle Creek. We stopped the car and got out. This, George said, was the Ruggles Boys Cut.

George stripped a manzanita limb of a handful of small gray berries, popped them into his mouth and attacked the heart of the matter that had taken us out the Middle Creek road. . . .

John and Charlie Ruggles were both in their twenties, personable in appearance, and well known in Shasta County as the sons of a respected and popular minister. George said that they had found out that this particular stage would carry a shipment of gold worth $40,000 from the Trinity diggings. (This point seems to be in dispute. George said there was $40,000 in the box and that that is what they got. J. W. Schoonover, a Southern Pacific employee in Redding at the time of the holdup—May 14, 1892— and now of Fernbridge, California, has quoted Dan Haskell, a Wells, Fargo shotgun messenger on the Weaverville-Redding run before and after the holdup, as saying "there was something less than $15,000 in the box." Rosena Giles, in her history of Shasta County, wrote that the box the Ruggles boys got contained waybills and stovepipe hats; the treasure box, containing $3,500, was hidden inside the coach.)

George walked down the dirt road, between the banks, and began his story.

"John Boyce, the driver of the stage, was on the box. Inside were Buck Montgomery, the Wells, Fargo messenger, and some passengers. The stage was drawn by four horses, and it came around that bend there"—he pointed down the road to where the road curved along the canyonside and approached the cut—"and Charlie was at the cut, hidden behind the manzanita bushes. John was on top of the bank, across the road, and they had bandannas on for masks.

"When the stage got about here"—he stood in the road, in the middle of the cut—"Charlie came up out of the manzanita and covered the stage with his pistol. 'Throw down the box,' he said. Somebody dumped the box down to the road. At the same time, Montgomery stuck his shotgun out of the stage and shot Charlie in the face. Charlie blazed back and hit the driver and a passenger in the legs. Then his brother John, from up on the bank there, shot Montgomery and killed him. Then the horses ran away, and ran wild to the Middle Creek Hotel, where doctors took care of the wounded.

"Back here, in this cut, John came down off the bank and took a look at Charlie and thought Charlie was a goner. He got the box and went down that path with it, through the manzanita and down the side of the gulch to the creek. And Charlie laid here in the road groaning."

George walked to the edge of the road and looked down the steep drop to the creek bed. "Before the robbery, they used to call this Henderson Gulch. Afterwards, it became the Ruggles Boys Gulch."

He said that the posse had found Charlie in the gulch the next day and that they had taken him to the jail in Redding where the doctors had treated his shotgun wound and he, George, had nursed him. As for the rest of the story, he would repeat what he overheard John tell Charlie one night, two months later, in the jail cell, after John himself had been captured in Woodland. Charlie's head was bandaged, and he was stretched out on his cell cot, and John leaned over him talking in a low voice.

"I saw you lyin' there in the road with your head full of bullets," George quoted John as saying. "I took the box down to the creek and got our ax and broke it open. I took a load of money and went and hid it.

"I was gone half an hour, maybe. I knew they'd be after us, and when I came back to the creek for the rest I saw you crawl down the side of the gulch and fall into a hole of water. Your face was bleedin' something awful. It was full of bullet holes. I laid you on a pile of rocks, knowin' you was goin' to die, and took the rest and went.

"I went up on to the old ditch—you know . . . ?"

A muffled "Uh-huh" came through Charlie's bandages, George said.

"I followed the ditch to the end, crossed over a little dam, and took up an old road by a graveyard. . . ." George's voice, imitating John's, was a low monotone, filled with John's troubled concern that his brother should understand everything that had happened, and everything he did. "I passed an old slaughterhouse. . . . I went over a mountain road west, and went down that. . . . I crossed a high flume over a creek, and went along a long ridge. . . ." In detail John described his flight past the towns of Anderson and Cottonwood. "I got to a town by a creek in time to catch a little train. . . . The train went on to Tehama and slowed down. I had about fifty pounds on me. . . . I jumped off the train and crossed the tracks and went west again. . . . Last month they caught me in Woodland. . . ."

Here, George said, John happened to look up and saw him sitting outside the cell. He stopped in the middle of a sentence, and said no more.

The way he got caught, George said, was that John's aunt in Woodland gave him away to the authorities. From Shasta County, a constable named Wycoff went to Woodland and cornered John in a restaurant.

He knew John was armed. He entered the restaurant and sat down opposite John, at the same table. When John picked up his knife and fork to begin to eat, Wycoff drew his gun and shot John in the right arm. Almost before he knew what had happened, John was in handcuffs.

The presence of the Ruggles boys in the Redding jail was more than a challenge to the friends of Buck Montgomery; it was a call for vengeance and frontier action swifter than the courts could provide. From all along the stage line they rode masked into Redding on the night of July 24, 1892, and broke into the jail and ordered George to hand them the key to the Ruggles boys' cell.

"The keys are in the office safe," George said.

The leaders went to the safe and blew it open. They got the keys, unlocked the cell and rushed John and Charlie out of the jail and down to the railroad tracks in back of Atter's blacksmith shop. Bolted to two pines and 12 or 15 feet from the ground, was a heavy crossbeam used for the lifting of freight wagons when they were having their wheels or tires fixed. The lynchers bound John and Charlie hand and foot, slipped the nooses around their throats, tossed the rope ends over the crossbeam and yanked the brothers into the air. They hung there, twisting and turning, for quite a while before someone came and cut them down.

That same year, during an autumn thunderstorm, a bolt of lightning struck the crossbeam, and tore and shredded it into a thousand splinters, and scattered the splinters on the ground, beneath the pines.

When George had finished with the story, we left the cut and drove the remaining mile or two into Shasta. I asked him about the money John said he had hidden in the gulch.

"I figure there's $30,000 there somewhere," George said. "Once in a while a fellow comes out here with a Spanish needle and follows it up and down the creek bed to see if it will point to the gold. But no one's found it yet."

We came up off the Middle Creek road and on to Shasta's Main Street and drove down the street to return to Redding on the paved highway. At the end of the street we passed Litsch's gasoline station, store, and museum. In front of the building was a rusty, ancient cannon.

"They say that cannon was brought by Frémont from Sutter's Fort," George said. "It was only used in Shasta once, and that time, with one shot, it won a war with the Indians. The men tied it on the back of a mule and went after the Indians. When they got close enough to them, they loaded it and fired it. Damned thing had such a kick, it blew the mule down the mountainside, plumb in the middle of all those redskins. Out of the thickets they came with their hands up. 'We're going to fight no white men strong enough to throw mules at us,' they said, and surrendered."

As he ended the story, George took off his hat and put his head out the window and breathed deeply of the soft warm air.

"Sure feels good, just to be here in Shasta," he said.

The car moved smoothly on, past the hills, the pines in the sun, the manzanita, a green meadow, and the sweet, fugitive song of a lark.

# CHAPTER NINE

# Yreka

THIS IS AN old Gold Rush town, the biggest town of the far Northern Mines that has survived, and so, as with all the other towns like it, living or dead, you can say if you like that its story began with the affair in the Coloma Valley, January 24, 1848, and the flake of gold James Marshall took from the millrace. But, to pick up this particular story, you can start with the situation in the north in the winter of '49 and '50, and the snow-bound winter camps of the Clear Creek diggings and Readings Springs, and those as deep in the snows in the country of the Trinity Forks. Except for the trappers' trails and the beginnings of the California-Oregon Trail that Lieutenant Emmons and Jim Clyman and the cattle-drivers had traveled (Lindsay Applegate's train had taken the first six wagons over the Siskiyous from the Willamette just the summer before; but they abandoned four of them, so rough was the going, at the head of the Sacramento Canyon, and turned around and went back to Oregon) the vast reach of

191

mountain ranges and forests and rivers to the north of the camps in the snow was absolute Indian country, belonging still to the Klamaths, the Pits, the Modocs, the Rogues, and the Shastans, whose centuries of savage sovereignty were now nearing their end.

It is said that when Peter Skene Ogden reached that north country with his South Brigade in '27, he was received in one of the Indian villages as very big medicine, and he and two of his men were ceremoniously shown to a large lodge where they might recline and smoke their trail-rope tobacco with the chief and rest.

With the coming of evening, three maidens of the tribe, shy, small-boned, and slender, entered the lodge. They pulled off the trappers' heavy trail boots, put on their feet beaded moccasins of soft doeskin, and gently stroked and combed their hair.

The next day, when Ogden and his men left for their camp, the beating of tom-toms rose over the village. It continued all day. At sunset, the drums fell silent. The medicine man of the tribe, daubed with paint and arrayed in feathers, danced a wild dance on the bank of the Shasta River, and into its swift-flowing waters flung three little man-dolls. To each doll was fastened a scalplock of hair that the maidens, during their tender ministrations of the night before, had cunningly cut from the heads of the three trappers.

Chanting, the medicine man and a dozen paint-streaked braves followed the dolls as they bobbed downstream, and with long sticks kept them floating free in the current. When the dolls at last outdistanced them and disappeared down the dusk-dark river, they returned to the village and the festival fire that blazed high under the lofty village pines. They ate elk meat that night, for it would be a night for the tribe to remember—the night the magic dolls cast a charm over the white men, and led them blindly down the winding river to a land so far away they could never find their way back to the country of Shasta, Wigwam of the Great Spirit.

Later, bitterness settled upon them as they saw that the charm of the scalplocks and man-dolls had failed. More and more white men kept coming within sight of the Shasta snows, trapping the beaver runs and passing on, or herding before them many cattle. Now, at last, in the winter of '49 and '50, all that remained to the life of their long and roving

race were a few months, and the hopeless struggle for the forests of their
hunting grounds and home. . . .

To those Forty-niners in the winter camps at Clear Creek and the
Springs and along the Trinity Forks came two strange and all but incredible tales. Prospectors drifted in with them from San Francisco and the
valley towns and the camps of the Mother Lode. When they saw that
they could go no farther until winter's end, they settled down in the tent
saloons, and it wasn't long before tall brandies and hot whisky punches
set their tongues wagging over what they'd heard down below about the
mine they called the Dead Man.

"Dead Man's Mine, that's what we've come to find," they said as they
poured themselves another and held their glasses high. "Here's to the
spring thaw and the Dead Man!" And their maudlin songs carried out of
the tent and over the camp and died away among the still, snow-mantled
pines.

As the winter wore on, it became clear that there were two Dead Man's
Mines, one in the mountains to the north, and another to the northwest, in
the shoreline foothills of the Coast Range. Pieced together from the fragments and the rumors, and sifted of their discrepancies and wild specula-
tions, they emerged as strikingly similar, yet fascinating tales that their
carriers swore were true. And by God, they vowed, when spring came and
they could move out of camp, they'd prove it.

The first, they said, began right in this very country, in the Trinity diggings, early last fall. There were three Forty-niners from the Wabash country of Indiana who came overland together and formed a partnership.
Two of them were older men named Cox and Benedict; the third was a
youth of about twenty named Compton. Deciding to try their luck in the
northern diggings, they set out over the valley trail, pressed on past Clear
Creek and Readings Springs and headed still farther north, for the wilderness of the Salmon Range, that lay between the Trinities and the Siskiyous.

Late one afternoon, not far from the highest headwaters of the Trinity
River's north fork, they pitched camp on a mountainside where a cold
spring bubbled from the roots of a great yellow pine. Cox and Benedict
immediately started out to prospect and explore, while Compton remained
on guard at the camp.

As darkness fell, Compton heard Cox and Benedict shout his name.

He hurried down the mountainside and found them in a high state of excitement.

They had wandered far from camp, they said, following the trail of an animal. As they rounded a point of rock, an immense grizzly bear reared up on its hind legs before them. They emptied their revolvers into the beast and it fell dead into a natural pit several yards in diameter. With a bear-steak dinner in mind, they leaped into the pit and began to skin the carcass. One of them found, on the pit floor, a lump of gold. They dug deeper, and found more.

Now, standing jubilant before Compton, they held out their hands. Their hands were filled with nuggets.

The next day they moved their camp to the pit. Six hundred paces east they built two cabins, one for themselves and the other for their provisions and equipment. After that was done they hauled the dead grizzly to one side and went to work on their gold mine.

For a month they dug gold out of the pit, enough to give each of them a modest fortune. Then, fearing the approach of winter, they stowed their tools away and drove their treasure-laden pack animals south. They blazed a trail as they went.

When they reached San Francisco, Cox and Benedict decided that they were through: they'd struck it rich, and that was what they'd come to California for, and anyway they were getting along in years for the mountain life. Compton could have the mine; they'd go home and live like kings for the rest of their days. There was no talking them out of it: they bought steamer passages, sailed out the Golden Gate, and left Compton to wait for the spring of '50 to melt the snows, so he could return to the cabins in the north.

But he never went back. That Christmas he contracted the deadly cholera. To a friend who had cared for him in his illness—a fellow Mason named Maxwell—Compton babbled his story, gave directions to the mine, and died.

One night not long after Compton's death, Maxwell drank too heavily in a Montgomery Street bar and talked, flashing some of the nuggets Compton had left him to prove his talk. Word of the bonanza spread swiftly. The next day, they were starting out from San Francisco. Within a week the story had reached the Mother Lode, and miners discouraged with the diggings there packed up their mules and were off for the north country. And so they had all come to the trail's end at Clear Creek and the Trinity, to wait for the breaking-up of winter and the day when they could search for a spring at the foot of a yellow pine, two cabins, and a gold mine that was guarded by the skeleton of a grizzly bear.

With them arrived some who had hurried north to look for another mine, and a treasure hidden somewhere in the country of the redwoods to the northwest.

These had heard tell that last summer a prospector crossed the Coast Range, east to west, near the mouth of the Klamath River, and hunted for gold in the foothill ravines near the ocean shore. He was alone and well supplied with provisions.

This miner—they did not know his name—hit a bonanza. So rich it was (their story went) it seemed to him as though the earth he struck with his pick must be of solid gold. Hastily he constructed a cabin shelter. Then, driven by the desire to amass a fortune and return to his home in the East, he worked day after day at a frantic pace. Each night he concealed what he had mined during the day in an underground hiding place near the cabin.

The mine had yielded him fabulous wealth, and his goal was in sight, when a roving band of Indians attacked his camp and left him senseless on the ground, to all appearances dead. Unable to find his hoarded gold, they set fire to his cabin and departed. After they had gone, the miner slowly recovered consciousness; but both reason and memory had deserted him.

In this condition he wandered out of the forest and found his way to a mining camp. There, sympathetic prospectors identified him and learned his native town and state in the East. (How this was accomplished was not exactly known; those who believed the story guessed that it was through letters found in his pockets.) The miners arranged for his passage home. A few months later he was back among his family and friends.

He still suffered, however, from the effects of the Indian attack, and it soon became apparent that he was dying. Miraculously, on his deathbed, his mind cleared. Calling his friends around him, he told them of the forest mine by the Pacific. He described minutely the location of the cabin, and told them how to reach the spot where they would find its ashes. He gave them precise directions to the secret vault that he had filled with gold and urged them, if they would be rich, to hasten westward and claim it for their own. At the end of his strange story, he lapsed into unconsciousness and died.

The friends journeyed to California as quickly as they could. But the tale had become generally known in their town, even before they left, and with them went adventurers bent on following them to the mine in the redwoods.

All of them were there now, in the snowbound camps of the northern diggings, waiting impatiently for the spring thaw. The gold was up there someplace; somebody'd find it; and maybe they'd be the ones. And if they weren't, they'd be close at hand when it was found and could stake out a claim of their own at the diggings.

Who knows? they asked themselves; such a claim might be even richer than any found before—richer than the promise of all their dreams.

Spring came at last, to the wild, rushing music of the snow-swollen creeks, and they and their pack mules were off for the virgin country beyond the ridge that Reading had crossed with his cattle and Indians in the summer of '48. A thousand, perhaps several thousand, strong, some going it alone and some united in clannish bands, they fanned down the draws and canyons to the south and north forks of the Salmon River, and struck across the Marble Mountains to the Scott River and the Klamath. Others traveled west and north for the Coast Range to hunt the treasure in the redwoods, and when they reached the littoral foothills, they found there before them prospectors who had come up to the landings of Trinidad Bay by sea.

Deeper into the forests they drove the Indians, and deeper into the wilderness, as they advanced, receded the will-o'-the-wisp bonanzas of the dead miners. In every long ravine, beyond the turn in every gorge and canyon and on the far side of every flat they looked for the tell-tale heap of ashes, the bubbling spring by the yellow pine, the skeleton of the bear, the two cabins, and the blazes Compton, Cox, and Benedict had slashed on the tree trunks as they made their way south the fall before. But spring became summer, the bloom fell from the wild lilac, and the higher hotter suns turned the mountain meadows tawny, and still they searched in vain.

The skeptical and easily discouraged soon abandoned the quest, saying they had known the stories were fables all along, and settled down and panned where they were; the dreamers, the imaginative, the superstitious —those with the mark of the mystic on them—kept on following the streams and the ridges and the light of their lucky star, confident that the mines lay waiting for them and for them alone. They became known as seekers after the Lost Cabins, and the mines they sought became known as the Lost Cabin Mines, and so to this day they remain in the legend of the California North.

By July, the miners who no longer took the stories seriously or who had dismissed them as Gold Rush fairy tales from the beginning were panning along the Salmon—at Pigeon Roost, Timber Turn, Bellyache Spring, China Slide, Paradise Flat, Clawhammer Bar, Dead Mule Gulch, and a hundred other riverbank settlements. From one of these camps, near the Forks of Salmon where the north fork and the south fork met, a party led by Edward Beam and J. M. C. Jones went north to the Klamath and followed the river east upstream to its union with the Shasta River. There, or near there, they had a brush with the Indians, and a day or so later were overtaken in camp by Rufus Johnson's party, and together, forming a group now of sixty or more, they fell south a few miles to a gently sloping flat 8 miles long and hard by a creek that flowed into the Shasta. This was a vale walled on the west by a high steep range that, farther west, became the Salmon Mountains. To the north, beyond the valley's end, were the Siskiyous. Along the quadrant north to east there was no barrier, and they could look from the creek bank east across the grass-grown lava hummocks of the Shasta Valley as far as Sheep Rock and Goosenest Mountain, that rose above the far side of the valley. From east to south one hog-backed ridge, covered with scrub oak, stood close between the flat and the valley, and obscured from view Mount Shasta—or Shasta Butte, as they called it—at the head of the valley, 40 miles to the southeast. Here on this flat, near the willows along the creek, the combined parties pitched camp.

They found there an Indian cache of dried salmon and rifled it until it was gone, and panned for gold and found traces of color, but not enough, they thought, to make it worth while to stay and seriously work the ground. After three days there, they raised camp and moved on.

A few months later, a party led by Adam Wolfe, bound north from the Salmon River country to Oregon for winter supplies, spent the night at the encampment by the willows. Before they left the next morning, a few members of the party discovered bits of coarse gold. Like Beam and Jones and Rufus Johnson, they shrugged it off: to two or three men who wanted to work like mules the flat might yield an ounce a day, but who wanted to work like a mule here, where there was all that fine dust over on the Salmon and the Klamath, and when John Scott, a week or two ago, had found an 8-pound nugget on Scott River, 20 miles west? They put out their breakfast fires, rode into the Shasta Valley, and by mid-forenoon picked up the California-Oregon Trail and headed north for Pilot Rock and the pass over the Siskiyou Summit.

It was the next February, in the late winter of '51, when a large party of Oregonians, bound for the Scott River diggings, raised their tents on the long flat and were held there by heavy rains. Among them were Dr. F. G. Hearn (a dentist), Jacob Wagner, Abraham Thompson, James Thornton, Charles J. Day, and a man named Bell. On the first fair day after the rains, they started for the spur of the western ridge and the trail to the Scott River Valley. Thompson, in preparation for the day's journey, led his pack mules off the trail to a small stand of ponderosa pine and incense cedar, and let them graze. Idly he watched them tug and nibble at the fresh young grass. One of them uprooted an entire tuft and Thompson saw, in the earth that clung to its roots, golden flecks. He dropped on his knees and yanked another tuft from the ground. Its roots also showed gold. Unstrapping his pan from one of the packs, he half filled it with the earth and carried it to a streamlet in a little ravine nearby, and washed it out. He washed a second pan, and a third. It was the same coarse gold that the others had found the year before, but more of it, much more—enough to bring a flush of excitement to Thompson's face.

He ran a few steps down the flat after the train.

"Come back!" he cried. "I've struck it!"

The others stopped and wheeled.

An hour later, their tents were up again, on a knoll half a mile from the creek, and they were staking out their claims.

In honor of the discoverer and because it was so far from the creek bank and water, they called it Thompson's Dry Diggings.

It was as if Thompson's triumphant shout had carried all the way to the Sacramento Valley and across the mountains, so swiftly did word of the new strike reach the camps of the Mother Lode and the Trinity Forks. Within a week bonanza-bent miners were pouring into the camp by the hundreds. Far down the flat their tents and brush shanties were strung out, and more kept coming in every day. Many had left wherever they came from so fast they hadn't bothered with equipment, and all over the diggings you could have seen them at work with rockers hastily hewn from oak trees, and riddles improvised from perforated deerskins.

Other camps materialized as the late-comers took one look at the crowd on the flat and headed for elbow-room in the nearby hills. A party bound for the gulches and canyons a few miles northwest of the flat met a dejected group of miners returning to Thompson's.

"We heard it's pretty rich over there where you just came from," said the members of the first party.

"Then what you heard is humbug," retorted the others sourly, and moved along on their way to the flat.

The first party continued northwest anyway, and, sure enough, struck pay dirt where the others had failed. They named their camp Humbug City and the creek beside it Humbug Creek; and the range of mountains that extended south from the camp became the Humbug Mountains.

South of Thompson's on the slope of a certain ridge, another band of independent prospectors toiled away at their claims for weeks and finally abandoned them as a waste of time. A newcomer, whose innocent air proclaimed him a "greenhorn," asked them where he could find a gold mine.

Rolling their quids and winking slyly at each other, they pointed out the ridge they had just left. "Right over yonder, son. We've taken out so much dust already we're plumb tuckered out and can't carry any more. But there's a pile left, and every ounce of it's your'n."

The greenhorn stammered his thanks and started for the abandoned claims.

A few days later, the old hands learned to their dismay that the greenhorn had made a strike. Back they rushed, and the camp that mushroomed on the ridge was called Greenhorn, and from that day forward the ridge itself was Greenhorn Ridge.

Meanwhile, the growing settlement on the flat had centered itself and consolidated along the creek near the water and in the shade and shelter of the cottonwoods and willows. By the middle of May it was a noisy, bustling boom town of 5,000 men and one white woman—the wife of a prospector named D. A. Lowery. With poles, shakes, and canvas, Sam Lockhart was building the camp's first business establishment, a saloon with a sandbagged, bullet-proof bar, and a Mr. Turner was building the first house, an 18-by-18-foot cottonwood log cabin. It had an *alcalde* in George C. S. Vail, and a constable in James Thomas, and an impressive new name, Shasta Butte City. When it became apparent that organization was needed in laying out the expanding town, Vail and other leading citizens settled the matter by pacing off the streets. So whimsical was the result that Lockhart's patrons, standing at the door of the tent saloon with gins and peppermint in hand, surveyed the new street lines and swore that they followed the trail of a drunken Forty-niner trying to catch a runaway pig.

Into the bedlam of the frisky, flourishing, up-country diggings rode, late that summer, twenty-nine-year-old Hiram Gano Ferris from Hancock County, Illinois, and David D. Colton, some ten years younger than Ferris and a native of the state of Maine (and, much later, a San Francisco financier noted as an associate of Central Pacific's Big Four). Both had quit Knox College in Galesburg to ride west from Council Bluffs in the summer of '50. Ferris arrived at the diggings with a bold and appraising look in his eye, a pistol in his belt, and a Bible and a copy of Shakespeare in his pack.

Two days after Christmas he wrote to *My dear friends at home* back in Hancock County's Fountain Green.

*I might as well in the first place tell you where I am,* his letter said. *This place is above the headwaters of the Sacraminto river near the northern line of Cal. . . . There is no mail carried nearer to this place than Shasta City a place midway between this and Sac City* [Sacramento]. *Hence we have to get our letters by private conveyance from below. The mines here were not discovered until last spring and since May last this town has been built containing 30 stores or more of different kinds. It is built in a beautiful valley among the mountains and nothing can be brought here from any other place but Oragon except on* pack mules. *Still our principal supplies are brot from Sac City. It is about 400 miles from Oragon City. They do come here with wagons from Oragon but is very difficult to do so on ac-*

*count of the mountains. I suppose we are not over 150 miles from the Coast but awful mountains are in between.*

Ferris went on to say that he didn't know how much longer he'd stay there in Shasta Butte City; it all depended on how his diggings went. But two weeks later, at the beginning of '52, he wrote to the folks at Fountain Green that he was interested in a quartz claim and it looked as though he'd have to stay through the next summer to get it operating.

So he was there the year that the Legislature cut Shasta County in half, and created a new county in the northern half and named it Siskiyou after the mountain range that separated it from Oregon. And when the first county elections were over, Shasta Butte City was the county seat, Ferris was the county clerk, and Colton was the sheriff.

The first white child was born in Shasta Butte City that year and was christened William Shasta Hill; and another thing that happened in '52 was that they changed the name of the town itself.

Shasta, the county seat of Shasta County some one hundred and twenty miles to the south, was often called Shasta City. The similarity between this and Shasta Butte City, and the resultant confusion, disturbed Ferris and the other county officials. One day, sitting under a tree far enough from town to have an unobstructed view of Mount Shasta, they talked it over. The town should have a different name, they all agreed, but what could they call it? (Ferris's son Joel, a Spokane, Washington, banker, told me this as the story he often heard at the dinner table later, when his father had returned to Carthage, Illinois, and had married and settled down.)

While they pondered the problem, a happy thought struck Ferris. Rising and walking over to a group of Indians nearby, he pointed to the snow-covered peak in the south and asked, "What do you call the mountain?"

"*I-e-ka*—'the white,' " replied the braves.

Then and there Ferris and the rest accepted Ieka as the town's new name. One of them volunteered to ride the 250 miles to Vallejo, then the State capital, to enter it officially in the records. By the time he reached Vallejo, however, the spelling and the sound of it had somehow evolved in his mind to "Wyreka" or "Yreka," pronounced alike. Of the two, he decided that it must have been the latter that he was supposed to register. That is what he did, and Yreka the town became.

(The frivolous-minded insist even today that the name "Yreka" was derived from "bakery" spelled backwards, with the "b" omitted. There is
now in the town a "Yreka Bakery" whose boast is that its name is spelled
the same "both going and coming." A more serious difference is involved
in the explanation of the county name. The one enjoying the heavier support of the authorities is that *siskiyou* was the Cree Indian word for "bob-
tailed horse." While scaling a mountain pass between Oregon and California in 1828, Alex McLeod, the Hudson's Bay Company fur trader, lost
many animals in a snowstorm, among them a highly prized bob-tailed race
horse. His men called the pass the "Pass of the Siskiyou," and usage soon
after applied it to the mountain range itself. The contending explanation
is that Big Mike LaFramboise forded a north-country river—perhaps the
Rogue—at a place marked by six stones. The French-Canadian trappers
came to know this as the ford of *Six Cailloux*. American mountainmen
shortened the vowel sounds, altered the spelling to an English approxima-
tion of the phonetic values, and so arrived at the name given to the mountain range and later to the county.)

As the months rolled on and the yield of the diggings rose into the millions, Yreka developed into as rough-and-ready and roistering a Gold Rush
community as any the Forty-niners ever found along the foothill creeks
of the Mother Lode. If there were fifty stores along Miner and Oregon and
Main Streets in the summer of '52, there were as many and more saloons:
and Jacob Wagner, who had been with Thompson the day his pack mules
plucked the gold-flecked grass roots from the valley floor, said in a letter
to his family back in Iowa, *There are more drunkards here than any place
I ever was before.*

There was also the confusion of the mule trains arriving from Shasta and
the Scott River Valley, and the dust swirling in clouds across the sagebrush
of the long flat, and the tramp of miners' boots along the plank sidewalks,
and the bursts of laughter and Gold Rush ballads from the open doors of
the saloons. Joaquin Miller, remembering later the stir of Yreka's Main
Street in '53 and '54, wrote: *A tide of people up and down, and across
from other streets, as strong as if in New York. The white people on the
sidewalks, the Chinese and mules in the street. . . . Brick houses on either
hand, two and three stories high. . . . I was utterly overcome by the magni-
tude of the place and the multitude of the people.* Amid all this character-

istic boom-town uproar, one sound was not yet heard: the tolling of a church bell. It was in '54 that the ladies of the town decided to act, and Mrs. Jerome Churchill found the story memorable enough to record it in her scrapbook of the annals of pioneer Yreka.

*There were few women in Yreka then,* she wrote, *but those few were women of nerve, mettle and conscience. Feeling an imperative need of some influence other than the saloon and gaming table, they resolved to secure funds to erect a place of worship. Regardless of sectarian dogma or prejudice, they united their forces and started out, armed with the courage of honest conviction and a subscription list. . . .*

From the initial success of the campaign, it seemed as though a wave of piety were sweeping the town and the days of hell-raising were over. All the workers—the Catholic Mrs. Callaghan, the Methodist Mrs. Lowery, the Presbyterian Mrs. Arnold, and the rest—glowingly announced the fulfillment of their subscription quotas. John S. Cleland, the butcher, had contributed $500; Charlie Herzog had given a fifty-dollar gold slug; miners had donated more than $1,000 in gold dust; Burns and Mayhew, the lumber dealers, had promised timber for the church, and the labor to build it.

But even as the church walls were going up on Courthouse Plaza, pros-

pectors of the Yreka flat and miners of the Greenhorn Ridge became involved in a bitter feud over water rights, and tolerance and brotherly love
were forgotten in the rush for sidearms and bowie knives. The situation
was just short of shooting when a Greenhorn miner cut the ditch that supplied water to the diggings on the flat. The court at Yreka ruled against
the Greenhorn men, and issued an injunction against further tapping of
the ditch. In defiance of the order, a Greenhorn prospector broke the ditch
once more. He was promptly arrested and clapped into jail, and the Greenhorn War was on.

The night that the Greenhorn miners picked to break open the jail and
liberate their friend and martyr was also the night that the ladies' committee sponsored a dedication supper in the new Union Church, now complete but for the installation of the pews. As smiling Sheriff Colton stood
at the head of the table, knife poised and ready to cut the festive ham, the
crack of pistol shots came from the direction of the courthouse. A man burst
through the church door. "Sheriff, come quick!" he cried. "The Greenhorns
are storming the jail!"

In a twinkling every able-bodied man in the room vanished out the
door and swarmed pell-mell after Colton, who sprinted hatless, six-gun in
hand, toward the Courthouse Plaza and a milling mob of 500 irate miners.

*Many ladies,* reported Mrs. Churchill, *ran out in excitement and curiosity,
but hearing a fusillade of shooting, mingled with the uproar of angry voices,
speedily retreated.*

In the pitched battle that followed, one man was killed; several, including Sheriff Colton, were wounded; and the Greenhorns succeeded in free-
ing their man from his jail cell.

When the shooting was over, the dead prospector buried, and the wounds
bandaged, the men returned to the church supper, apologized for the un-
pleasantness and resumed their places. After the meal there was an auction
of pies and cakes, and the ladies had no trouble at all in raising another
$1,800, which was quite enough for the pews, and for a bell that would ring
out over the flat on Sunday mornings.

This bell, perhaps, was just what Yreka had needed, for it wasn't long
before most of the frontier roughness dropped from its life and disappeared.

It was true that 3,000 Yrekans trooped out to Butcher Hill a mile or so
from town and there witnessed the stringing-up of Sampson Crowder, who

*Sailor Jim hung lifeless against the blue July sky*

had killed a man named Lewis over at Scott Bar, across the Humbugs. That was in '56, and the next year they all trooped back again for the hanging of Sailor Jim, John Burke's murderer. This one they remembered for a long time, because the noose failed to tighten on the first drop. "For God's sake, men, don't do that again," said Sailor Jim to his executioners. They said they were sorry; they would do better the next time—and, as a matter of fact, they did. The readjusted noose functioned perfectly, cracking the vertebrae of the neck, as it should, and Sailor Jim hung lifeless against the blue July sky.

But as they all said, and correctly, there had been nothing wild or lawless about it, no capering drunks and festive bonfires as, for example, there had been at Columbia when John Barclay swung from the Gold Spring flume. The condemned had received a fair trial in open court, and death was their sentence, and the two affairs at Butcher Hill represented the final fulfillment of the process of justice.

A summer evening would come when it would not be quite like this, but now such an evening was forty years away. . . .

What happened to all the Gold Rush diggings, all the happy camps, happened to Yreka. The bonanza that Abe Thompson had struck that March day yielded what it had to yield—$60,000,000, or maybe $70,000,000 —and then as time passed, summer sun succeeding summer sun shone down on ditches drier this year than they were the last, diggings more desolate this August than the August the year before, shanties whose roofs, damaged by the winter storms, no one bothered to repair now that summer had come again, because no one had lived in them since last year when the dust was finally all gone, and no one would ever live in them again. No smell of burning juniper boughs and manzanita drifted down the banks of Humbug Creek or along Greenhorn Ridge on the summer evenings. The gold was taken out, the outlying camps deserted and as silent as the long pine shadows that fell across the empty clearings.

But the town itself survived. It had for many years what Shasta had: the mule pack trains that came up from the Sacramento Valley, and later, when they built the wagon road through the Sacramento Canyon and over the Devil's Backbone, the freight wagons and the California-Oregon stages that made the long wilderness run from Sacramento to Portland.

They lasted for a long time, but not forever, though in those years of the '60s and '70s many a true Yrekan died believing they would. The railroad finally reached north from Redding, and in 1887 was advancing up the Shasta Valley, passing Yreka 8 miles east on the valley floor. There, as a terminal, the railroad surveyors laid out a town they called Montague, in honor of C. W. Montague, a civil engineer of the road.

This staggered Yreka, as the same fate had staggered Shasta, but by then Yrekans had another kind of stake in the country. All around them, in Shasta Valley to the south and east, and in Scott Valley to the west, the land that had given up its gold was rippling fields of oats, barley, wheat, and alfalfa; and to the north, in the Klamath and Siskiyou forests, the axes were bringing to earth the tall, thick stands of fir and pine.

The stores and mills of Yrekans formed the busy trading center for these valley farms and forest lumber camps, and there had been time to watch Shasta die, after the building of Redding 6 miles east. Yrekans decided that the C. & O. couldn't by-pass them, they wouldn't stand for anything like that, and twelve months after the driving of the Gold Spike at Ashland, they finished laying the tracks of their own 8-mile line from the flat, around the base of Butcher Hill and across the Shasta River and valley to Montague. Bell clanging, whistle tooting, the first puffing wood-burner of the Yreka Western Railroad made the line's maiden trip January 9, 1889, in the sprightly running time of a few seconds less than twenty minutes. (Six months later, when Montague's Fiock Hotel caught fire, Yreka firemen received a call for help. They hauled their hose trucks and pumpers to Yreka Western flatcars, and Wood-burner No. 1, running wide open all the way, got them to Montague that day in thirteen minutes. They were too late to save the hotel, but the road had hung up a record that no wood-burner of the line ever bettered.)

With the completion of its short line, Yreka itself was, in a manner of speaking, a railroad terminal, and nothing has ever again threatened its existence. The stages kept the wagon road open—it veered northwest from the C. & O. right-of-way at Grenada, 9 miles below, and passed into the flat between Greenhorn Ridge and the hog-backed rise, known now as Flagtree Hill, and went thence to Yreka Creek and into town—and when the State built Highway 99 up the California Valley to the Oregon line and Pilot Rock, it, too, veered northwest at Grenada, skirted the base of

Flagtree Hill, and passed along Yreka's Main Street, and continued north to Hornbrook, Hilt, and the Siskiyou Summit.

So, the way things developed, Yreka had a railroad, and a place on the trunk-line highway as well. It couldn't ask for anything more, and it didn't, and it was lost forever to the Gold Rush ghosts that had been waiting for its ruins.

The year was 1948, and although the one hundredth anniversary of Abe Thompson's strike wouldn't arrive for another three years, Yrekans were having a Gold Rush celebration anyway.

It was the typical, lively folk festival that Californians in the foothill and mountain towns always produce when the theme is the "Days of '49" and the spirit of the pioneers. For four days Main Street was a bright arcade of bunting. American flags, vivid in the blazing June sun, stood out from half a hundred flagstaffs before the invigorating breeze that blew down from the snow-covered slopes of Mount Shasta. Visitors by the thousands, many of them from the mountains, gulches, and bars of the Klamath and Salmon River country, thronged down the narrow, irregular streets.

Itinerant fiddlers played old-time tunes beneath the sidewalk awnings of Miner Street and in the shade of the locust trees bordering Courthouse Plaza. Peddlers, their display boards hung with miniature gold pans that flashed in the sun, hawked their souvenirs up and down Broadway. Snatches of song and juke-box music drifted from the saloons to mingle with the blare of an Army Air Force Recruiting Service sound truck and the whistle of a merry-go-round calliope from the carnival grounds down by Yreka Creek. Swarthy Indians of the Klamath and Shasta tribes, oddly conventional in their store-bought clothes, roamed the streets and stared bemused at the antics of their white brothers when the latter, moved either by the festival spirit or long shots of forty-rod, were inspired to kick up their heels in a sidewalk jig or sing a ballad that their grandfathers had learned along the Overland Trail.

In the shop windows you saw the community memory externalized—the preserved form and substance, at least, of fragments from the stream of community consciousness: faded photographs, showing scenes of the Big Snow of 1890, when Yrekans tunneled through drifts to cross Main Street; showing the six-horse stages that crossed the westward ridge to Fort Jones

on their way to Shasta, and the canvas-topped freight wagons that used
to come up through the Sacramento Canyon; showing Captain Jack, Shack-
nasty Jim, Bogus Charlie, Steamboat Frank, the massacred Rev. Eleazer
Thomas and General Edward Canby and other leading figures in The
Tragedy of the Lava Beds, which was what they had all called the Modoc
Indian War when, in '73, it was taking place 80 miles to the east; showing
Klamath Peggy, the Indian woman heroine whose timely warning to
Yrekans had enabled them to frustrate an attack on the town by slaughter-
bent braves of her tribe. There, too, were to be seen the snowshoes that the
pack-train mules wore crossing the Salmon Mountains in wintertime, hand-
hewn washboards, ruffle-fluters, muzzle-loading rifles and powder horns,
silver trumpets of the old volunteer fire department, the caps of the men
of Klamath Engine Company No. 2 and Siskiyou No. 1, the brass-bound
broom awarded to the pumper crew that threw the highest and strongest
stream on the Fourth of July, 1888, and the department's motto-lettered
banner, saying, *Prompt is the response of all to any point that duty calls.*

As I looked at the relics and the photographs, I saw three pictures whose
stories I knew. One was the photograph of a stuffed bear; the second was
a crude sketch of a night lynching, with four men hanging from an improvised gibbet, and the third was a picture of the Indian Rain Rock of
Fort Jones. . . .

The bear was Clubfoot, the most famous grizzly in California history.
For nearly fifty years this gigantic beast roved the north country preying
on the sheep and cattle of the ranchers and resisting until his death man's
advance into the domain that had once been ruled by him and his kind.

When he was finally tracked down and killed in 1890, some fifteen miles
north of Yreka, his slayers took from his scarred and massive carcass a
quart measure of lead bullets, and considered it small wonder that many
hunters had believed Clubfoot a forest phantom, and indestructible.

Clubfoot is still one of the living legends of Yreka and all the north country. The pioneers called him the Scourge of the Siskiyous, and they say
there that it was this bear that stampeded the horses of Frémont's expedition when it passed through southern Oregon in the 1840s.

Ten years later, the great grizzly was trapped. Not far from their Klamath River cabin his captors, two brothers named Greive, heard his roars

of pain and rage. As they approached with their dogs for the kill, the bear tore his right forepaw free, leaving in the trap three claws and a part of the foot. Before they could take aim and fire, he disappeared into the woods and, in spite of his wounded paw, outdistanced the following hounds. But the mutilation, and the distinctive trail he left because of it, earned him the name by which he was known for the rest of his life.

As time went on his tracks were found around slaughtered cattle from the Mad River redwood country along the coast to the extreme eastern slopes of the Siskiyous 150 miles and three watersheds east. With great craft and cunning he avoided the traps set for him, and when hunters succeeded in wounding him, he vanished into the forest so swiftly that he baffled pursuit.

In the spring of 1882 a sheepherder watched with awe and fascination as Clubfoot descended like a fury upon a band of grazing cattle and attacked a calf. When the calf's mother tried to protect it, Clubfoot felled her with a savage swipe of his paw. A bull charged at Clubfoot and tossed him into a manzanita thicket. Clubfoot arose with incredible swiftness and closed on the bull with a ferocious rush. He seized the bull by the muzzle and with one wrench of his mighty jaws broke its neck.

Eight years after that, a young hunter named Pearl Bean and his companion, William A. Wright, came upon Clubfoot's trail in the snow near Camp Creek, a few miles from Hornbrook. They set out after him and at length caught sight of him several hundred yards ahead. Upwind and unaware of their presence, he lumbered along the trail toward a distant ridge, pausing every now and then to raise his majestic head and search the breeze that blew lightly down the slope and across the snow.

Bean and Wright aimed their 50-70 Sharps rifles and fired. The old bear wheeled. For a split second he hesitated, as if, against the snow, his age-dimmed eyes were trying to find their silhouettes. Then he saw them, and hurtled toward them down the slope. Bean and Wright kept firing. Twenty yards away, the monarch's stride faltered. The bullets plowed into his throat and massive skull. Clubfoot stumbled forward, and toppled dead at their feet.

Not long ago, George R. Schrader, acting supervisor of Shasta National Forest and one of the founders of the six-year-old Siskiyou County Historical Society, became interested in the story of Clubfoot. He talked with descendants of the Greive brothers, who still have one of the three claws Clubfoot left in the trap on the Klamath River in 1856. He held the claw in his hand, and set and sprang the immense 40-pound trap. He talked to Pearl Bean's widow, who has the quart measure of bullets her husband took from Clubfoot when he and Wright skinned their kill, and handled one of the guns that the hunters used the day they shot the bear.

His efforts to discover what became of Clubfoot revealed that the pelt, 8 feet from nose to tail, was taken to Ashland, Oregon, where it was stuffed by amateur taxidermists. From the size of the skin, woodsmen estimated the bear's weight to have been anywhere from 1,850 to well over 2,000 pounds.

For more than a year Bean and Wright exhibited the crudely mounted bear up and down the coast. In 1892 they sold him for $500 to a Doctor Jordan, who took him to the Chicago Exposition, set him up in a side-show tent and, for an admission charge of ten cents, displayed him to tourists as a superior specimen of "a man-eating grizzly from the mountains of the Wild West."

There, the trail of Clubfoot grew dim. Schrader's search ended with two scraps of information: one, divulged by an old newspaper clipping, was that Doctor Jordan had taken Clubfoot to Europe for an exhibition tour of the continental capitals; the other was the unconfirmed, and unconfirmable, report that Clubfoot was in San Francisco at the time of the 1906 earthquake and fire, and was destroyed.

As for the sketch of the lynching, it stated simply that, like San Francisco and many other California towns, Yreka had a grim and violent side to its past. Like most San Franciscans, Yrekans are not ashamed of it, but neither are they proud of it. They place it where it belongs, both in time and circumstance, and there, for better or worse, it remains.

One must admit, however, that they have clung to the frontier spirit quite a bit longer than San Franciscans, who began to discard it in the middle 1850s, for only about fifteen years have passed since a killer named Johnson was lynched from a pine tree a mile out of town on the road to Fort Jones. Eugene S. Dowling, a past president of the Siskiyou County Historical Society, still has a section of the rope—stout, half-inch hemp. The tree has been cut down because it interfered with the erection of power lines, and when, driving to Fort Jones, I saw the stump, it stood by the side of the road amid a patch of yellow poppies, helping to hold up a barbed wire fence.

The mass hanging took place in Courthouse Plaza in August, 1895, and it was Dowling who told me the story as we sat, on a hot afternoon of one of the celebration days, on the low retaining wall that surrounds the square.

The plaza today, as it did then, encompasses the Siskiyou County Hall of Records and the courthouse, an expanse of smooth green lawn and walks bordered with roses, petunias and marigolds. It is a pleasant, peaceful place, not much different now from what it was in 1895, except that then the walks were lined with locust trees that rose to a height of thirty or forty feet. Across Fourth Street from the square and on a corner, is a small brick building that houses the Siskiyou County Free Library; in 1895, this was the county jail.

The principal characters in the north-country drama were William Null, forty-five, a miner from Ohio; Lawrence H. Johnston, fifty-nine, a Scotsman; Louis Moreno, forty, a Mexican; and Garland Stemler, a nineteen-year-old Arkansan.

Over a period of four months preceding that August, each of these men had committed a murder: Null had shot his partner in the back at their cabin at Callaghan's; Johnston, a blacksmith, had stabbed his wife at their home in the Scott Valley; Moreno and Stemler, two itinerants, had shot a Hungry Creek miner in an attempted holdup at Bailey Hill, 20 miles north of Yreka.

As the months passed and the law did nothing about Null, who had committed his crime in April, and the murderers accumulated in the county jail, the ranchers and miners in the Scott and Shasta valleys, and those living in the Bailey Hill region at the foot of the Siskiyous grew restive. It was high time, they told each other, that justice was done. Toward the end of July, with that in mind, they organized and laid their plans.

To the four murderers lounging in their cells, that day in August was just another quiet Sunday. Through their barred windows came the measured footsteps of churchgoers, and the tolling of the bells of St. Mark's Church, St. Joseph's, and the Methodist Church (built on the site of the Union Church of the Gold Rush), all of which, like the jail, faced Courthouse Plaza.

But in the surrounding valleys and mountains, the vigilantes were gathering for the task ahead of them. There were about two hundred of them, all mounted, all masked. Their identifying password was "Mud." The sun was setting as they started for the Yreka flat.

At nine o'clock sharp, they threw blockades across all roads leading into Yreka and stopped and held all travelers approaching or leaving town.

At ten, picked squads entered the stations of the town's volunteer fire department and tied the bell ropes high out of reach so that no emergency alarm could be sounded.

Shortly after midnight another group rode to a blacksmith's shop on the Oregon Road and commandeered some iron bars, several sledgehammers, and a length of rope; others rode to the Yreka depot and there obtained a railroad rail. Simultaneously, two of the vigilantes, unmasked, knocked on the door of Town Marshal Erskine Parks, babbled an excited story of a fight at Yreka Creek and enticed him out of town, far from Courthouse Plaza and what was about to take place there.

It was about one o'clock in the morning when Deputy Jailer Harry Brautlacht heard the murmur of voices outside the jail door. As he opened it to investigate, a masked man covered him with a Winchester and said, "Give us the keys to the cells of those murderers."

"I haven't got them," replied Brautlacht. "You'll have to get them from Deputy Sheriff Radford over in the courthouse."

A dozen vigilantes left the group outside the jail, crossed the street, and banged on the door of the sheriff's office. "Radford, we want the keys to the county jail cells. Hand them over."

There was a moment's silence. Then Radford's voice came cool and even from behind the closed door. "I've got two guns. You're not going to get the keys until those guns are empty. If you want them that bad, come and get them."

Five minutes later, while several stood guard over Brautlacht, the vigilantes smashed the cell-door locks with sledgehammers.

Meanwhile, having discovered the ruse which had taken him to the creek, Marshal Parks hastened back to town to sound an alarm. When he found that he could not ring the firehouse bells, he ran to the plaza. He was promptly surrounded and held helpless at rifle point. Sheriff Hobbs, whom someone had roused from bed, rounded a courthouse corridor, and stared down the barrels of half a dozen waiting Winchesters.

From the iron rail, the ends of which were supported 10 feet from the ground by forks of adjacent locust trees on the courthouse lawn, Johnston was the first to hang. He died pleading for a fair trial. Next was Null, and third was Moreno, who was stoical to the end. The youth Stemler was last. He asked the vigilantes to remove his shoes; he had promised his mother when he went West that he wouldn't die with his boots on. They complied with his request, and he swung shouting, "Tell my mother I am innocent!"

Not more than twenty minutes elapsed between the time that Brautlacht first opened the jail door and the moment when, their work done, the vigilantes rode swiftly out of town.

At two o'clock, Coroner Schofield cut the bodies down and took them to the fire station of Engine House No. 1. He unpinned this note from Johnston's shirt: CAUTION. *Let this be a warning, and it is hoped that all cold-blooded murderers in this county suffer likewise. (signed) Tax-Paying Citizens. P.S.—Officers: Ask no questions. Be wise and keep mum.*

A few days later, a coroner's jury found that the four victims *came to their deaths on the 26th day of August, 1895, in this county by strangulation. They were hanged by the neck by parties unknown to this jury.* The case of the State of California *vs.* Null, Johnston, Moreno, and Stemler was closed.

It is curious, when you remember the lightning bolt at Redding, that not much longer than a year after the lynching, something happened which mystified and troubled the citizens of Yreka: while all around them trees and flowers grew healthy and strong, the two locusts which had supported the lynching rail began to wither. Expert tree surgeons were called upon to save them, and they did everything that they could, but in a little while, the trees were dead.

There was justification for the picture of the Rain Rock in the shop window on Miner Street, for the rock that year was a wonder and a riddle to the people of Yreka and the Scott River country. Some believed in it; some proclaimed it a well-organized hoax. Others wrote off its seeming magic as a coincidence in which the sponsors of the rock received whimsical and timely cooperation from the elements. It was, in any case, a lively topic of conversation, and before the Gold Rush celebration was over more than one partisan measured his length in the sawdust of the Yreka saloons as disputes reached the point where a small, localized riot seemed to be the only way to settle the matter once and for all—or, at any rate, for the next fifteen minutes.

Hoax or not, there the Rain Rock stood, as the picture showed, at one corner of the little museum at Fort Jones, tarpaulin-covered, lest it should work its medicine and cause the clouds to gather and the rain to fall from the sunny June sky.

The rock was a two- or three-ton piece of soapstone uncovered by a road-scraper in 1947 at Gotville, on the Klamath River. Indians of the region said that they had known of the rock, and that it had been of cere-monial import for many centuries. The rock was dug up and trucked to Fort Jones, which lies 18 miles southwest of Yreka between the Humbugs and the Salmons, and on the old pack trail and stage road from Yreka to the Trinity Mountains and Shasta. There it was placed on a stone base near the museum.

Those responsible for the removal of the Rain Rock to the museum were members of a group of historically minded Fort Jones citizens who called themselves Squaws, Inc. Its members included W. T. Davidson, chairman of the Siskiyou County Board of Supervisors (an elective body which ad-ministrates the county government); Harry Bryan, George Milne, Arland Walker, and Eddie Edgecomb.

Soon after the arrival of the Rain Rock at Fort Jones, Scott Valley ranch-ers noticed peculiarities in the weather. Some of them blamed the Rain Rock. Davidson took a Quartz Valley brave aside and asked his opinion.

"Keep the rock covered," warned the Indian, "or it will rain and snow all summer."

For a while, Davidson regarded this as sheer superstition. But unprece-dented behavior on the part of the weather during the winter of 1947–1948 —rain when there should have been snow, snow when there should have been rain, sleet when there should have been clear weather, and clear weather when it should have stormed—gave him cause to ponder the In-dian's remark more seriously.

In the middle of May, 1948, a howling snowstorm struck the Scott Valley. A few weeks later, an unseasonal downpour rained out one night of the Siskiyou County Sheriff's Posse Rodeo. Davidson and Squaws, Inc., de-cided that the Rain Rock had plenty of medicine. The next day they cov-ered it with canvas.

From then on, Scott Valley and the weather got along together pretty well. But as time passed, Davidson became more than ever convinced that the Rain Rock worked. Once he uncovered it to oblige a friend whose irrigation ditches were running dry.

"I took the cover off at 6 P.M.," he said. "By 8 P.M., it was raining bucketfuls. I put the cover back on right away, but it took three days for the sky to clear."

The Rain Rock's fame spread across the county line. Desperately hoping for fair skies over the Fourth of July week end for its Gold Rush celebration, the Chamber of Commerce of Oroville in Butte County, 200 miles to the southeast, wrote the Siskiyou Board of Supervisors and asked for a guarantee that they would keep the rock under cover during the week of the holiday. Officials of the State Fair in Sacramento filed a similar request. Both petitions were received that June, and Davidson said the board had voted to grant them.

It was one of the first Sundays of summer that Joel Ferris and I talked to Davidson, and the main street of the little valley hamlet was quite deserted. Lush green meadows, the white bloom of elderberry and long lavender banks of wild lilacs reached across the valley floor to the foot of the Salmons, that lifted their rugged, snow-capped summits 8,000 feet against the sky. The smell of new-mown alfalfa lingered in the quiet air. To Davidson, all this was commonplace. His concern was with the rock.

"Hope this doesn't cause a cloudburst," he said, with a worried glance at the flawless sky, and pulled away the protective tarpaulin.

There stood revealed an irregularly shaped stone whose greatest over-all dimension was perhaps 5 feet. Its surface was pitted with holes, seventy-eight of them, Davidson said. Here and there were scratched Indian "bear signs," or six-toes bear tracks.

It was, undoubtedly, an authentic survival of an age-old supplicatory rite. For centuries, Klamath River Indians had resorted to this stone when they were in need of rain.

A few weeks before, Davidson said, Harry Bryan of Squaws, Inc., had interviewed Dick Pepper of Happy Camp, northwest of Fort Jones on the Klamath River. Pepper, a high official of the Karok tribe, was said to know as much about the Rain Rock as any Indian in the county. Bryan asked him how his ancestors used the rock. His reply, as taken down verbatim by Mrs. Jewel Smith of Fort Jones, secretary of Squaws, Inc., was as follows:

*Winds come up after pounding on rock, just keep pounding, sometimes big hole, keep on pounding, wind brought, keep pounding, after while rain come. If don't stop raining, put dirt in holes to stop rain.*

With regard to the bear tracks, Pepper explained: *Them days, sometimes maybe not have anything to eat, can't get nothing to eat, make a track so can get luck, so can get bear or anything. Make mystery on rock, maybe he can get acorns. Bear track pound out, have good luck.*

Pepper and other Indians said that one year their forefathers pounded a hole in the rock for rain, and their plea was answered with such thoroughness that the resultant torrential downpour caused a disastrous flood along the Klamath River channel. Rather than run the risk of a similar disaster, they buried the rock at Gotville.

There were Indians of the region, Davidson said, who went to Fort Jones and stood all day looking at the rock with stolid and impassive faces. Additionally, its disinterment had caused mutterings of discontent among the older members of the Klamath tribes: they believed that it should have been left where their ancestors buried it.

As we were preparing to leave for the drive back to Yreka, Ferris and I watched Davidson draw the tarpaulin across the rock and lash it tight.

"Before we go, Mr. Davidson," said Ferris, "I want to ask you one thing, point-blank: Does the Rain Rock really work? When you need rain, and uncover it, does it rain?"

Davidson was unruffled. "It worked all spring," he replied, shaking his head, as if to say that it was beyond him, but it was the truth. "To me it was a freak of luck that it didn't work today. Just last week, a pilot from Sacramento landed his plane near here and came into town to see the Rain Rock. I uncovered it, and while we were standing looking at it, it commenced to rain, and rained for about a minute. Damnedest thing I ever saw."

He bent over, reached down, and carefully tucked in a corner of canvas, and concealed from sight and the Sunday sky the last visible portion of the Rain Rock, a small expanse no bigger than his hand.

On the last day of the four-day celebration there was a parade, and after the parade was over Yrekans and visitors to the town streamed out Yama Road by the hundreds to a 15-ton granite boulder half a mile or so northwest of the center of town. On the boulder was a new bronze plaque which shone in the bright afternoon sunlight. It had been determined that the place where Abraham Thompson had made his strike ninety-seven years before was on the shelf of a small ravine, about sixty feet from the monument. The ceremonies and the dedication of the plaque, which were about to take place, would commemorate that historic event.

In relief, at the top of the plaque, was a stylized representation of a miner panning gold. His pack mule grazed nearby. The lettering read:

*Gold was discovered here in March, 1851, by Abraham Thompson, member of a party which was enroute from Oregon to Scott Bar. Following a heavy rain storm, particles of gold in the roots of grass pulled up by pack animals caused Thompson to wash three pans of gravel. The results convinced the party that the area was rich enough to work. In the party were Dr. F. G. Hearn, Judge Silas J. O'Day and a Mr. Bell, Thompson's partner. All staked claims on these flats, thirty feet square, and it was named "Thompson's Dry Diggings." Within six weeks 2,000 prospectors rushed here to mine, but need of water caused the settlement to move to the creek, and it became known as Shasta Butte City. The name, being confused with Shasta, in Shasta County, was changed to "I-e-ka," the Indian word for Mt. Shasta, now "Yreka," in 1852. Erected by Siskiyou County Historical Society—1948.*

Behind the gathered people, some of whom wore buckskins and dresses of calico, lay the town which was that day asserting its claim to a Gold Rush heritage as authentic as that of any California town of the Mother Lode.

Where Lockhart's shake-and-canvas saloon and Turner's cottonwood-log cabin used to stand were up-to-date sandwich shops and soda fountains. Smoke poured from the tall stacks of the lumber mills south of town. Ranchers from the rich valley farms, not prospectors down from Humbug or the Greenhorn Ridge, walked its streets and patronized its stores, and only as the climax of a rare holiday (such as this one had been) could an old-timer in from the hills ride his pony up the stone steps of the Yreka Inn into the lobby and with a Pit River war whoop empty his six-gun at the ceiling. The little Siskiyou short line—now using locomotives that once hauled freight cars along the State Belt tracks of San Francisco's water front—still chuffed 8 miles across the floor of Shasta Valley, and linked the town with the main-line freights and streamliners of the Southern Pacific.

Diesel trucks, bound north on Highway 99 for Portland, or south for San
Francisco, rumbled along Main Street, which had known the long mule
trains and Concords of the California-Oregon Trail.

Beyond the crowd lay this town and the long flat, Greenhorn Ridge and
Flagtree Hill; to the west rose the Humbugs, and far to the east across
Shasta Valley the smoke-blue, 8,000-foot summit of Goosenest, and to the
north the Siskiyous.

Grouped there on the flat, they listened with reverence to the measured
invocation, the reading of commemorative poems, and the ringing speeches
of sons of the pioneers (most of them had known the orators all their lives);
and watched with pride on their faces the raising of the American flag on
the new, freshly peeled staff of the plaque site, and the ceremonial unveiling
of the plaque itself.

When it was over, they smiled and applauded, and stood around chatting
with friends and the participants in the ceremony and members of the
Historical Society and officials of the town and county.

In a little while, they wandered away, back down Yama Road toward
the town.

The stately incense cedars and the ponderosa pines along the bank of the
ravine were motionless against the mid-afternoon sky. No breeze stirred
the flat's gray sage and yellow poppies. And the deep, lonely, north country
quiet settled over the trees, the sage, these wildflowers and the level clearing, where stood the granite boulder and the gleaming bronze tablet.

CHAPTER TEN

# The Mountain

No MATTER HOW they approached the California North, there came a day, a certain moment on the trail, when they saw it, a white, far-off enchantment against the distant blue sky. What it represented, when at last it loomed low on their horizon, was determined by who they were, and where they came from, and where they were going, and why they were going there.

Hunting beaver skins in a wild unknown land and praying for his own and his brigade's safe return to the Columbia, the trapper Ogden thought of what he knew, of friendly landmarks seen from familiar trails: *There is a mountain equal in height to Mount Hood or Vancouver, I have named Sastice.*

Lieutenant Emmons, leading the government exploring expedition, hastened past it southward, for he knew that it marked the end of the country of hostile Indians. Nevertheless, as he skirted its base, he conscientiously jotted in his journal notes on its general physical characteristics for his superior officer, Lieutenant Wilkes, and, later, Lieutenant Wilkes included them in his report of the expedition:

*The Shaste peak is a magnificent sight, rising as it does to a lofty height, its steep sides emerging from the mists which envelop its base, and seem to throw it off to an immense distance; its cleft summit gave proof of its former active state as a volcano. The snow lies in patches on the sides and part of the peak of this mountain; but there is a great difference in the position of its snow-line from that of Mt. Hood or St. Helen's. Its height is said to be fourteen thousand three hundred and ninety feet, but Lieutenant Emmons thinks it is not so high.*

That was in 1841, and in another four years the country was better known and better mapped, and travelers were coming to relate it to that country. Jim Clyman, taking Marshall and the others of his party south from Oregon in '45, knew that it would bring him to a good campground in a small valley beside a river, where the Hudson's Bay men camped every year; and so on a June day, after the Siskiyou crossing, he led them south *steering for a Tripple shaped high round peaked snowcapd Montain known by the name of Snowy Bute. . . .*

Their Sastice, their Shaste, their Snowy Butte was Shasta, which in a few years, to the emigrants who had driven their wagons west over the Lassen or Applegate Trails, would mean journey's end—an end to danger and the long ordeal—and the start of the new life for which they had traveled so far and endured so much. When their throats were desert-parched and their eyes were dry, stinging, and bloodshot from the arid desert winds, and at last they saw Shasta on their western skyline, a hundred miles beyond deserts and mountains yet to cross and with its far snows cool and dazzling white, it was a sight that melted their hearts with gratitude and thanksgiving. For there it was, the embodiment of their struggle won and of a myth that at last they knew was no myth at all.

Later, after the wagons had ceased to creak and rock along the emigrant trails, and pastures grew green and apple trees bloomed in the peaceful valleys at its northern and western base, and the small settlements were clustered far below its timberline, Joaquin Miller—a poet, who had come from nowhere and who was going nowhere—looked at it, and saw a loneliness that reminded him of the loneliness of God.

On the map you can see how it stands 60 miles across the Devil's Back-bone from the head of the Sacramento Valley, at the latitude where, in the west, the Coast Range is breaking up into the Klamaths and the Trinities. The Sierra have ended, the Cascades have not yet begun, and geologists do not seem to agree as to whether Shasta is a Cascade mountain, or the last northward peak of the Sierra, or a mountain that is somehow common to and a point of union of all three systems—the Coast Range bearing north-east, the Sierra bearing northwest and the Cascades reaching south—all meeting here at Shasta, at the valley's end.

Melting snows sink and fall through the mountain's porous lava mass from its five glaciers and its snowfields, and emerge in bubbling springs at its base. Two of these, that the Hudson's Bay trappers found gushing from the earth 15 and 20 miles southwest of the summit, in the Sacramento Canyon, came to be called, because of their carbonation and mineral con-tent, Upper and Lower Soda Springs. Other springs flow broad, free, and clear from great veins at the foot of the mountain and are the highest head-waters of the Shasta River, the McCloud River and the Sacramento.

The first of these rivers runs north to the Klamath, through a broad valley that the people of the north country call the Valley of a Thousand Hills, for the grass-grown lava hillocks that lie two and three hundred feet high across the valley floor. The big springs of the McCloud River are on Shasta's eastern flank, and this river once flowed into the Pit, which in turn flowed into the Sacramento. The main Sacramento rushes wild, sparkling, and ice-cold from a crevice beneath Spring Hill, 12 miles southwest of the summit. From here it winds swiftly south through a valley called Straw-berry because of the wild strawberries that used to grow there, picks up its north, middle, and south forks and tumbles singing in rapids to the long gorge of the Sacramento Canyon, which carries it across the Devil's Back-bone to the head of the long valley beyond.

Towering majestically above all these river valleys, above all the miles of forests of tall pine and fir and gray-green brushfields, the far ridges, and the hundreds of square miles of the McCloud River flats, is the solitary, brooding, beautiful, snow-crested cone of Shasta, sweeping up a sheer 11,000 feet from the valleys and the flats that are themselves 3,000 feet above the sea.

The beaver brought the white man to the forests and rivers and creeks at the foot of the mountain, but those who came looking for gold did not find it here. Abe Thompson found it 40 miles north; John Scott found it 40 miles west in Scott Valley, beyond Rainbow Ridge and the Eddy Mountains that separated that valley from Strawberry, and Reading found it 60 miles southwest, near those other springs. But lava country is not gold country. It is not a place where the earth yields bonanzas, and tent cities grow overnight. There are salmon in the swift rivers, and deer feeding along their grassy banks; lupine, the April redbud, whitethorn, and October goldenrod along the meadows, and ponderosa pines and stately Douglas firs across the forest flats; and high up the slopes you can hear the harsh cry of a Clark's crow—look for these things and you will find them living above the age-old lava fields of Shasta, but look for gold and you will look in vain.

In the first years of the excitement, therefore, the mountain was the high "Snowy Butte," the trailmark looming above the north country and the north-country trails between the Sacramento Valley and the Yreka diggings, and the territory still farther north in Oregon. The peril for the freight wagons to avoid was the rugged Sacramento Canyon passage, and drivers tried, in '54, the breaking of a wagon road athwart the eastern base of the mountain from Pit River Falls across the McCloud flats to the Sheep Rock pass, the Shasta River Valley, and Yreka. It turned out that on this road they never knew when they'd be safe, or when the war-painted Pits would slaughter them and burn their trains. They abandoned it a year or two later for the other less dangerous road that took them from the town of Shasta across the Trinities to Scott Valley, and thence to Yreka and the Oregon border.

But prospectors traveling light and traveling fast hit the trappers' trail across the Devil's Backbone and through the canyon, camping on the river flat by Lower Soda Springs beneath the lofty gray spires and pinnacles of Castle Crags, on the next flat 6 miles north at Upper Soda Springs, and, beyond the canyon's end, along the green meadows of Strawberry Valley.

As time passed settlers opened trading establishments at these points, and these settlers are the men and women the local historians call to mind when they reflect on the quiet, leisurely beginnings of the communities into which the posts and resorts developed many years later with the coming of the railroad.

Mountain Joe Doblondy, the frontiersman and Frémont guide, was one of them. In the '50s, he started a post at Lower Soda Springs, and it was he who, in '55, led the winning fight against the Indian maurauders in the Battle of Castle Crags, the encounter in which Joe's friend, young Joaquin Miller, took an arrow in the throat and was carried down off the crags in a buckskin bag on an Indian woman's back, to rest and recovery beneath the riverbank cedars. Another was Wash Bailey, who bought the Springs in '58 and ran a resort there for thirty years, until he sold it to Leland Stanford for a summer home after the railroad was built through the canyon, north to Oregon. Not far from where Mountain Joe's cabin once stood, the Pacific Improvement Company, in 1892, erected the Castle Crag Tavern that was known to travelers from all over the world for its hospitality, its curative waters, its mountain air, the swift river beside its green, sloping lawns, and the awe-inspiring minarets of granite that soared 4,000 feet above its canyon site. Eight years later fire destroyed the hotel, and because the era of elegance and opulence that it represented was dying with the death of the '90s, it was never replaced.

Two other settlers were Ross and Mary McCloud, whose name, confused with Alex McLeod's, came to be applied to the river rising east of the mountain. The McClouds (he had been elected the first county surveyor of Siskiyou County) went to the canyon in '55, bought the flat at Upper Soda Springs from squatters, and built there a two-story inn and a river toll bridge. Four years later he built a sawmill north in Strawberry Valley and was thus a pioneer in a lumbering industry that for nearly a century would thrive on the stands of pine, cedar, and fir that grew thick and tall about the mountain's base.

Another two settlers would be Isaac Fry and Richard Mannon. It was said that Fry had been a Mississippi riverboat captain, and Mannon had been a professional gambler on Fry's steamer. Nobody seemed to know why or how they formed their partnership. They came down from Oregon and built a cabin near the inn of the McClouds, and when the McClouds and their children, Ross, Jr., and Elda, went to the Shasta Valley to live, in '64 or '65, they left Fry in charge of their resort. McCloud died in the valley, and a few years later his widow and Fry were married.

Fry and Mannon (whom the canyon people now called "Uncle Dick") built a new hotel hard by the Springs, a long, impressive, two-story building that, they said, resembled a riverboat because of the verandas that ran, like decks, along the four walls of both stories.

It was in the '70s, after the stage road from Yreka had been completed through the canyon and after both Mr. and Mrs. Fry had died and Uncle Dick was managing the hotel for the children, that he had the trouble with the panther.

One day Mrs. George Campbell (her husband was Mrs. Fry's brother) was standing on the hotel porch watching her four-year-old son at play upon a low hillside above the Springs. All at once, to her horror, she saw a panther leap from an oak tree, pounce upon the child, and bear him to earth. She ran screaming to the boy's rescue. Uncle Dick followed her with his rifle, pursued the panther into the woods nearby and killed it. The animal, half grown and lean with hunger, had torn the boy's throat and cheek and clawed his back, but the wounds were not fatal.

It was the first time that a California panther had attacked a human since the 1830s, when one of them carried off and presumably killed an Indian boy playing in the backyard of Jacob Leese's house in the pueblo of Yerba Buena (later to become San Francisco); and the story brought nationwide attention to Uncle Dick and Upper Soda Springs.

Another incident of note was the naming of the big trout that angler-guests at the hotel caught on the other side of the mountain spurs, in the McCloud River. It happened that a favorite book of Uncle Dick's was Dickens's *Barnaby Rudge,* and he spent hours of delight listening to young Elda McCloud as she read it to him. (Elda's son, Charles Masson, remembers her saying that she once read it to Uncle Dick as he shingled the veranda roofs, standing below him and moving with him as he progressed along the chalk lines.) Dolly Varden, the winsome daughter of the locksmith who saved Barnaby's life, captured the hearts of Uncle Dick and Elda and during one of those summers Elda wore with great pride and pleasure a fashionable Dolly Varden dress of a light, lavender-spotted material. One day a fishing party returned to the hotel and arranged a large catch of the McCloud River trout upon the hotel lawn for the admiration of the other guests.

"Precisely what do you call these fish?" asked an inquisitive guest.

"Well," one of the anglers replied, "they're a kind of trout. We don't know what to call them. Just McCloud River trout, I guess,"

Elda was suddenly struck by the resemblance between the material of which her dress was made and the speckled marking of the fish. "I've got a name for them!" she exclaimed. "The Dolly Varden trout!"

The name, everyone agreed, was an inspiration: from then on, it would be the Dolly Varden. And thus, among fishermen, at least, was perpetuated the locksmith's pretty daughter and the popular style of the '70s that bore her name.

In 1886 Uncle Dick fell ill. One July day he called Elda to his bedside, told her his money was hidden beneath the toolbox in the woodshed, said good-by, and died, at the age of seventy-three.

Meanwhile, the California and Oregon tracks had reached north from Redding to the Sacramento Canyon, and there, just south of Upper Soda Springs, the road had put down the switching yards, the roundhouse, and shops of a division point. The year that Uncle Dick died, a post office was established by the Springs and named Mannon after the kindly innkeeper. A few months later, however, young Alex Dunsmuir, son of Robert Dunsmuir, the wealthy British Columbia coal magnate, stopped at Mannon to take the waters of Upper Soda Springs. Invigorated by their tang and effervescence and enchanted by the mountain town, he persuaded Colonel James Scobie, a railroad construction official, to give his family name to the settlement. In 1887 the railroad's influence effected the change; Mannon as a name was dropped, and the post office and the town became Dunsmuir. The year after that Alex's father gave the town a small iron fountain, to represent his appreciation. When you make the canyon passage today on Southern Pacific's streamliner *Shasta Daylight,* you can see the fountain on the small green lawn, just south of the Dunsmuir station.

The beginnings of Strawberry Valley were just as quiet, pastoral, and slow, and there the remembered names are those of the Sullaways, whose men were the early ranchers and the stage drivers of the line south from Yreka; and that of Justin Hinckley Sisson, a Connecticut-born school teacher who went West with the Gold Rush from Illinois. In the early '60s he and his bride, the former Lydia Maria Field of Vermont, settled there in the valley, in a log cabin. They hired Indians to pick strawberries and huckleberries for them, and sold the berries at Yreka and the Soda Springs, and thus for several years made their living from the meadows. In 1865 Sisson built a hotel facing east to Mount Shasta, and on its register, during the next quarter century, were inscribed the signatures of thousands of mountaineers, travelers, scientists, and vacationing city-dwellers who stopped in the valley for ascents of the mountain, hunting, fishing, and all the diversions of the old resort life. Another name still recalled is that of Sophia Jane Fellows. Widowed by the death in Ohio of her first husband, she had crossed the Isthmus with her two young daughters in 1860 and had gone to Yreka, where she married Joseph S. Fellows. A few years later, they settled by the stage road in Strawberry Valley and began one of the valley's first commercial enterprises, the J. S. Fellows Pail and Tub Factory.

When a tiny post office called Berryvale was built there beside the road and the stage station, Sisson was the first postmaster and "Aunty" Fellows, as the valley children called her, was the second. On the death of her husband in the '70s, Aunty Fellows herself opened a resort and travelers' rest, and those who stopped there took away with them enduring memories of her hospitality and her kindness to the children of the ranches, and always remembered the picture her plump figure made sitting in the little phaeton that she drove along the stage road, drawn by a frisky brown horse wearing a betassled fly net, on her trips to Soda Springs or to the homes of friends who lived north in Butteville. They remembered, too, her white donkey, Balaam, which she would ride across the fields on her way to fish for trout in the valley creeks.

But by the time Sisson died, in '93, and Aunty Fellows died, in '98, the valley was not the same as it had been in those years of the swaying Concords, when the summer guests came to picnic under the oaks, and gathered berries and wildflowers in the long afternoons of the gray-gold haze at the mountain's base.

The railroad reached here as well, in its progress north from Dunsmuir, and wanted a town a mile east of the stage road, and that was where it was built. The post office was moved from the stage road to the town and was renamed Sisson. Soon, all along the advancing rails on the mountain's western slope, timber fallers were at work bringing to earth the mountain's tall trees for the new sawmills that were supplying ties for the railroad and cordwood for the wood-burning locomotives, and the lumber for the new box factories and sash-and-door mills that, on the completed C. & O., would ship their products north to Oregon and south to the markets of San Francisco and all the West.

It was in truth a great day for the Sacramento Valley and the California north country, that day in December, 1887, when they drove the Gold Spike at Ashland, Oregon, where the rails south from Portland met the rails north from San Francisco.

To the stirring music of a brass band and the cheers of the crowds that had come to see her off, the eleven-car excursion special left Oakland at 4 P.M., December 16, and started its historic journey for the Ashland union and the city of Portland.

The consist of the train included the diamond-stacked wood-burner No. 125 with Engineer Phil Garrison at the throttle; a baggage car; a kitchen car and a flag-bedecked dining car; five Pullman Palace sleeping cars for the 150 paying passengers; the Palace car *Tahoe* carrying Governor Waterman of California and officials of California cities; the *Sacramento,* reserved for the press and J. A. Fillmore, superintendent of the road; and, finally, the luxurious private car of Charles Crocker, vice-president of the Southern Pacific, parent road of the C. & O.

Large and jubilant throngs gathered on station platforms to sing, cheer, wave flags, set off firecrackers, and toss their hats in the air as the excursion train chuffed through Sacramento, Marysville, Chico, Red Bluff, and Redding. Early on the morning of the 17th, pulled now by three engines in tandem, it headed into the canyon, its piercing whistles echoing up and down the gorge and the canyonside gulches, and its labored panting stilling the sound of the swiftly rushing river. It puffed through Dunsmuir and Sisson, passed Mount Shasta and rattled the length of the Valley of a Thousand Hills, scattering the cattle in fright across the meadows as it advanced on Montague. The sun was setting that afternoon when it left behind the tunnels and trestles and loops of the Siskiyou crossing and brought the excursionists safe to Ashland.

There they greeted a similar group of Oregon officials and citizens, and proceeded at once with the commemorative program. Orators hailed the thrilling occasion as an event equalled in importance in western history only by the northward march of Captain Gaspar de Portolá in 1769 and the discovery of gold by James Marshall in 1848.

*Today,* declaimed Joseph Steffins, president of the Sacramento Board of Trade, *Mount Shasta greets Mount Hood. The waters of the Sacramento whisper to the waters of the Columbia. The magnolia, the orange and the*

*laurel shed their reciprocity greetings of fragrance to the rose, the apple
and the pine.*

At the climax of the ceremony, Vice-president Crocker stood over the
last rail and, as the crowd applauded, swung a silver hammer three times,
and as many times struck the Gold Spike squarely on the head.

The three taps were repeated by every telegraphic instrument along the
Southern Pacific system from Portland to the Gulf of Mexico, and by the
fire bells of Sacramento, San Francisco, and New Orleans. In a dozen communities, the signals touched off wild and exuberant demonstrations.

Church bells pealed in Albany, Oregon; factory whistles blew in Marysville; flag-waving mobs milled in the Sacramento streets. In Chico, the sudden detonation of celebration bombs so frightened the horse of Supervisor
E. T. Reynolds that it ran away with its carriage, spilling Mrs. Reynolds
and her two children into a ditch. Mrs. Reynolds suffered a broken collar-
bone and multiple bruises of the head and shoulders.

Back at the scene of the *wedding of the rails,* as the papers called it,
Crocker nimbly climbed to the table that served as a speaker's platform,
and in a voice that rang with pride promised the lands of the Pacific shore
a new, undreamed-of era of development and prosperity.

South of the Siskiyous, as the purple mists of the December dusk gathered
in the valleys and deep in the river canyon, and the alpenglow softly flushed
the Shasta snows, the stage drivers of the California-Oregon road were
bringing their teams to the stations for the last time; the Concords were
rolling their last mile of the old run; the bugles were sounding soft and clear
the journey's end.

As change had come to the happy Gold Rush camps, as time had drawn
out their destinies, so change came to these settlements in Shasta's morning
shadow, these settlements in the quiet valley of the rushing river, and beside the bubbling springs.

The railroad brought a new and vital aspect to Dunsmuir and Sisson
(whose name was later changed to Mount Shasta City). Sawmills sprang
up until there were forty and more along the right of way in the 20 miles
north of Dunsmuir. But the resorts at the Springs and in Strawberry Valley
had still a few years left to them. Parents who had been coming for years
with their growing families to escape the heat of their home towns in the

big valley south still spent summer weeks at the Soda Springs Hotel and Sisson's. Even though the wood-burners filled the canyon with smoke and clatter and the shriek of their whistles, there were still vacationers through the '90s, elegantly fishing for the Dolly Varden, or gathering the mountain lilies, or picnicking by the riverbank, or singing in the moonlight to mandolins.

In *Steep Trails,* John Muir, the naturalist, tells how they came to Sisson's Hotel in Strawberry Valley, *whence as headquarters they radiate in every direction to the so-called "points of interest"; sauntering about the flowery fringes of Strawberry Meadows, bathing in the balm of the woods, scrambling, fishing, hunting; riding about Castle Lake, the McCloud River Soda Springs, Big Spring, deer pastures, and elsewhere. Some demand bears, and make excited queries concerning their haunts, how many there might be altogether on the mountain, and whether they are grizzly, brown, or black. Others shout, "Excelsior," and make off at once for the upper snow-fields. Most, however, are content with comparatively level ground and moderate distances, gathering at the hotel every evening laden with trophies—great sheaves of flowers, cones of various trees, cedar and fir branches covered with yellow lichens, and possibly a fish or two, or quail, or grouse. . . . Fresh roses come to cheeks that have long been pale, and sentiment often begins to blossom under the new inspiration.*

It was all very genteel and very naïve, and a way of leisure life that failed to exert an enduring charm over the children who spent their growing summers there beneath the mountain. As they came to lead their own lives, they spurned their parents' ways and pleasures, and in their automobiles took their own families traveling farther afield. This was the reason for the decline of the resorts by the Springs and in Strawberry Valley, according to Charles Masson. He lives in Dunsmuir, beside Highway 99 and on the canyonside above the site of the old Soda Springs Hotel; and he told me one evening last spring that when people got automobiles, they all wanted to travel.

"They used to come here, entire families, with trunks, and spend three or four weeks," he said. "But with the automobile, no one wanted to spend his summer vacation staying in one place. He wanted to be on the move and see the country, two or three hundred miles of it a day, every day. The old-fashioned resort was through."

In 1915, Sisson's Hotel burned to the ground. The local historians can take you down the old valley stage road and show you the expanse of road-side meadow where it stood, and the row of trees that once shaded its summer lawns. Six or seven years ago, Uncle Dick's Soda Springs Hotel, with its picturesque double-decked veranda, fell to the wreckers' ropes and hammers. There was no place for it any more. Up and down the canyon beside Highway 99 the motels and tourist cabins were getting all the trade, from car-borne travelers who arrived at dusk and were fifty miles along the highway when the sun rose clear of the Shasta spurs the next morning.

To thousands of men and women California is the soft slow fog coming in through the Golden Gate when the day is almost over, or lights twinkling on the hills of San Francisco on an evening in spring, or the smell of foot-hill pines and Gold Rush ruins in the sun, or a grove of weeping willows far across a valley, beside a winding river. But whoever these men and women are, they are not north-country people. To north-country people, their part of America, their part of California, is the sublime and lofty mountain that guided their grandfathers and grandmothers down the trails and that, in their own time, they have looked up to every day of their lives.

It was off there, against the sky, when as children they gazed from their schoolroom windows. They knew as children the flaring snow banners streaming from the distant crest, the blue shadows that lazy summer clouds cast across the vast, snow-filled glacial channel they called The Heart, and the shifting, weaving planes of gold and rose that played across the summit, a far 2 miles above them, long after the sun had set and the shadows were gathering in the valleys.

They have known and loved the mountain all their lives, and they die if they can at their windows, drawing serenity, repose and strength from the mountain and wanting it to be the last they see of this world.

It was in their grandfathers' time that white men first accepted the chal-lenge of the Shasta Summit and climbed above the timberline and across the moraine and snowfields to the highest peak of the mountain, whose slopes the Indians before them had shunned as sacred to the Great Spirit.

Timberline is at 8,000 feet, and the official height of the mountain is 14,161 feet. You can say that at its base in the valleys it covers an area of about 144 square miles. It rises to its greatest height in a sharp, mighty sweep which carries the last 8,000 feet to the crest in a horizontal distance of 4 miles. But scaling it in summertime requires no alpine work, if you avoid the glaciers on the north and east, and ascend the western face to Thumb Rock, thence to Misery Hill and the summit.

This, roughly, was the route followed by Captain E. D. Pearce, who, on August 14, 1854, with a party of thirteen men from Scott Valley and Yreka, made the first recorded ascent of Mount Shasta. They found the mountain's crater filled, and the summit a fairly level area a mile and a half broad; and there, in a stone cairn, they deposited copies of the *New York Herald,* the *New Testament,* and the constitutions of the Sons of Temperance and the International Order of Odd Fellows. At precisely twelve noon, according to Captain Pearce's account, they *unfurled the Stars and Stripes, and raised the standard to its long resting-place amid the deafening cheers of the little multitude.*

On the descent, three hundred feet or so below the summit, they discovered *a cluster of boiling hot sulphur springs about a dozen in number, emitting any amount of steam, smoke, gas, etc.* They took the temperature of the springs and found it to be 180° Fahrenheit. Then they sat down on what Captain Pearce called their "unmentionables," and, with their heels as brakes and their walking sticks as rudders, slid down the mountain snow slope.

*. . . The like I never saw before in the shape of coasting,* Pearce said. *Some unshipped their rudders before reaching the quarter (there was no such thing as stopping), some broached to and went stern foremost, making wry faces, while others, too eager to be the first down, got up too much steam, and went end over end; while others found themselves athwartships, and making 160 revolutions a minute. . . . No one knew what time we made the four miles in; however, it was concluded by all that we were not over five and a half minutes on the snow.*

Once the mountain had been conquered, others were ready and quick to try the struggle to the summit, and in the years since that time thousands have climbed it: scientists, travelers, professors, schoolteachers, ranchers,

*With their heels as brakes and walking sticks as rudders, they slid down the mountain snow slope*

hikers, high-school youths—representatives of every class and walk of life. Many of them went to satisfy some objective interest in the mountain, or to test their powers of endurance, or both. Many, undoubtedly, went simply to say that they had been to the summit, or to see what the world looked like from up there, and still others could not have said why they went. These scrawled their names in the mountaintop register, with an emphatic, "Never again!," and huffily turned to the descent with scarcely a look at the view. A few have climbed it with a curious light in their eyes: these are the mystics bent on discovering the secret of Shasta, unlocking its mystery, and solving the cosmic riddle of which they believe it is the form and substance.

There have been some memorable ascents. . . .

Anton Roman, the bookseller of the town of Shasta, was one of the first to follow Captain Pearce. He made his climb in 1856, in April, and was able to testify for the rest of his life that that was a little early in the year. As he toiled up Misery Hill a few hundred feet from the summit, his fingers grew so numb with cold he could no longer hold his thermometer. The last time he looked at it before it slipped from his hand and broke, it registered 12° below zero.

Six years later, the first ascent in the interests of science was made by State Geologist Josiah Dwight Whitney, William H. Brewer (who afterward became renowned as professor of agriculture at Yale's Sheffield Scientific School), Chester Averill, and three men from Strawberry Valley and Soda Springs. Short of time and equipment and encountering at the top a temperature of 26°, they accomplished little more than determining, within a few hundred feet, the mountain's altitude, which until then had been estimated as high as 17,000 feet. It was snowing through a dense fog as they descended Misery Hill and passed Thumb Rock, Brewer wrote in his *Up and Down California*, . . . *and so cold that our beards were white as snow, mustaches frozen, and faces blue.*

The Shasta glaciers—Hotlum, Bolam, Whitney, Wintoon, and Konwakiton (also called the McCloud)—were discovered in 1870 by Clarence King during his Survey of the Fortieth Parallel. King made the ascent with Samuel F. Emmons, Frederick A. Clark, and Albert B. Clark, spending one night on the crater rim of Shastina some two thousand feet below and west of the main summit, and a second night at the hot springs. In his classic *Mountaineering in the Sierra Nevada,* King described the sunset from the highest crest, on the late clear afternoon—a strange and eerie sight:

*Afar in the north bars of shadow streamed out from the peaks, tracing themselves upon the rosy air. All the eastern slope of Shasta was of course in dark shade, the gray glacier forms, broken ridges of stone, and forest, all dim and fading. A long cone of cobalt-blue, the shadow of Shasta fell strongly defined over the bright plain, its apex darkening the earth a hundred miles away. As the sun sank, this gigantic spectral volcano rose on the warm sky till its darker form stood huge and terrible over the whole east. It was intensely distinct at its summit, just as far-away peaks seen against the east in the evening always are, and faded at the base as it entered the stratum of earth mist.*

*Grand and impressive we had thought Shasta when studying [it] in similar light from the plain. Infinitely more impressive was this phantom volcano as it stood overshadowing the land and slowly fading into the night.*

Before they left the crest for their bivouac at the boiling springs, King and Fred Clark climbed upon the peak's highest pinnacle, a slender needle of rock. It was *so small we could barely balance there together, but we stood a moment and waved the American flag, looking down over our shoulders eleven thousand feet.*

The experience of John Muir and Jerome Fay in April, 1875, was less exhilarating. Trapped on the summit by a terrifying fury of thunder, lightning, hail, and snow, they spent the below-zero night without food or blankets beside the springs, which scalded them on one side while they all but froze on the other, and threatened them with asphyxiation from carbonic acid gases should they doze in their numbness and fatigue. They remained there thirteen hours; and in the cold morning sunlight waded through the summit snow on frostbitten feet, slid, stumbled and pitched down the white slopes, and at ten o'clock reached the timberline and safety.

That same year, Capt. A. F. Rodgers of the United States Coast Survey set out for the mountaintop with a pack train that carried, in sections, a galvanized iron shaft. At the 11,000-foot level the sections were transferred to the backs of Indian porters, who took them the rest of the way. Captain Rodgers then assembled them into a cylinder 14 feet high, set the monument's base in concrete 2 feet below the level of the ground, and capped it with a nickel-plated conoid reflector. It was his plan to establish long-distance survey lines from Shasta by means of the sun signals that would be struck from the reflector. Weathering and tarnish, however, frustrated the Survey's aims. The reflector remained there, bleak and oddly incongruous, until 1905, when lightning tore it apart and sent its fragments sailing over the summit's eastern precipice. (The cap was somehow salvaged, and sits today atop a file cabinet in the office of Orbell Apperson's *Mount Shasta Herald,* Mount Shasta City.)

Effective signals were achieved from the peak in 1878. In the July and August of that year, B. A. Colonna of the United States Coast and Geodetic Survey lived on the summit for nine days and nights and during that period exchanged flashes by heliograph with scientists stationed atop Mount St. Helena, an airline distance of 192 miles south. This experiment, perhaps the most sensational in Shasta's early history, left the public wondering which accomplishment was the more impressive, the establishment of the longest line of observation known to man, or Colonna's dramatic vigil in the clouds.

*There is no reason,* wrote King, *why anyone of sound wind and limb should not, after a little mountaineering practice, be able to make the Shasta climb. There is nowhere the shadow of danger, and never a real piece of mountain climbing—climbing, I mean, with hands and feet—no scaling of walls or labor involving other qualifications than simple muscular endurance.*

The old *Mount Shasta Register,* now at the University of California's Bancroft Library, bears the signatures of some Shasta climbers, however, who would have had their relatives certify them as raving maniacs before they repeated their experience. More than one of them, having scanned the pages of names of those who had preceded them, wrote, *I have one reason to be thankful I climbed Mount Shasta: I discovered I am not the only damned fool in the world!* A note of genuine terror crept into the penciled remarks of others. *It is growing dark. God help us to make it to safety,* they wrote. Or, *Hands too numb to write clearly. We're going to try to get back.*

In contrast, there is for September 10, 1883, the entry, *Gilbert Thompson, Geographer, U.S. Geological Survey; Thomas Watson, and two saddle mules, Dynamite and Cropper.* As far as can be determined, Dynamite and

Cropper were the first animals ever to scale the mountain, and ever since north-country people have been asking, if a mule can do it, why can't you?

Mr. Dowling of Yreka, the gentleman who reviewed for me the Yreka lynching of '95, has in his possession a photograph. It shows the boiler-plate monument; two bearded and obviously weary men, one sitting in the snow and the other standing beside the cylinder; and a light-colored horse upon which, seated sidesaddle, is a young woman in a flowing dress and a black sailor hat. The significant feature of the picture is not the monument, the men, or the woman, but the horse—the first and perhaps the only horse to reach the summit. The date of the ascent was August 18, 1893.

On the authority of Frank Montgomery, whose father founded the *Mount Shasta Herald* in 1887, the men have been identified as Thompson's companion Watson, who was a professional mountain guide, and William Beam, the owner of a Dunsmuir livery stable. The lady was Miss Alice Cousins of Sisson, and the photograph was taken by W. S. Valentine of Redding.

Penned on the back of the picture are a few notes about the historic horse. It was six or seven years old and owned by Beam. Its name was Jump-up. And, the notes said, it was never the same horse from that day forward. To Watson, Beam, Valentine, and Miss Cousins it had all been a lark and an excursion, but Jump-up *became stiff and stove up and though doctored, was finally killed.*

It is said that on another occasion members of a patriotic miners' band from Yreka struggled to the summit with their instruments, and, at a jaunty wave from their leader's baton, struck up what they intended as a spirited rendition of *The Star-Spangled Banner*. Though they puffed themselves red in the face, the only sound they made was a long-drawn, sibilant hiss. In the high thin atmosphere, the wind instruments were so many pretty pieces of brass, incapable of producing the merest toot. So they sang the anthem instead and contented themselves with the thought that, anyway, it was probably the first time in American history it had ever been sung at an elevation exceeding 14,000 feet.

But those who have agreed all along with King that *anyone of sound wind and limb* could make the climb, have a more persuasive argument than Dynamite and Cropper, Jump-up, and a miners' band that packed trumpets and tubas to the mountaintop: in August, 1923, hikers and mountain climbers of California's Sierra Club made an ascent to the summit. With them went Geraldine Mazza of San Francisco, believed to be the youngest person ever to climb the mountain. Geraldine, on that August day, was eight years old.

Once you have seen it at certain times of the day or year, or in the light of a particular moon, it will not be difficult for you to understand why some believe the mountain to be inhabited by a race that is stranger to our own, or by beings who exist upon a plane impossible for mortals to attain.

You will understand, then, that to all who listen the mountain speaks. To some it speaks of grandeur and distant majesty, to some of longing, to others of mystery. It is these last who people the mountain's forests and glacial caves with alien beings, to represent the mystery embodied and personified.

When, only twenty years ago, reports circulated that such beings had been seen on the mountain, the reaction demonstrated that the fantastic, attributed to Shasta, was the credible: men, women, and children traveled in large numbers to the mountain towns, to see, if they could, the weird creatures for themselves, and to find, if they could, the gold whose sources the creatures were said to control.

In 1931, the Supreme Grand Lodge of the Ancient Mystical Order Rosae Crucis published at its headquarters in San Jose, California, a book called *Lemuria, The Lost Continent of the Pacific.* The name of the author was given as W. S. Cervé, said to be the nom de plume of Dr. H. Spencer Lewis, first Imperator of the Rosicrucian Order of North and South America.

The first eight chapters of this book were devoted to a lay and not unentertaining review of the ancient history of the submerged land mass and its people. They were based, the author said, on rare old manuscripts brought from secret archives in Tibet and China by a representative of the Rosicrucian brotherhood.

His ninth and last chapter, however, was entitled, "Present Day Mystic Lemurians in California," which some believe to be a remnant of Lemuria that escaped inundation by the Pacific Ocean. Most of this chapter was devoted to an anthology of hearsay and north-country folk tales from unnamed sources. If they were true, the author said, it would appear as though somewhere on Mount Shasta, perhaps in the forests of the McCloud River flats, there lived a surviving colony of Lemurians.

*Many years ago,* he wrote, *it was quite common to hear stories whispered in Northern California about the occasional strange-looking persons seen to emerge from the forest and the dense growth of trees in that region, and who would run back into hiding when discovered or seen by anyone.*

Sometimes, according to these tales, one of the weird strangers would appear in Dunsmuir, Mount Shasta City, or Weed—a lumber town a few miles north of Mount Shasta City—and exchange gold nuggets or gold dust for merchandise. They would be glimpsed along the highways—tall, grave, garbed in white robes and sandals. When approached by tourists bent on photographing them or speaking to them, they would flee into the woods, or simply vanish on the spot. Storekeepers who heard them talk reported that they spoke perfect English, with a slight British accent. All wore a special decoration over the center of their foreheads, presumably to conceal a Lemurian organ of sixth sense which enabled them to communicate among themselves by means of mental telepathy.

Other uncanny occurrences, assertedly told by persons with firsthand experience, were reported by Cervé. Ceremonial fires of a blazing white light burned in the forests at night and illuminated hidden palaces of marble and onyx with golden domes. Eerily beautiful chants were carried on the winds to nearby towns. Anyone rash or bold enough to approach the Lemurian fastness would be intercepted and hustled away by *a heavily covered and concealed person of large size,* or would be arrested by peculiar vibrations which permitted him to move in no direction but back whence he had come.

Cars moving along Forest Service trails were known to have been suddenly brought to a stop, as if by a failure of their ignition system. Their occupants succeeded in starting them again only after they had pushed the automobiles back down the road a hundred feet and turned them around. Amphibious craft were seen floating up from Shasta, silent blimps that the Lemurians apparently powered by means of radioactive stones; at high altitudes they would make for the Pacific, where they would descend to the ocean's surface and proceed as ships. When forest fires threatened the flats east of Shasta, strange vapors drifted from the center of the wilderness and smothered the flames.

*Lemuria, The Lost Continent of the Pacific,* received a wide distribution, not only in the United States, but in Europe and Asia as well. Not long after its publication, readers by the hundreds began to converge on Mount Shasta City, Dunsmuir, and Weed and demand to be conducted to the colony of the Lemurians. The only reply that most of the natives could give was a startled, "What Lemurians?"

With a flourish of Cervé's book, the visitors told the natives they didn't know what was going on right in their own backyards, and struck off up the mountain or into the wilderness east of the mountain. In the years immediately following the book's appearance, Lemurian-hunters arrived in the mountain towns from several European nations, and from Africa, New Zealand, and Australia.

From their expeditions to the mountain some returned saying that they had been hoodwinked. Others said that they had "made contacts," but when asked with whom replied that their lips were sealed. Still others came back saying nothing at all.

Last spring, Orbell Apperson, owner of the *Mount Shasta Herald,* recalled this curious passage in Shasta's history.

"I figure," he said, "that either someone put something over on them, or they came up here to put something over on us natives.

"We tried to tell them at first that there was no such thing as a Lemurian colony on Mount Shasta, or anywhere near Mount Shasta. Sometimes they came here, into my office, asking about 'the little people' who lived on the mountain, and we told them there weren't any 'little people,' either.

"One day a husky blond fellow came in and asked me if I had seen any of them, and I said no, I hadn't, and he wanted to take me out into the street and beat me up. After that," concluded Mr. Apperson, "I stopped telling them anything."

Mount Shasta is located in the million-and-a-half-acre Shasta National Forest. Letters of inquiry arrived steadily at the Forest Service headquarters in Mount Shasta City. Forest Service officials dutifully answered each one. The Lemurian stories, they said, were sheer fantasy. Every inch of the mountain and the McCloud River flats had either been explored on foot or photographed from the air. No Forest Service man had ever encountered the vaguest trace of a Lemurian.

Nevertheless, one group of searchers spent an entire summer hunting for the white-robed men, and gasoline service station operators and storekeepers in Weed were so badgered by requests for directions to the gold-and-marble palaces in the wilderness that they put up signs outside their establishments reading, "We Will Answer No Questions About Lemurians."

As time went on and the Sunday supplement stories about the mountain colony grew colder, the Lemurian-hunters dwindled. Toward the end of the 1930s, the summers brought only a few of them to the Shasta slopes.

In 1932 Shasta became an occult symbol of importance through the publication of *Unveiled Mysteries* by Godfré Ray King (pen name of the late G. W. Ballard, founder with Mrs. Ballard of the St. Germain Foundation).

In this book Ballard related an experience he had had in the summer of 1930 on the eastern flank of Mount Shasta. He was walking in the woods in the vicinity of the McCloud River, he wrote, when someone in the form of a hiker, like himself, appeared to him out of the forest, gave him a milk-white elixir to drink and talked to him of the white "Light of God." Toward the end of the interview the young man revealed himself to Ballard as St. Germain, one of the Ascended Masters of the Brotherhood of Mount Shasta. From this and subsequent talks with St. Germain, Ballard derived the tenets and decrees for the nationwide religious organization known as the "I AM" Activity of the St. Germain Foundation.

In 1948 Mrs. Ballard established at Mount Shasta City the world headquarters of the "I AM" Ascended Master Youth. A permanent colony of members now lives in the community.

The leader of the Mount Shasta youth sanctuary last spring was an attractive, twenty-year-old graduate of Northwestern University. The mountain bore a special significance to her and members of the activity, she said. "There are retreats all over the world at which Ascended Masters are working for the good of mankind. Mount Shasta is such a retreat, where certain members of the Brotherhood of Masters live and do their work."

"Can you see them?" I asked.

She shook her head. "They live on another, higher plane. To us, most of the time, they are invisible, but very real, because of the assistance they give in helping us bring greater good into the physical world. They can and do become visible and tangible whenever they choose."

Thus the mountain camps and the mountain people have come and gone, and the people have always looked at Shasta with awe and wonder and have made it a symbol of many various things that are outside of history, outside of time.

The country of Dunsmuir today is a country of the Sacramento canyon and river gorges, of tall pines and firs standing high on mountain ridges against the sky, of logging camps and loaded lumber trucks pounding down 99, of earth-shaking Mallet engines shattering the canyon stillness, of tourist cabins beside the road, of sharp pine-scented air, swift fishing streams, and hills that hunters love. At the canyon head the country of Mount Shasta City is valley meadows, the mountain, Rainbow Ridge, and the Eddys to the west, and across the northern ridge, beyond the dark cone of Muir's peak, the Valley of a Thousand Hills.

The people who are there today know their country's past; they learned it from their grandfathers and grandmothers who settled there many years ago, when you could still see the trails the trappers blazed. And they know the mountain; all their lives they have studied its lineaments, its lights and shadows, its changing moods. The poorest cottage beside the road has its picture window facing Mount Shasta.

They understand the myths and legends. They know that in the high, special air you can see spectral things. Charles Masson, climbing Shasta with Grant Towendolly, the son of a Wintun chief, looked over his shoulder not far above the timberline and saw a group of riders upon a lava ridge, silhouetted against the sky. "Look!" he said, "there is a band of horsemen." The keen-eyed Indian followed his pointing finger. "The spirits have got you," he said. "There is nothing there." Masson looked again, and the riders had vanished.

They know, too, that the winds moaning along the desolate lava slopes can sound like voices singing in the distance, or like the far-off roar of the phantom truck that the lowlanders sometimes swear they hear coming up the road, but that never arrives. They know that the sunlight, glancing off the blue, translucent roofs of the glacier ice caves, can make you think you see flickering lights, or minarets of light, or, sometimes, the golden gables of a mountain temple.

But when they think of the greatest miracle of all, they are thinking of the rivers flowing wild and free from the springs of Shasta, the McCloud and the Sacramento, flowing south to the great Shasta Lake that now lies behind Shasta Dam, spinning the turbines of the dam's hydroelectric plant; then flowing south once more, as the Sacramento, to become the giver of life to the fertile fortunate valley that lies south between Shasta and the sea—and thus to fulfill the promise of their fathers' Promised Land.

·   ·   ·

From the iron grillwork of a shuttered brick building in a Mother Lode
town, a crested jay breaks over a still, deserted street, and flies away. The
wind rustles through the ivy that has climbed the ruin walls. The grass
grows tall over the overland trails; and since it all began, the glaciers of
Shasta have moved—how far? one mile, perhaps—down the high desolate
reach of the summit slopes.

There is gold in the hills yet, the old men say, as they sit and smoke in the
shade of the country catalpas and locust trees. And as they say it, and sagely
nod their heads, the swift, lovely, life-giving rivers run to the sea, the sunlight shimmers along the far-off highland pines, and the peaches and
apricots hang heavy in the valley once called Buenaventura; the Shasta
turbines whine keen and high, the cars and trucks move across the great
bridges of the great bay, the long, lonely whistle of a mountain freight
echoes down a distant canyon and fades off and away.

There is gold yet in the hills, they say, and as they say it, one more shake,
dry and weathered by a century of sun and rain, falls to the floor of a
cabin by a caved-in mine shaft, in a long-forgotten gulch. This happens,
and the sky of El Dorado arches blue and soft above, as it did before there
was any cabin there.

# Index

245